"MIRROR, MIRROR, ON THE WALL . . . CAN I REALLY HAVE IT ALL?"

YES!—*If* you learn how to master the envious feelings that can sabotage your chances for happiness. *The Snow White Syndrome* talks to famous women who have overcome the envy trap and reached their full potential. Here are some of *their* views on ENVY . . .

Gloria Steinem: "I experience envy as a barrier between me and other women, women I want to reach. I feel lonely, like someone has set me apart . . . It certainly does not feel good."

Sally Quinn: "Envy is the most frightening, the most ugly emotion when it surfaces in friends or relatives. It is so scary to me that it actually makes me not want to be successful."

Julie Harris: "Envy is a confining, enslaving emotion. When you are envious, you try to suppress it. Any emotion you suppress most of the time goes inward and gives you bile. Envy has a bitterness, a rancor, that makes you sick."

Billie Jean King: "I can't let someone's envy put me into a tailspin and not perform well. Sure I'm hurt. I'm human. But after the match I'll be more upset with myself if I let petty remarks get to me . . . If you play like a donkey . . . nobody wins."

THE SNOW WHITE Syndrome

All About Envy

BETSY COHEN

JOVE BOOKS, NEW YORK

All events in this account are factual.
However, in an effort to safeguard the
privacy of certain individuals, I have
changed names and, in some cases,
disguised identifying characteristics.

This Jove book contains the complete
text of the original hardcover edition.
It has been completely reset in a typeface
designed for easy reading, and was printed
from new film.

THE SNOW WHITE SYNDROME

A Jove Book / published by arrangement with
Macmillan Publishing Company

PRINTING HISTORY
Macmillan edition published 1986
Jove edition / August 1989

Jove Books are published by The Berkley Publishing Group,
200 Madison Avenue, New York, New York 10016.
The name "JOVE" and the "J" logo
are trademarks belonging to Jove Publications, Inc.

PRINTED IN THE UNITED STATES OF AMERICA

10 9 8 7 6 5 4 3 2 1

I dedicate this book to Faye, Albert, Dashiell, and Harvey.

Contents

Acknowledgments

I need to thank Kim Chernin for her structural editing. I met her two years ago in a sauna and told her my idea for this book. She assured me she could help make it happen, and she did. Judith Tannenbaum was an encouraging, perceptive, hard-working assistant with interviewing and editing throughout the project. Linda Purrington was a terrific initial editor. Sherry Helmers provided word by word review, child care, and hand-holding late into the night.

This book could not have come to life without Macmillan Publishing Company's belief in me. To them, especially Arlene Friedman for her outstanding editorial contributions and steady boosts, and her associate editors Melinda Corey and Emily Easton, I thank you for hanging in there with all the details.

Elizabeth Lay also trusted in this project from the very beginning. She and her co-agent, Carole Mann, have been behind me throughout.

Other professional helpers have been steadfast and caring: secretarial, Dorothy Consodine and Jan Buoc; transcribing, Antoinette Constable; typing, Francis Wilcox; library research, Mary Ann Hooper; editorial, Linda Purrington; attorney, Ted Lyman; psychiatric consultation, Florence C. Irvine, M.D.; theoretical consultation, Hal Sampson, Ph.D., and Stephen Joseph, M.D.; research statistics, Liz Hartka; photography, Jill and Pat Stevens and Russ Fushella; computer repair, Stephen Michel; spiritual advisor, Gail Stewart.

THE SNOW WHITE SYNDROME

Two of the first dwarfs were Mimsy Goodman and Enid Goldstein who made sure I got off the ground. Claudia Anderson was a "sister" before she met me. Same with Laurie Glen.

I am indebted to my close friends for their careful and critical reading of the manuscript through its many changes: Kathy Miller, Judith W. Klein, Gale Bailey, Barbara Baer, Beth Barmak, Roberta Maisel, Mary Montez, and Jane G. Cohen. Roberta Seid, Marcy Jones, Betsy Maisel, Terry Nathan, Lonnie Prince, Corey Joseph, Jill Stevens, Roger Thompson and Emilyn Page all came through for me when I needed them. To Karen Harber, Anita Noennig, Pam Valois, Sharon Gillin, Fred and Elke Behrens, Barbara Cohen, Clay Axelrod, Susan Waterfall, Melinda Nix, Jane Burka, Joan Cole, and all the other unnamed friends who called with interest and nurturance, I thank you. I also appreciate two campers at the Lair of the Bear, Dick Lemon and Judith Hersher, who assisted with copyediting the manuscript during a vacation.

I extend my gratitude to all the women interviewed and surveyed. You gave of your time openly and freely to benefit other women.

I thank my siblings, Don, Paul, and Tom, and Fern and Tal for their enthusiasm. Two others can't be forgotten: late night cafe au lait from the French Hotel, and the faithful encouragement, love, understanding, selflessness and pride from my son, Dashiell. Thank you, all.

Betsy Cohen, L.C.S.W.
Labor Day, 1986

Introduction

Are you afraid of becoming too successful?

Are you afraid your best friend won't like you if you do too well or look too good?

Do you hold yourself back from fulfilling your potential?

Are you afraid to make others feel bad by surpassing them?

If so, you are suffering from the Snow White Syndrome.

This book is about envy. This book is a useful tool to help understand feelings we may have every day in our lives. It offers an awareness of something powerful that we usually don't let ourselves think about.

Webster's New World Dictionary of the American Language says that envy is "the feeling of discontent and ill will because of another's advantages, possessions, etc; resentful dislike of another who has something desirable." In other words, envy is wanting what someone else has and feeling bad about yourself for not having it. We rarely tell anyone that we feel envy—we don't even want to admit it to ourselves. We were taught not to envy or talk about envy, to keep envy in the closet. But envy is a natural emotion. Everyone feels it.

However, envy could be getting in the way of your success without your knowing it. Let's look at how.

Envy is being threatened by another's success and believing you shouldn't feel that way.

Envy is looking at another woman's body, wanting it, and hating your own.

Envy is finding yourself being catty, downright mean to someone you really care about.

Envy is longing for the excitement you imagine your daughter has, while criticizing her ability to take care of both her job and her children.

This book is also about being envied.

Are you afraid something terrible will happen to you if you have too much and so you play down what you do have?

Are you afraid someone will want what you have?

Are you afraid to tell your best friend, who didn't get a promotion at work, that you just got one?

Do you avoid your colleague in the restroom for fear she won't want to be your friend once she finds out about your success?

Have you been afraid to speak too eloquently at a PTA meeting in front of 100 mothers? Do you wear an old hand-me-down rather than the stylish rayon dress you bought yesterday? Do you stutter and need to drink a lot of water? You could be afraid of being envied.

I have been a psychotherapist for sixteen years and know that most women suffer from envy. Many of my patients had envious mothers and before our therapy, had no idea their mothers could possibly feel such an emotion toward them. They learned how envy makes them afraid to be a threat to anyone. You, too, will learn about this fear and what to do about it.

The Snow White Syndrome will provide clues that tell you if you are feeling envious or if you are being envied. You will be encouraged to discover hidden envy in yourself and others. It will show you how to easily recognize what envy is and what to do about it.

And, you will see that well-known women—Gloria Steinem, Billie Jean King, Julia Child, Rona Barrett, Susan Anspach, Julie Harris, Sally Quinn, Sharon Percy Rockefeller—to name just a few—have had problems with envy. Being in the limelight, these women have had to learn to handle being envied. I will show you how to handle it, too.

What does Snow White have to do with all this? Haven't we had a lot of books about fairy tales and syndromes lately? We have. But Snow White offers us an important message we need to receive if we want to be comfortable with success. Snow White liberates herself from her fear of being envied and you can do the same.

In *The Snow White Syndrome*, you will read stories about women whose lives in one way or another parallel the life of Snow White. You will enter the real lives of the 300 women interviewed, women from 48 states, from different walks of life, all of whom have struggled with envy. 150 women answered questionnaires and 150 were personally interviewed. These women all responded because they recognized the role that envy played in their lives.

You will find yourself in this book. You will realize you are like everyone else. You will learn how to transform the pain and shame of your own envy into a positive, motivating force. Since envy has been such a taboo, you may not even know that you are suffering from this emotion. Even if you're sure you have never had an envious feeling, you will soon be able to recognize envious people around you, and learn how to work with them. You will learn how to deal comfortably with envy in all aspects of your life.

Familiarize yourself with your own envy; answer the questionnaire in the appendix before reading the book, then see if your answers change after reading the book and/or compare your answers with those of the women surveyed.

In order to understand *The Snow White Syndrome*, you do not need to be an expert in psychology. All you *do* need is a willingness to learn about yourself. Learning to deal with envy is not a simple task, but it can be managed in a positive way.

After reading *The Snow White Syndrome*, you will no longer envy in solitude. You will be able to talk about your envy openly, not be ashamed or embarrassed, and maybe even laugh about it.

Of course, envy is not the only way to look at problems between people, but it needs to be brought into the light. When you can admit to your envy, you're less likely to hurt yourself or the person you envy.

If you are a woman who wants to be successful, and you want to enjoy that success fully, you'll need to know about the Snow White syndrome.

The Snow White Syndrome will teach you to use your envy to go after what you want.

CHAPTER 1

Let's Remember
Snow White

THE STORY OF SNOW WHITE

"Snow White" is the story of a victory. We will look at this fairy tale as an important myth of our time and see how it has touched the lives of millions of women.

Walt Disney's *Snow White,* from 1936, presents a cultural ideal and stereotype of the passive housewife who comes to life only with the prince's kiss. The story of Snow White was first written down by the Brothers Grimm in the 1800s. Looking more closely at the original fairy tale, we can see Snow White as a woman liberating herself from her mother, and moving into the world of work and relationships by getting to know herself better.

What lesson does she teach us?

The story of Snow White is an example of a mother's extreme reaction to being replaced. The tale illuminates the motive behind such an extreme response: Envy is the hidden drive that moves this story along.

The following is a modern retelling of the Brothers Grimm version of the tale:

THE FAIRY TALE RETOLD

One wintry day, when the snow was falling, a queen sewed. As she gazed dreamily through the window framed in black, the needle happened to prick her finger, spilling three drops of blood onto the snow. The red blood provided a bright contrast to the white snow, and the queen thought, Would that I had a child as white as snow, as red as blood, with hair as black as the wood of this window frame.

Her wish came true. Soon she gave birth to a baby girl with skin as white as snow, hair as black as ebony, and cheeks as red as blood. She called her baby little Snow White. Shortly thereafter, the queen died. (In modern psychological terms, this queen was the good mother.)

When little Snow White was one year old, her father, the king, remarried. He chose a beautiful woman who was proud, arrogant, and contemptuous. Because her self-worth depended on her outer appearance, Snow White's new stepmother needed to be more beautiful than anyone else. She kept track of her competitors by means of a magic mirror which provided an instant opinion rating any time she asked the following question:

> Mirror, mirror, on the wall,
> Who's the fairest of them all?

As long as the new queen remained youthful, the mirror always answered,

> You, O Queen, are the fairest of them all.

The queen, who knew her trusty mirror never lied, could then breathe a sigh of relief.

Six years passed. Snow White was quietly growing up and becoming more and more beautiful. But the queen was getting older, and eventually her worst fears were realized. When she asked her mirror if she was still the fairest in the land, the mirror replied, "No, Snow White is the most beautiful."

The wicked queen was shocked, upset—green with envy. She

had to face a bitter reality. Her hope of remaining forever young was destroyed. From that moment on, whenever she looked at Snow White, her heart hurt with the hatred she felt toward her stepdaughter.

The feeling of hatred pervaded the queen's days and gave her sleepless nights. Eventually, the wicked queen ordered a hunter to take Snow White into the forest and kill her. (In modern psychology, the new queen represents the bad mother.)

As proof that he had done what she ordered, the queen told the hunter to bring Snow White's lungs and liver to her. The hunter, who felt both guilt and pity, considered Snow White too beautiful to kill. (He played the role of a father who cannot directly say "no" to his wife, who could help his daughter only behind her mother's back.) The hunter killed a wild animal instead and brought the animal's lungs and liver to the wicked queen. She ate them hungrily, enjoying what she thought was her final victory. In this way, she hoped to take on the youth and beauty of Snow White.

Instead of being killed by wild animals, Snow White found safety in the woods. (As she ran into the forest, and therefore deeper into her own nature, she ran further away from a confrontation with her stepmother's envy.) When night fell, to her surprise, she came upon a small cottage and fell asleep inside. The owners of this cottage, which was neat and clean, were seven dwarfs.

In the morning, the curious and friendly dwarfs peppered her with questions, and Snow White explained her predicament. Hearing the sad tale, they asked if she would become their housewife and live with them free of charge. (This conventional woman's role spared Snow White direct confrontation with her mother's envy—for the time being.)

Because she was alone all day, the dwarfs were concerned for her safety. (They saw their duties as fatherly—working hard during the day and offering advice and concern at night.) They warned her not to talk to strangers, for they thought her stepmother would soon appear. (They felt it would be impossible for Snow White to avoid confronting her stepmother's envy. They knew the strength of that envy would pursue Snow White even into her quiet forest retreat.)

And they were right. Back at the castle, the wicked queen asked the mirror to report the good news. She discovered that Snow

White was alive and well. Aghast, the queen could think of nothing but how to kill Snow White. Envy allowed her no rest.

The queen dressed as an old peddler woman and tempted Snow White with a lacy silk bra and corset. As she showed Snow White the undergarment, the old woman commented that Snow White looked as if she had not received much attention from a woman lately. Snow White accepted the old woman's offer, perhaps because she wanted to acknowledge her girlhood with the proper undergarment. (Also, she was lured and tempted by motherly concern. She needed caring from a woman, having been raised by an envious stepmother.) But the wicked queen laced her up so tightly that Snow White lost her breath and fell down as though dead.

The dwarfs returned home shortly and untied the lace. Snow White began to breathe and slowly life returned. The dwarfs knew the old woman had been the wicked queen, and they warned Snow White not to let anyone in again.

At the castle, the queen once more asked for the mirror's good word. But the mirror told the truth. The queen again disguised herself as an old woman. (By assuming this disguise, the queen may have been attempting to deal with the unthinkable—getting older.)

This time the queen took a poisonous comb for Snow White and offered to comb Snow White's hair properly for once. Snow White accepted the offer and the moment the old woman put the comb to Snow White's beautiful ebony-black hair, Snow White fell down as if dead.

Again, the dwarfs returned home shortly. On taking the comb from her hair, they saw her return to life. This time they were adamant that she open the door to no one.

Predictably, the queen rushed home to the mirror. But the mirror did not lie. The wicked queen shook with anger. "Snow White shall die if it costs me my life." Life meant only one thing to the queen—being the most beautiful of all. She now used her witchcraft to make an unusual red apple. Half of it was poison, and the other half was not.

The queen painted her face as a witch and again traveled to the cottage. Snow White refused the apple: "I cannot take anything." Snow White feared poisoning, and this witch seemed to understand: "Are you afraid of poison? I will bite from this half, and you can have a bite from the other." Snow White's wish for the nutritious apple, and for a good mother, was irresistible. Seeing the old woman eat a bite, she was no longer afraid. She bit into the poisonous half and fell down as if dead.

Unable to restore her life, the dwarfs thought about burying her, but her cheeks were still red, and they could not bear to place her underground. Instead, they built a glass coffin and gently set her inside. They used glass instead of wood or metal so she would be visible from all sides, and they could continue to watch and protect her.

They set the coffin on the mountain, and the dwarfs kept a constant vigil. (These psychic helpers were the support she needed for this period of quiet in her development. Only seven years old, she was not yet ready for the prince. She needed time for herself in a nondestructive environment. She needed protection, helpers. She needed to prepare herself for the sexual and envious world.)

The years passed. Snow White grew up in her glass coffin. By chance, a king's son came by, saw the coffin, and could not take his eyes from her beauty. The prince begged the dwarfs for the coffin. He felt he could not live without seeing her. (In our reading of the tale, the prince was not a separate person in his own right. He was a part of Snow White, a male part that would become her own: her initiative, her aggressiveness, her pursuit of goals and ambitions.) The prince spoke so lovingly that the dwarfs pitied him. Like good fathers, they knew they would have to allow her to grow up and leave them, and they let him take the coffin.

As the prince's servants carried the coffin away, they stumbled. The coffin shook, and the poisonous apple was dislodged from Snow White's throat. (As is often the case, a crisis has to occur before there is an awakening.) Snow White suddenly opened her eyes, raised the lid of the glass coffin herself, and sat up, alive. The prince spoke of his love, offered to marry her and to make his palace their home. She accepted.

The couple invited Snow White's wicked stepmother to the wedding as an honored guest. The faithful mirror had given the wicked queen the bad news that Snow White was alive. The queen was driven to face her competition because there seemed no other way to find peace. She accepted the invitation. As soon as she saw Snow White, her daughter and enemy, the queen stood motionless with fear and rage.

Snow White and the prince had planned their revenge. Iron slippers were on the fire, waiting for the evil queen. The queen was forced to wear these red-hot shoes and to dance at the wedding party until it was *her* turn to fall down dead. (The queen

was forced to face her own mortality, the inevitability of death. As
Snow White rids herself to her envious stepmother, she is, at the
same time, next in line to become a mother herself—more able,
we hope, to deal with envy than her stepmother had been.)

WHAT THE TALE MEANS FOR YOU AND ME

"Snow White" is not a story about a real girl who is chased into
the forest by her wicked stepmother. Instead it is the story of a
girl's development into a woman. It reveals a psychological
pattern many of us face in our families of origin, in our growing
up and struggling for independence.

Snow White is not a psychological essay, nor a prescription for
behavior; it is a fairy tale. The tellers of fairy tales know that
emotions like envy are considered taboo; we are usually forbidden
to acknowledge and talk about them. Therefore, fairy tales tell
their stories in the way our dreams tell their stories, revealing what
is unacceptable.

In fact, you can think of the fairy tale as a shared dream. The
language of fairy tales and dreams is that of imagery and
metaphor. Many women share the dream that is Snow White.
Important issues about mothers and daughters lie in the fairy tale
in disguised form. By listening to the language of this dream, by
analyzing the tale, paying attention to the universal elements in
this story, you open yourself to a new look at your own life. Thus,
you can change in ways that will allow you to be more successful,
joyful, and victorious.

Mirror, Mirror

Mirrors illuminate the hidden emotions in this story. As you
know, mirrors are important for a woman's self-esteem. A mirror
has wrecked many a good day because women learn to let the
mirror define who they are.

"Snow White" is not only a story of the wicked queen's actual mirror, it is also the story of the absence of her motherly "mirroring." If the wicked queen were a good mother, *she* would be Snow White's mirror. She would then reflect Snow White's beauty, offering Snow White a positive image, a positive mirror of herself.

A child needs an attentive, accepting, sincerely complimentary, supportive parent in order to learn to perceive, experience, and trust her own feelings. Snow White did not have such a parent. Snow White had what is commonly called a "narcissistic" mother—a self-centered and self-preoccupied mother. In the fairy tale, the queen is either looking in the mirror or trying to kill her daughter. She notices her daughter only when Snow White becomes a threat.

Snow White may have felt her own thoughts and emotions did not matter, for until the end of the tale, she seems like a nonperson, without anger or direction. Snow White is clearly wounded by her lack of mirroring. A toddler who is adequately mirrored is more likely to develop a life full of goals and ambitions, feeling she has the right to have what she wants. Such a child has an easier time becoming independent in the world.

When a mother is unable to reflect her daughter's fine developing qualities, the daughter does not know that she has these qualities. This daughter will not see her own image in the mirror—she will see her mother. Not only is the envious mother unable to reflect her daughter's unique qualities, but she is actually blocking their development.

The Snow White–daughter, whose good qualities are not mirrored, believes she has little right to achieve in the world, and hence lacks initiative. Snow White cares for others but initiates no action of her own. She turns to a man for the affirmation of herself, for her self-esteem, hoping to find herself through this man. She must find her own mirror, her own reflection of herself.

The Wicked Queen

What is fascinating about the Snow White fairy tale is that every mother is like the wicked queen at certain *moments* in her life. Most mothers wish the best for their daughters, try to provide their daughters with what they never had, try to make their daughters' lives better than their own. But when the daughter does develop a better life, envy comes tagging along behind. *The mother envies her daughter when she sees her daughter has opportunities, freedom and fun that she, the mother, never had. The mother may not even be aware of her envy.*

In Snow White's home there is no heart-to-heart talk—Mom just sets out to kill. Most little girls can't believe that their much loved mom could become so frighteningly angry. The first way a child tries to handle the shock of her mother's anger is to split up the image of her mother in her mind: "Good Mom loves me. Bad Mom doesn't. So Bad Mom isn't really my mom."

The fairy tale reflects this split. Snow White's real mother, her good mother, dies. It is the stepmother who embodies evil. Repeatedly, Snow White hopes to be cared for by a good mother, but instead she encounters the bad mother. Only after four life-threatening attacks is Snow White forced to accept the facts: "My stepmother has been out to get me."

Snow White's stepmother is insecure and vain. She can't let the importance of her daughter's life triumph over her own insecurity. This mother hates to lose.

Every woman confronts her envy of youth and beauty as she grows older. This envy is most intense when she regards her own daughter as her rival. The wicked queen, who represents the extreme of all mothers, deals with her envy in the worst possible way—she acts out her fantasies.

What is the effect on the Snow White, the budding beauty, in all of us, when we have a mother who is sometimes like the wicked queen? If your mother is envious too much of the time, you feel it is not safe to feel good as you grow up. Because you don't want to make your mother feel bad, you limit your success and pleasures. You keep the lid on. You don't show your own happiness. You don't trust yourself. This pattern is what I call the *Snow White syndrome*.

The daughter who is caught in the Snow White syndrome feels a need to keep herself at a level the same as, or worse than, her mother. If she surpasses her mother, this daughter fears she will arouse her mother's envy and insecurity. This daughter feels she needs to take care of her mother by not becoming too successful. Actually, she needs to leave her envious mother behind so she can become an accomplished, happy, and peaceful woman.

The Snow White syndrome has two parts: the envier—the queen, and the person envied—Snow White. The relationship between the two leads to the fear of being envied, the fear that if you're too successful, you won't be liked. The consequence of this fear is that you hold yourself back in life—for fear of being the target of envy. You hold yourself back because you, like Snow White, don't want to be hurt or feel that you are intentionally hurting anyone. Then, because you are limiting your own possibilities, you are more likely to get caught up in envying the talent and success of others.

Many women are caught up in the Snow White syndrome. They comment, "My mother envied me and I now restrain myself, my boisterousness, my potential, my joy." Or, "I'm afraid to be powerful because my mother might retaliate." Or, "Right in my own home, I was taught that success is not safe."

Since the stakes are so high—life or death—why doesn't Snow White follow the dwarfs' warnings and accept the fact that her wicked queen mother wanted to kill her? Because Snow White, like any one of you with an envious mother, wants to deny the obvious, to protect herself from truth that is too painful to bear. Too painful, because Snow White needs her mother—needs her precisely because she never had a nurturing mother. Therefore, Snow White keeps seeking the mothering she lacks, the mothering that died with her "good mother."

For anyone with a wicked queen mother, the battle to become a full, adult woman is as strenuous as the battle facing Snow White.

Absent Father

Where was Snow White's daddy? Where was the king? The fairy tale tells us nothing about this man. The intensity of the drama between Snow White and the wicked queen plays itself out in his absence.

Daddy's out. He's at the office, at work, at war, on the road, at a conference, fixing the car, running a marathon, watching TV in the den, and "He mustn't be disturbed, dear." Daddy was out when Snow White's stepmother gave the orders to have her killed.

If Snow White had had a good father at home taking care of her, he might have alerted Snow White to the danger ahead. Or he might have told Snow White, "Face it, kid, your mother has a problem here. Don't take her seriously. She's always been hung up on her looks. Your grandmother was, too. Your mother can't help it." Or he might have helped his wife by reassuring her of his love despite her getting older. Or he and his wife may have divorced if there were no other solutions, and he could have taken care of Snow White himself more of the time.

He could have helped Snow White deal with an envious mother. He could have been a balance to her mother, a countervoice to the queen's. He could have told his daughter, "Honey, I'm so proud of you, you are wonderful." But the only messages Snow White heard at home were negative ones from her mother.

Also, a mother like Snow White's, a woman who has trouble sharing, might keep her daughter from having a good relationship with her father. Would the wicked queen have wanted closeness between Snow White and the king? A good relationship with a father is a primary way to foster a young girl's sexuality, as the father looks fondly at her, and gets pleasure from her company. Snow White had to find the dwarfs in order to begin to know her sexuality.

The Magical Helpers

The dwarfs, Snow White's rescuers, are the helpers who seem to come into our lives magically, just at the moment we need them. In the "real world," these helpers may be therapists, friends, relatives, mates, ministers, or just a stranger on the bus.

In the story of Snow White, the dwarfs are humble, nonthreatening, empathic, understanding, nurturing men with qualities that present a true contrast to those of the wicked queen. The dwarfs are miners. They dig deep into the earth, seeking precious gems and metals. They help Snow White mine for what is precious in herself.

The dwarfs bring Snow White down to earth. They watch over Snow White and try to guard her from her envious mother. They warn her, support her, and give her a role, a purpose in life. They teach her how to have a "good relationship" with them. The dwarfs tell Snow White the truth: "Your mother does not love you, care about your needs, or put your interests first. She is out to get you. Be careful!" Snow White and the dwarfs actually mother each other. Snow White is learning about the world, about much that she had never known before.

Since Snow White needed to separate from her envious mother

to figure out thoughts and feelings that were hers and not her mother's, these dwarfs are essential in enabling Snow White to become an adult woman. They also provide an earthy environment in which Snow White's sexuality can develop. They don't try to steal the show, as her mother had done.

The Glass Coffin

Why is the coffin made of glass? It's not the usual material for coffins, is it? Coffins contain decay, which is not put on display. This coffin is more like a greenhouse which nurtures a young plant until it can brace the winds outside.

Because the coffin is glass, Snow White is not walled off. She is not dead. The coffin is a container, a vessel, a healing place for her to change. She is safe. Snow White had never been alone with her own thoughts and feelings. In the coffin, she is finally able to have her own quiet space—her own room, so to speak. Change can occur in a safe and healing place, such as in therapy or in a close relationship with someone.

Snow White needs this long period of sleep. Sleep is often connected with rebirth. Dreams refresh us. We awake from sleep often feeling as though we can start the day anew. A good night's rest heals the soul.

The coffin is also made of glass because it symbolizes the stepmother's mirror. *Snow White looks up at the glass and sees her own reflection*. She is finding her own "mirroring." She had never been able to see herself before; she could only see her mother's reflection.

The glass is unique. Not only does it reflect Snow White, it allows her to see *out* as well. This looking out beyond herself, more into the world of birds and sky and flowers and insects, is also what she needs.

Looking out into the world, connecting with your friends and classmates, is what girls traditionally do during the years Snow White spent in the coffin. Dr. Bruno Bettelheim, psychiatrist and interpreter of fairy tales, believes that Snow White's stay in the coffin corresponds to the traditional psychoanalytic period of "latency." The word "latent" means hidden, and we don't know much about what happens during these years precisely because so much is hidden. The task for children in latency years is to look

outside of themselves and form meaningful connections with
peers, to discover activities and interests. Latency is a time when
you pay less attention to your parents. Dr. Bettelheim believes that
Snow White needs the coffin during her latency years because it
represents a protected place where she can develop her sexual
adult self. She went in at about age seven and came out at puberty,
when she was supposedly ready for union with a man.

The Prince

Snow White looks up and finds, instead of her own reflection, the
prince. She sees a symbol, not a real man. The prince is a symbol
for qualities that Snow White has been lacking. He represents the
"inner male," part of herself, the ripening of her own powers,
powers her envious mother did not allow her to develop. To give
one interpretation, in connecting with the prince, Snow White is
connecting with qualities of her own that have been dormant.

Historically and culturally, men have cornered the market on
the ability to be assertive, aggressive, directly desiring, wanting,
and asking; they have had the lion's share of independence,
competitiveness, and ambition. The prince is active; he governs
his land, shows desire. These are qualities Snow White needs in
order to become fulfilled.

In discovering these qualities, she awakens from her state of
self-absorption. She is ready to leave the coffin, to move out into
the world.

Killing the Wicked Queen

What does Snow White do when she reenters the world? She plans
her wedding and decides to invite her stepmother. Is it a vengeful
Snow White who plots her stepmother's murder, wanting to
punish her for the harm she's caused? If so, Snow White hasn't
learned much from the dwarfs, from her time in the glass coffin,
or from her union with the prince. If revenge is all Snow White is
after, she has been destroyed just as surely as if she'd died from
the poisonous apple.

I claim, however, that Snow White has learned from the

dwarfs— she's come down to earth, she's had time alone in the coffin, she's been calm with her own thoughts. In this reading of the tale, Snow White successfully unites with her male self and "wakes up." Her act of murder is dream language, fairy-tale language for her experience of confronting the negative and envious mother, a mother that every woman fears. In order to avoid becoming a wicked queen herself, Snow White needs to separate from and kill off this destructive force inside of her. The adult Snow White is not going to need a mirror to affirm her self-worth. The death of the wicked queen allows Snow White to truly celebrate her marriage, the bringing together of herself.

SNOW WHITE VICTORIOUS

How Snow White's life unfolds from this point on is not clear; that is not the subject of the fairy tale. What is clear is that Snow White has achieved a hero's victory. She undergoes the many trials set for her. She masters them. Essentially, she says, "Don't be afraid. If I can do it, someone as passive and sweet as I have been, so can you. Don't be afraid of your mother's envy. There is hope." She teaches us to persevere in the face of parental envy.

As in most fairy tales, Snow White's story is one of extremes: an extremely good mother who dies and thus can give no nurturing, an extremely evil stepmother who is governed by envy. Most real lives are less extreme. Most of you have mothers who nurtured you some and envied you some. Although Snow White's story outlines the basic issues, we will look at real lives, not a fairy-tale life. However, before looking at how envy shows itself in real life, it will be helpful to examine just what envy is.

CHAPTER 2

What Is Envy?

The envious will die, but envy never.
—MOLIERE, *Tartuffe*

If envy were an illness, the world would be a hospital.
—SCHOECK

"Envy is a far dirtier little secret than sex or money," says contemporary writer George P. Elliott.

A thirty-six-year-old psychotherapist reports, "At my job at the mental health clinic, I can't even use the word 'envy' with my clients because it would seem that I am accusing them of something horrid. I have to find other words to use instead."

Why don't we want to use the word?

Envy, after all, is a sin, a sin against the Tenth Commandment, which tells us in Exodus 20:17:

You shall not covet your neighbor's house,
You shall not covet your neighbor's wife, or
his manservant, or his maidservant, or his ox,
or his ass, or anything that is your neighbor's.

Envy also appears as one of the seven deadly sins in Dante's *Inferno*. Of the seven deadly sins (lust, sloth, wrath, avarice, gluttony, envy, and pride), only pride was considered deadlier than envy. With such a curse against envy, is it any wonder that we bury it?

Even though we try to repress it, envy is a normal human emotion—disagreeable, but unavoidable.

Social psychologist Maury Silver says, "I can't imagine anyone who has not experienced envy at one time or another." He continues, "To be human is to compare ourselves with others. People can be comparable in work, salary, almost anything. That is the basis of envy."

Popular psychologist Joyce Brothers agrees: "There's one failing each of us shares and hates above all else to admit. There's not a man, nor a woman, alive (nor a child either) who hasn't at some time felt the sharp stab in the heart that results when someone else gets something that we covet." She adds, "Envy is a prime cause of the discontent many people feel about their lives. Yet we are so ashamed of envious feelings that we seldom pull them out into the light where we can get a good look at them."

Our first step then is obvious. We must bring envy "into the light." It is a dark and hidden emotion but easily disarmed. When unacknowledged, envy is dangerous. Bring it into the light, use the word, and it becomes less potent. We must call it by name—envy.

Well, then, what *is* envy?

Envy is the unpleasant feeling of wanting what another person has and feeling bad that you don't have it. How do you know if you're feeling envy? Here are some clues:

ARE YOU FEELING ENVY?

1. *Do you feel pain because of another person's success?*

Sally, a twenty-nine-year-old speech therapist, says, "What I have envied most recently is financial security, a certain level of affluence—when I drive through parts of Marin County I get green around the gills, and that's pain."

2. *Do you compare yourself with someone more successful and feel bad or threatened because of their success?*

Cheryl, a forty-four-year-old architect, envies women who are in relationships. "When I envy someone, I put myself down:

'How come she's got a relationship and I don't? There are lots of people who are screwed up, but *they* have relationships.' People tell me, 'Just get yourself together, and then you'll fall in love.' But instead of getting a man, I'm just getting older."

3. *Do you feel you have a right to have or be what you envy?*

You envy someone when you feel that person has what you deserve. The wicked queen felt entitled to be and remain the "fairest in the land." Pamela, a fifty-five-year-old photographer, admitted, "I ought to have the same fame and success as my friend has. I'm just as good as she is. I envy her."

Envy results when there's a big difference between "who I am" and "who I think I ought to be."

4. *Do you want to put down the person who is more successful than you are?*

Micky, a forty-eight-year-old postal worker, wrote, "I find myself being mean to women whom I envy. I say bad things to them, and then I feel worse about myself."

5. *Do you want to take away from the person what you envy about her? Do you want to hurt her?*

"He that cannot possibly mend his own case will do what he can to impair another's." So wrote Francis Bacon, back in 1625.

Arlene, a successful New York writer at age forty-four, confessed, "Envy is wanting what another person has and, if you're real honest with yourself, admitting you'd do almost anything to get it. Sometimes I feel I would even want to wreck someone else's success if that would make me more successful. When I envy someone and I hear about their misery, I feel better."

6. *Is your vision half-blind?*

Anaïs Nin said, "We don't see things as they are, we see them as we are."

I interviewed someone who envied a particular television producer. Then I interviewed the television producer. *She* envied a woman who is self-employed as a television consultant, who earns more money and has more free time. Haven't you noticed? The grass is always greener over there.

In *The Inferno,* Dante suggested a fitting punishment for the envious: that their eyelids be sewn together. Dante figured that if you could not see what you did not have, you would not be envious. However, an old Russian proverb says, "The envious sees with his ears as well."

Envy's eyes are greedy and see only what they wish to, in a distorted, partial way. Envy does not see a person's handicaps or the costs of success.

The following joke illustrates envy's blindness. It is a story of cutting off your nose to spite your face or shooting yourself in the foot because someone else is winning the race. Some people go to enormous extremes when their envy takes over.

Two women, Shirley and Ruthie, go scuba diving. They are lifelong friends—and lifelong rivals. Shirley is wearing lots of gear: cap, goggles, snorkle, wet suit, fins, oxygen tank, underwater watch, and bathing suit. But Ruthie, wearing only a skimpy bathing suit, flashes past her, going much deeper and faster.

Shirley is furious, thinking to herself, Of all the nerve! She's going farther and deeper than I! Shirley quickly swims deeper to catch up with Ruthie and gurgles enviously, "Ruthie, what the hell are you doing down here so deep?"

Ruthie gasps, "I'm drowning!"

7. *Do you believe that you will gain from another person's loss?*

Snow White's stepmother thought that if Snow White lost her youth and beauty, then she, the queen, would naturally come to possess it. The wicked queen thinks that if she eliminates Snow White, her stepdaughter's youth and beauty will come to her. In fact, since she is aging, someone younger would probably be considered the fairest in the land (at least in *this* land).

8. *Are you in a no-win situation?*

If you are an envious person, you may envy your friend's fur coat. If she gives it to you, you might enjoy wearing it. But then you may envy your friend's generous nature or the fact that she has much to give and you have little.

9. *Are your cravings endless?*

We're familiar with the woman who envies her friends who live in a better neighborhood. She buys a new home in their neighborhood, with payments slightly above her means. Now she envies their being able to afford gardeners, painters, interior designers, window dressers, and maids. It is hard to reassure an extremely envious person.

There are ways to deal with this envious hunger. You will learn them. The truth is, envious people often hurt themselves. Envy wants the other person to suffer, but you, the envier, usually suffer the most. As my friend's mother put it, envy does more harm to the vessel in which it is stored than to the object on which it is poured.

THE CONTINUUM OF ENVY

How Much Envy Do You Feel?

You can see that envy, like other emotions, is experienced in varying degrees. Here's one way to visualize this:

The Continuum of Envy

DESTRUCTIVE   POSITIVE
The Wish to Harm→Self-Hatred→Resentment→Covetousness→Admiration→Emulation

The wish to harm. Envy, at its worst, is wanting the person you envy to suffer; you want to wreck what she has. Often you want to spoil precisely what you think is most admirable and valued.

Hatred. Beware of envy's darker side. "I hate you, I hate what you have, I hate that you have it. But most of all, I hate myself for not having it."

Resentment. A milder form of envy is resentment: "I envy you for having a better job in the company than I do. How come you're the preferred one?" You resent the other's good fortune, fortune you're sure you'll never have.

Covetousness. "The man who covets is guilty of robbery in thought," says the *Treasury of Jewish Quotations*. Covetousness is also a mild degree of envy. "I crave and long for what you have. I wish it were mine."

Admiration. "He who goes unenvied shall not be admired," wrote Aeschylus in the ancient Greek drama *Agamemnon*. Admiration is often a feeling of the moment—"I envy you, I think you did a fine job. I wish I could do as well." When you admire someone, you envy but do not want to harm.

Emulation. Alexander Pope once wrote, "Envy, to which the ignoble mind's a slave, is emulation in the learned or the brave." Although *Webster's New World Dictionary* defines emulation as "a desire or ambition to equal or surpass," most of the women interviewed used the word with less focus on surpassing. Instead, they emphasized "striving for what the other person has, using the envied person as a role model." It is in this context—learning what you want by paying attention to what you envy—that I use the word "emulation."

When you see a person get a job you want, and you try for the same type of job, you are emulating that person. Emulation is a healthy part of personality development. It helps you accomplish what you want in life.

Which of these words describes your envy? One indicator is how much anger and bitterness you feel. At one end of the continuum, you feel a great deal of anger. However, if you admire and emulate, there's very little anger connected with your envy. Within admiration and emulation is envy that is under control and has found a positive channel. *The more you admire, and feel the possibility of getting what you admire, the less you need to hurt the person you envy.*

Looking at this continuum, you can see that envy has two poles. One woman I interviewed was definite: "Envy is both a way to put myself and others down and a way to find out what I want more of."

How Can Envy Be a Positive Guide?

Envy can help you form positive identifications. Envy helps us form what psychologists call a "positive identification" with someone—to begin with, our parents. This urge to identify with someone means taking on the qualities and the values of a person you admire, copying and modeling yourself after him or her. A little girl learns to become a woman by forming a positive identification with her mother. The little girl sees Mommy having what the little girl wants but doesn't have. She takes in what she desires from her mother, what the little girl needs to be the person she wants to be in the world.

Thirty percent of the women in the survey reported envying their mother at one time. Here is a response:

"Yes, I envied my mother for having my father's love. I realized I had better identify with my mother if I wanted my father to love me. I liked Brussels sprouts because she did, I wore the same color shoes, liver disgusts me and I would force myself to eat it and say I liked it. Then, when I found out my father didn't love my mother, oy-vey!"

Envy can help you learn. One part of making a positive identification is "taking into" yourself qualities the other person has that you want. Joyce, a thirty-four-year-old poet, explained it this way: "There was a poem by Anne Sexton that I loved. I felt it was the poem I was meant to write, but she wrote it. It was the first poem I memorized because I loved it so much and wanted it to be mine. In the process of memorizing it, and saying it, I found that I no longer envied it because I possessed it."

Envy can be a warning sign. Envy can serve as a warning that your own life is not as you wish it to be. You can look at what you envy and focus on developing that quality in yourself. Envy can be a directional sign on the road map toward self-improvement.

Envy can be a goad, a stimulus for change. Envy, while usually felt as a lack in yourself, also provides the hope of someday getting what you want. "If she can do it, I can, too."

Eleanor, a forty-five-year-old psychology professor, says that envy gives her hope. "Envy is a kind of primitive, primal wanting. It is healthy to want. Some people shut down before wanting. Envy is a good thing to work with. It tells you that what you have is not enough."

Envy can become a way to get something for yourself. Jungian psychologist Judith Hubback says, "Envy is necessary for normal personality development." To grow up with a positive sense of yourself, to learn from others how to act in the world, you need to emulate others. The wanting, hungry, emulating part of envy *pushes you toward developing your wants, your needs, your personality:* "Envy spurs me to develop my own talents, to become more productive."

If you use envy as a positive guide, rather than to diminish yourself or hurt the person you envy, you are fully receiving the advantages envy has to offer.

Jealousy

Why isn't jealousy on this continuum? Envy and jealousy, though related, are not the same emotion. It's no wonder people confuse the two. We say we are "green with envy," or "green with jealousy." How do they compare?

When I envy, I want what you have. When I'm jealous, I'm afraid I'll lose what I already have. I may *envy* you your brass bed, but I'll rage with *jealousy* if you invite my lover to a pleasant afternoon in that bed!

Both emotions stem from a lack of self-esteem, from "not having my needs met" and "not feeling good about myself."

Envy, like our word "invidious," comes from the Latin *invidere*—to look hatefully at someone; hence the common phrase "to make invidious (hateful) comparisons." Jealousy, like the word "zealot," comes from the Greek *zelos*—vehemence, eagerness.

Envy is alive in two-person situations; jealousy involves three people. Jealousy dwells in the eternal triangle. In jealousy there is always the *rival*, the person I suspect of taking away my loved one.

Envy was born earlier and is more basic, more primitive. Psychoanalyst Melanie Klein says the earliest form of envy is the baby's envy of the mother's capacity to nurture and feed the infant. In abnormal development, a person never moves past this infantile envy. In normal development, envy becomes a wish to be as nurturing as your mother, to become a good mother yourself. Jealousy develops later in the baby's life, when the little girl wants to take Daddy from Mommy (or vice versa with the little boy).

Envy is the broader, more encompassing emotion. For example, Sally was married to Pete for seven years. She and Pete got divorced last year. Sally's friend, Julie, recently got married to Jeff. Sally is *envious* of Julie for being married, for having the status of a married person, for having a good relationship. However, Sally is not jealous. She doesn't have romantic feelings for Jeff.

What about when you feel envy and jealousy at the same time? A friend of mine calls it envy-gel. You hate your friend for having the beauty you feel you don't have and for trying to take your man away at the same time. If you can't handle envy, you're really in trouble when you've got envy-gel.

MASKS OF ENVY

Although there is a full range of envious feelings, we tend to see all envy as harmful. Because you were taught to rejoice in another's success and not to be upset, you may despise yourself for these feelings. As one writer expressed it, "I hate myself so much for feeling envy, that after the first pangs which alert me to recognize it, my impulse is not to control my envy but to deny it—to *hide* it from myself and others."

Unfortunately, hiding it does not work. Hidden envy turns against the self and keeps you from achieving your goals. That's why so many women thanked me for interviewing them and giving them a chance to respond to the "Women and Envy" questionnaire. One woman who enjoyed answering the questionnaire wrote, "Before, only God and my husband knew about these envious feelings. Now I can talk about these feelings with others."

Envy always costs something—some serenity, comfort around colleagues, sleep. Another cost is shame. Most people try to conceal the costs of envy by masking these feelings. As long as you mask your envy, you do not have to admit you are envious. The following methods are most commonly used to disguise your envy from yourself:

WALLOWING IN SELF-PITY

Do you use expressions like "Poor me, look how bad off I am, and look how lucky she is"? If so, you are masking your envious feelings by wallowing in self-pity. As one woman told me, "Instead of admitting my envious feelings, I run around crying, feeling put out and stamping my foot in a little girl's temper tantrum which doesn't work."

The mother of a patient of mine feels sorry for herself. She complains that her friends go on vacations while she has to stay home and take care of the pets. This mother gripes about how busy she is (which is why she can't take a vacation). She needs to sound busy because in fact her life feels empty. One reason her life feels empty is that she spends so much time hiding from and masking her own envy. In just feeling sorry for herself rather than addressing the problem, she cannot mobilize herself to make her life more meaningful or more fun. This same mother told her daughter, "I'm not envious. If you're envious, you never get ahead in life." That can be true: envy can be incapacitating.

WAILING ABOUT LIFE'S INJUSTICE

Envious people may disguise their true feelings by bewailing "the injustice of the world." "She did better than I did; I practiced hard—what a cruddy world I live in; life's not fair!" That's true. Life is not fair. The person who looks at what others have, and whines about what she doesn't have, is an envious person.

PRETENDING NOT TO CARE

In order to mask your envy, you pretend you are indifferent to the situation. For example, my mother is never able to take care of my child because she is bedridden. Therefore, I may be resentful of a mother who can help her daughter in this way. I pretend it doesn't bother me that my friend Sandy's mother can take care of her grandchildren whenever Sandy needs her to.

AVOIDANCE

A woman who is limited by her finances says, "I don't go shopping much. I don't look at the luxuries I can't have. I avoid situations that will provoke my envy." This is an appropriate response to her situation.

But using avoidance to an extreme can limit your life. After a period of pretending not to care about Sandy's helpful mother, I avoid Sandy and her mother when they are together. I miss my friendship with them.

Joan, a speech therapist with an envious mother, said that when she was growing up, she was envious of kids who came from "good" families. "I could not tolerate being with people who had nice mothers. I avoided many people I liked, people who could have provided me with a better life."

CRITICISM

When Marilyn Monroe was awarded the *Photoplay* Top Young Star Award in 1953, Joan Crawford commented, "Marilyn Monroe is a menace to family entertainment." This response of criticizing the successful person is very common. If you feel bad because of someone else's success, you might prefer to criticize that person—with the hope of feeling better about yourself. For example, I envy my close friend Kathy, who works out with weights and has "defined" muscles in her arms and legs. I critically say, "Look how she wastes time on her body when she could be helping others." Maury Silver, an expert on envy, tells us that if a criticism is designed to undercut rather than be constructive, it comes from envy.

Fake Praise

"It is hard to envy with style," says writer Harry Stein. If you try to praise and congratulate people you envy, you could wind up sounding insincere. Envy is sneaky; it shows itself when you least desire it to. Let's say I did terribly at my flute recital while my friend Susan was a big success, even though I had practiced much harder than she had. I congratulate Susan, but my congratulations come out sounding phony. It is difficult to fake my happiness. Susan can see that I am envious because I am not really expressing pleasure at her success.

Gossip

A familiar way to disguise your envy is to discover some failing or misfortune that has befallen the person you envy. That is why gossip—focusing on a person's human failings or weaknesses—may give you a momentary sense of relief and power. You try to feel better about yourself by devaluing the person you envy. Since you feel small, you try to be bigger by making the one you envy small. It's called "cutting someone down to size."

Evoke Envy in Others

People who make others feel envious are often protecting themselves. They evoke envy in others, exhibiting the "see how great I am" syndrome, the "don't you wish you were like me?" pattern. Such people arrange things so they do not have to experience *their* envious feelings. Instead, they get people to envy *them*. They are thus saved from the truth of their own negative feelings. Sometimes, of course, the attempt appears pathetic because it is too obvious to be effective.

I know about evoking envy. When I was fourteen and my brother was twelve, he took French lessons and I did not. But I was better at learning languages than he. Feeling insecure for whatever reasons and not wanting to admit my envy of his being a boy and therefore "special," I wanted him to envy me. When he wasn't noticing, I memorized the French poem he had such difficulty learning. I would go around the house singing the French phrases, infuriating him, but also rubbing it in that I was better at languages.

IDEALIZE THE PERSON YOU ENVY

Another way not to admit your envy is to rush at the person you envy, shouting, "Look how great *you* are!" You idealize the other person and make her more wonderful than she is. If she is so terrific, then she is out of reach of competition. If you can never match her, if she is "too good to be true," then she is not true, and you can thus avoid real feelings of envy toward her.

If you focus on how wonderful the other person is, you do not have to feel any ill feelings toward her or yourself. A woman from New Brunswick, New Jersey, writes, "I resent that some enviers denigrate my accomplishments, almost as much as I resent the other type of enviers fawning on me and getting vicarious thrills. The vicarious types (fawners) are worse, because they confuse me, and because if I mistake them for real friends and honest admirers, I get badly hurt when I realize that they (1) will not tolerate any failure in me and still be friends, and (2) are secretly hoping for me to fail."

A related form of idealization is the exaggerated wish to help the person you envy, the urge to take care of her. Doting, fawning, and doing everything possible to make her feel good are all ways not to experience what may be your deeper motive—envy. After all, you only wish to help.

Beware the person who "only wants to help," because people often hide their self-interest. If someone wants to help you, while wanting nothing for herself, she may be deceiving herself and might bear a grudge later. She might secretly end up envying you for receiving so much kindness.

Project Your Envy Outward

An important way we mask feeling envious is to pretend that someone else is the envious person. This mechanism, putting our envious feelings onto someone else, is called *projection*. For example, Andrea says she does not envy Janet's money. Instead, says Andrea, "It's my spiritual values that are important."

However, Andrea's attention is constantly on the details of Janet's spending. She can tell you how many pairs of earrings Janet owns, how much money (down to the last cent) Janet spent on mini-blinds, and (down to the last peso) how much Janet spent in Puerto Vallarta last winter. Yet Andrea insists that Janet envies her spiritual values.

Janet, the extravagant spender, never mentions the wish for a more spiritual life. She is not complaining. It becomes obvious that the envious one is Andrea, not Janet.

The Envious Snob

We all know a snob—someone who acts as though she were better off than you, someone who walks around with her superior nose in the air. A snob is two-faced. One side is superiority; turn her around, and you will find envy.

Take this story. My friend Terry is a snob. He won't eat at fancy Berkeley restaurants like Chez Panisse because they are "too cute." Without the finest seat at the opera, he complains. As for movies, an Academy Award means nothing—the only passable movie is a "sleeper" with Pauline Kael's *New Yorker* certification. He notices if your clothes are from Saks. If so, he tries to get to know you better. He wouldn't be seen at a laundromat. When Terry quotes Marcel, you are, of course, supposed to know he means Proust. His overheating car has been a source of embarrassment, but he won't buy an affordable American or Japanese car. It must be a BMW.

Terry is not happy. His snobbishness stems from feelings of inferiority and envy. He needs to put down people he considers unsophisticated. Secretly he thinks these people have more fun than he.

He first realized this pattern while visiting Norway, sailing down the fjords on a boat with a friend. A group of American tourists were on board, the leader of whom was a brittle little woman in a tour guide's uniform complete with a hat advertising "Bennett Tours." Terry and his friend felt immediate contempt for these loud, crass tourists. They felt, These people are beneath us. We are glad not to be a part of their group.

As they scoffed at her, the tour guide put on a show for her group. Standing at the edge of the boat, she extended her arm, holding up a cracker, waiting expectantly for a seagull to come and grab it. The seagulls circled, hovering over the cracker for some time before one was brave enough to swoop down and attack the cracker. The whole boat was watching with interest, but Terry and his friend merely smirked to themselves, "What silly little pleasures!"

The group got off the boat at the next stop while Terry and his friend continued down the fjords. But as soon as the ship set sail once again, lo and behold!—Terry and his friend couldn't wait to put a cracker out for a seagull. Soon a flock of seagulls were following the boat as Terry and his friend enjoyed their "silly little pleasures."

Terry then understood that he had envied the tour leader's sense of play. Instead of confessing their envy, he and his friend had put down the little woman with the Bennett Tours hat and acted like snobs when they'd really wanted to share in the fun the woman was having. Now Terry laughs when he sounds like a snob.

Look for envy beneath the contempt of a snob.

BECOME A CLONE

One way not to acknowledge your envy is to become just like the person you envy. If you *become her,* then (you reason) you won't have envious feelings toward her. The problem here, of course, is losing your identity and becoming a clone. In addition, the person you envy often reacts with hostility, since becoming a clone is, in effect, encroaching on someone else's territory and individuality. What you are saying is, "I want to be you. I don't want *you* to be you." Emulation, on the other hand, is a compliment; it's saying, "I want to be *like* you, similar to you, but different."

An article by Judith Viorst in *Redbook* magazine gives an example of this tendency to become a clone. Joan envied Emily so much that she acquired Emily's mannerisms, her hairdo, her perfume, her politics, and her type of car. Emily had a cocker spaniel and Joan bought one too—with the same colorings. Said Emily, "I swear that if Joan could have, she would have opened her shopping bag and put everything from my apartment inside it, including me."

The wish to be exactly the same as the person you envy can produce eerie feelings—in the person. A forty-two-year-old San Francisco lawyer told me about another lawyer, Karen: "Karen was so envious of me for being creative and having a low-key attitude toward life that she just attached herself to me, became a chameleon, took on my qualities and interests." To be envied is often to be carefully and closely observed. "I felt it was all very creepy, like my life was literally being invaded. She was trying to become me, and *I* was having a hard enough time being me in the first place."

Suffer Quietly

One familiar method of masking envy is to leave your successful friend alone and keep your mean feelings to yourself, to suffer in silence. You feel bad but pretend you've withdrawn for some other reason. "I just might ignore my envy, but then I feel worse," said one woman. "It doesn't work when I withdraw and don't talk to anyone about it. When I'm ashamed of it, and alone in it, my envy increases."

Remember, the experience of envy does not define us as individuals. It's what we do with this feeling that counts.

Wicked Queen Envy

As our continuum illustrates, envy involves both resentment and desire. Resentments can be small, or they can become all-consuming. What makes the difference? As an envious person, you cannot stand the idea that someone else is more successful, luckier, richer, prettier, happier, smarter, more powerful, or more interesting than you are.

Envy becomes a problem when it is no longer suffering quietly or a feeling of the moment. As one woman described, "It becomes envy when it lasts more than a minute." You imagine your future will be the same as the present. You dread you will *never* have what the other person has. This can drive you to desperation. *The fear that things won't work out for you, that you will never have what you want, creates envy.*

When envy becomes the core of your being, and you cannot think of anything else, it has become poisonous. Be careful when you look around and you envy everyone you see. You are feeding yourself the poisonous apple of envy.

What begins as simple envy of the moment can lead you through a vicious cycle: from envy to self-pity to aloneness. Suzanne McNear, writing in a *Cosmopolitan* article, illustrates this: She envied a woman who published a book, while hers was being rejected. Then she told everyone the book was a success because it was crass and her book was a work of art.

After that I began to envy every friend who'd ever written a book, then friends who had good jobs, then people who could afford to travel. It was like poison ivy. I loathed myself. Other people can write and I can't . . . What else can I do? Nothing. But I have to work because I have no one to take care of me. Poor me. What I really need is a vacation, but where can I go and with whom will I go? Maybe I'll go alone, but then nobody would pay attention to me, because I'm old and fat and pale and uninteresting. I could ask people for dinner but the apartment is uninteresting and I can't cook anyway. Everyone else is taking Chinese cooking lessons, and I can't even boil rice.

DESTRUCTIVE ENVY

At its most extreme, envy doesn't only hurt you—you pass the poison apple to someone else. In his book *Envy: A Theory of Social Behavior,* Helmut Schoeck has devoted a whole section to murders resulting from envy. In northern California, we recently read about the trial of Bernadette Protti, who stabbed her schoolmate, Kirsten Costos, to death. Why? Bernadette, fifteen years old, embarrassed by her parents and her home and feeling excluded, envied pretty, popular Kirsten who, testimony revealed, had become a symbol of the "success and popularity Bernadette could not achieve" (*San Francisco Chronicle, March 14, 1985*).

Envy is Universal

Destructive envy, the kind that leads to murder, is clearly not typical. But envy itself is everywhere.

Anthropologist George Foster has studied envy in many primitive and peasant societies. He finds that all human beings envy, that envy is visible in every society.

Sociologist Helmut Schoeck believes that "envy lies at the core of man's life as a social being." He points out that people are always potentially envious. As he puts it, envy is one of the "most disturbing and carefully concealed, yet most basic facts of human existence at all levels of cultural development."

Why does everyone envy? Because everyone wants to feel good, to have his or her needs met. If you see someone else having what you want, you respond with natural self-interest. You want what you feel will make you satisfied. The list is *endless*. You can forever find in someone else what you feel you do not have.

One woman reported: "I envy women who have achieved the goals I would like to reach: the old lady, with her tiny cottage, walking the beach at dawn; people laughing; lovers in the first stages of discovery; the herb lady high in the mountains; anyone with more knowledge and insight than I possess; and a white-haired woman driving a red XKE convertible."

What do you envy?

I asked three hundred women what they envy. The list of answers filled fifty single-spaced typed pages. Here are a few of the responses.

Job status • job satisfaction • income • business savvy • free time • not having to work • travel • inherited money • lottery winners • good health • being able to pull yourself out of despair in middle age • ambition • being uninhibited • knowing what you want • fame • boyfriends • supportive and successful husbands • being articulate • a lasting marriage • appreciative children • generous relatives • a parent's unshakable faith and love • grandchildren • being able to combine professional and personal lives with ease • culinary prowess • being a woman your daughter admires • assertiveness • competence • being relaxed about sex • high cheekbones • being heterosexual and able to hold hands with and kiss a lover in a shopping mall • friendliness • self-discipline • athletic ability • self-esteem • inner calm • a nice house • material possessions • style • being organized • personal success • nurturing friendships • leadership qualities • ability to spend money easily • happiness • power • beauty • a good figure • musical talent • a man's freedom to be out alone at night • popularity • creativity • intelligence • knowing how to flirt • education • happy childhood • youth • not caring about what others think • love • and the ability to find simple pleasure in day-to-day life *without envying others*.

WHY YOU ENVY

Psychologists make a fuss about exactly what causes envy and when it begins in the child's life. *No one really knows*. But we do know what is common to all psychological theories of envy and why some people are more envious than others.

What Is Common to All Theories of Envy

Some psychological theories hold that envy begins at birth, that a baby is born with envy. British psychoanalyst Melanie Klein was the first to be convinced, from observing newborns, that envy is constitutional and innate in the infant. Klein believes that the infant envies the mother's breast (or bottle) because it is the source of food; when the breast is taken away—there you have it—envy.

Psychiatrists such as Heinz Kohut, D. W. Winnicott, and Leslie Farber believe that envy comes later in life, after the baby and the mother are more separate, after the infant has truly felt deprived. I agree with them. After all, for some infants, the breast is there when needed. Sure, the infant wants what the mother has, but I don't believe this desire is envy because at first the infant is too blended and fused with the mother. Envy develops gradually, as a child has more and more frustrating experiences and develops a sense of who he or she is apart from the mother. Envy arises as the child is able to fantasize and imagine what it would like to have. For some children, toy envy is stronger than breast envy.

All theories agree that you envy because you feel a lack of something. You imagine that what the other person has will make you happy, will provide something missing in you. Envy comes from not getting what you need and from feeling humiliated.

"How appetizing is the fish on the other man's table," says an old proverb. In a restaurant, do you ever long for the food on the platter whizzing by and wish you had ordered that instead?

To envy, you must first compare and then, in the comparison, find you lack something. The wicked queen compared, she felt a lack, and she couldn't stand the pain of inferiority. Psychologists call this feeling of inferiority a "lack of self-esteem." They talk about an "actual self" (who you feel you really are) and an "ideal self" (who you want to be). It is the *comparison* between your actual self and your ideal self that makes you envy.

In your comparisons, you find differences. You see your friend, boss, employee, lover, child, or parent as the person you want to be. You feel she or he has the "goodies," and the felt difference between you hurts.

In addition to a feeling of deprivation, envy is also the wish for more.

"I wish I were six inches taller," explained Elise. "I could play better tennis. I wouldn't have to look at everyone's belly button in an elevator. If I were blond, I wouldn't have to shave my legs every day. You see, I envy women who are tall and blond." I asked Elise how she might better handle her envy. "I would grow six more inches and bleach my hair!"

How the Drama of Envy Unfolds

Have you ever wondered, "Why am I so envious? Why are some people more confident and less envious than I am? How did I get to be like this?"

Primarily, you envy because *you look outside of yourself to feel good about yourself.* As a child, you were not taught that you are a good enough person. You did not feel loved for who you are, but, rather, for how you compared with your sister, brother, neighbor, or parents' ideal of who you should be. You falsely believe that good feelings will come from acquiring new things or from being like so and so, but what you long for are only symbols of parental love, symbols of self-love.

You do not feel self-worth because you were not given essential "mirroring" as a child. As psychoanalyst Alice Miller tells us, the child needs "mirroring" to be seen, to be made to feel important, admired, understood, echoed, affirmed. By "mirroring," the mother gives the child a positive reflection, a positive interpretation of who she is. The mirroring is what Snow White needed, but her mother stole the show—and the mirror.

As the child who is positively mirrored grows up, she needs the mirror less because she knows, inside herself, that she is somebody of value. This child has less need to envy.

An example of good mirroring: A child brings a drawing home from nursery school. The loving mother takes the time to look at it, comments on the color, asks the child a few questions, shows the drawing to other people, sometimes frames it and puts it up on the wall or refrigerator.

This gives the child a sense that she is important and that her work is important. She thinks, Why, I can draw! I am somebody. And later in life, if her mother offers enough good mirroring, the acquired self-worth can translate as, "I don't need Sally's riches, beauty, acclaim, new running shoes, or a membership in Club Med to feel good about myself. I am satisfied as I am."

Many present-day psychologists recognize the importance of mirroring for a child. Dr. Heinz Kohut, Freudian psychoanalyst and founder of self-psychology, was one of the first to emphasize mirroring's function. His example of a good mirror/mother is of the toddler and her mother at the park. The toddler begins to walk slowly away from her mother, then looks back and sees her mother smiling at her with pride. This child feels, I am somebody even while I'm going away from my mother.

The child who is adequately mirrored feels:

- My parents see me as I am, rather than their fantasy of who I am.

- My parents understand me when I try to express my feelings, and they don't laugh at me.
- My parents have their own talents and courage, and they do not depend on me to boost their ego and make them feel good about who they are.
- When I am happy, I act happy. When I am sad, I act sad. I do not have to look cheerful for anyone else. . . . I can be angry, and no one will get a headache or die because of it. . . . I can rage without losing my parents.

The child who does not receive adequate mirroring is more likely to get caught in the Snow White syndrome because when she leaves her mother, her mother fails to be proud and approving. The mother may pretend to be proud. But the daughter, overly sensitive to her mother's reaction, feels the mother's distress about being surpassed and left behind.

Of course, it's impossible to provide ideal mirroring *all* the time. But if the mother is self-centered, as the wicked queen certainly was, and uses the child for her own needs, we have a child who does not experience her own uniqueness or specialness. Hence, an envious child.

Perhaps the mother who is not a good mirror did not receive adequate mirroring from her own mother, from her mate or friends, or (as is true in most cases) from the prevailing patriarchical culture with its focus on women's looks, bodies, and other external features. This mother now seeks what she lacks from her own young daughter, a child who can be controlled, who won't desert her for years, who is centered on her. This child remains in the Snow White syndrome, fearful of surpassing her mother. And this mother uses the child to be the mirror she never had.

Such a child feels there is something wrong with her, especially if she is not able to make her mother happy. So she compares herself with others. She thinks others seem more fulfilled and happier than she is. Because she feels empty, she envies what she imagines as someone else's abundance. She is angry at her mother for not giving her good feelings about herself, and she is angry at herself for not feeling good in the first place. As this child becomes an adult, she feels powerless and looks more and more outside herself for the positive reflection for which she feels so desperate.

This reflection really needs to come from within. The things our grown-up child wants only symbolize the good feeling she longs for, which has to come from a feeling about herself and who she is, not from outer possessions. This is why her envy is endless. She whines, "Mabel drives a Cadillac. Mabel seems to be happy, to feel good. Maybe if I drove a Cadillac (or a Mercedes or BMW), I could be happy." It doesn't work that way.

Why Do Some People Envy More Than Others?

If you feel that envy rules you, you may not have received adequate mirroring. But there are many other reasons that people feel envy.

- *Your parents may have made you feel* too *special and superior*. This attention gives you an exaggerated picture of yourself. You might envy someone's peace of mind, inner calm, lack of a need to show off. If so, you still did not receive adequate mirroring, because your parents did not give you a realistic appraisal of who you are. You can't accept being ordinary, regular, average. You now have inner standards of excellence and perfection that are hard or impossible to meet. You envy anyone who seems to be more nearly perfect, or more comfortable being imperfect than you are. Your expectations for happiness are probably too high. You fail to accept your existential condition: life is fraught with disappointments, sadness, illness, and death.
- *You may have experienced a sudden change in a situation or relationship*. A major cause for envy arises when two people have been relatively equal, and a change in status occurs. For example, two women have been equals at work. Suddenly one is promoted, the other is kept at the same level. This abrupt change will likely provoke envy in the woman who is not promoted.
- *You are affected by how envious your parents were and whether they could admit their envy*. If they did not admit their envy, but it was obvious, you are more likely to be envious yourself.
- *You envy because there are basic limitations in life*. As a child, your parents may not have earned enough money to

afford the comforts your friends had. You envied those friends because you wanted the financial security that they had and that you were deprived of. Or, if you have a physical disability, you may envy the person who is strong, whole, athletic, muscular, and active. I interviewed five women with life-threatening diseases. They envied the good health of others, and understandably so. Or you may be part of a minority group that has experienced unequal opportunities in our society. Envy screams at limitations, especially when something essential is denied you.

But what about people who had adequate mirroring or who are healthy and have every opportunity? What about a person in business who was truly loved by his or her parents, yet out of envy is willing to do anything to get ahead? Why do these people envy? In addition to the more individual and personal causes of envy, there are also social and cultural reasons for our current envy epidemic.

CHAPTER 3

The Current Explosion of Envy

Your great-great-grandmother felt envy; so do you. But she probably felt much less envy than you do; and your grandchildren may suffer even sharper pangs than the two of you put together. What's going on? Why is there an explosion of envy in our 1980s American society?

Examining envy from the perspective of our personal histories is not enough. Envy is also a cultural and social problem.

If I ask you, "Are you equal to everyone else?" you will probably retort, "You bet." This is the land of opportunity, where for over two hundred years people have sought the American dream on streets supposedly paved with gold. But the American dream is a movie run on the projector of envy. Our society not only encourages envy, it actually requires envy to maintain itself. We encourage everyone to earn more money, to look better, to do better, to learn more, to have more. Our society creates inevitable comparison and inevitable dissatisfaction. If you're at the bottom of the pecking order, you'd better pull yourself up by your bootstraps; if you've risen to the top, you'd better start worrying, because you've got more than your share and someone is bound to envy you, maybe even try to take it from you.

Our American society promises equality; we're told everything and anything is possible. With this promise comes envy, because we do not provide the equality we promise.

Let's look at the reasons for our current explosion of envy.

We are a nation of immigrants coming to the land of

opportunity. From the time of the *Mayflower* through the days of Ellis Island through the mass immigration of the last decade, people have flocked from all over the world to seek safety and fortune on American soil. With the exception of the Native Americans, whose home this was, and the black slaves, who were brought here in chains, people have always come to this land with the expectation that life would be better than it was in the places they'd left behind.

People today are still leaving homelands because of war, revolution, or lack of opportunity. They see what is possible for them here, and envy those who have what they hoped to find.

Increased visibility between classes of people. At one time in history, servants were servants and lords were lords. Sons and daughters expected to become what their parents were. A slow historical change took place after the French Revolution through the Industrial Revolution through the Age of Jacksonian Democracy. Wealth became more accessible. Servants thought they could become, if not a lord, then at least rich and famous.

It might seem as though you would feel more envy if you knew that you had to remain a servant. However, envy is more intense when there is a possibility of getting what you desire, when there is *less* social distance between you and the person you envy. Today, our national expectation is that any child can grow up to become president. We are told we can become anything we want, regardless of race, religion, class, or sex.

In America, there was an attempt to reduce class boundaries by allowing everyone a supposed equal access to money, education, and opportunity. People thought they could move freely from one class to another, but it wasn't so easy; some feared there wouldn't be enough for everyone, that they couldn't have the same as everyone else. This is the fear of limited good and anthropologist George Foster believes it to be the cause, economically and psychologically, of envy.

Most societies consist of the "haves" and the "have-nots." However, in preindustrial societies, the have-nots rarely sat down to lunch with the haves. The have-nots did not watch the haves devour steak while they ate rice. Foster believes that envy is more prevalent in "deprivation societies," where rich people with well-being and power are all too visible to those who have less. The United States is definitely a deprivation society.

Most of us value the increased work opportunities and increased wealth our society offers, but there's a price to pay: envy. With increased social mobility between classes of people, wealth and prestige become more visible. People want what is visible and close at hand. But the problem is still one of failed expectations. The truth is, that although we are told the poor can become rich, the distribution of wealth in our country has remained relatively unchanged for more than fifty years. The poor generally do not become rich, but they might become less poor. And they certainly become envious.

What is true about the breakdown of class distinctions is also increasingly true in the realm of race and sex. Previously oppressed groups, like racial minorities and women, have seen what's available and want to equal those at the top.

The movement of the past one hundred years has been away from a patient waiting for equality toward an active fight to be more equal to the haves of society. Keeping segments of a population segregated is a powerful way to reduce envy. It's hard to envy what you don't see.

Our consumer economy. In nineteenth-century America, people placed a tremendous importance on hard work, self-discipline, and saving for the future. A worker labored not only to provide for himself and his family. He also felt a moral obligation to produce what society as a whole needed.

Today we've moved from this production economy toward a consumer economy. Now a worker toils primarily to have money to buy the fruits of his labor. People focus on individual success and accomplishment, and enjoy their own superiority. Many define their worth by what they own and what they look like, rather than how hard they work, or their contribution to the community. This self-preoccupation provides fertile soil for envy.

For many reasons—religious, social, economic—people in the nineteenth century did not particularly believe in the possibility of satisfaction in their lifetime, only after death. Now we assume that instant gratification is a birthright. Our technological advances have led to more goods, more material wealth, more leisure time, and greater access to information and entertainment.

People place tremendous importance on fulfilling their needs— "I want it, I want it now!" You are told that your needs will be satisfied by purchasing the latest product. But satisfaction remains always just beyond your reach. As soon as you satisfy a need by buying something, the object is outdated or the fashion has changed, and you're left still wanting. You're also left envious of the person who has just acquired the newest model.

Unrealistic expectations. Those of us in the "me generation" are post-World War II babies. Fewer of us lived, as earlier generations had, in close proximity to our grandparents and extended families. The attention of our parents and all the benefits of post-war prosperity were lavished upon us. Many middle-class children were given everything, including the message that they should be the best. Mothers looked to their children to fulfill their own dreams and aspirations. Fathers also wanted their children to be the best at everything they tried.

What we were not given is what earlier generations and less affluent members of society knew from birth: there are limits to what one human being can have and achieve. Since we expect it all, we tend to feel envious when someone else has achieved what we feel we have not. There's also a gnawing feeling that there is something wrong if we don't have what the Joneses have, so why not push a little harder?

Advertising. Advertising reminds you that you don't have what your neighbor has. This six-billion-dollar-a-day industry in the United States alone whets your appetite in order to keep the economy going. Today's economy needs envious people who will buy now. Advertising tells us what our "needs" are. Look at the sleek blonde in her sexy Mercedes with her new face cream. Look at a world full of beautiful objects that you, too, can possess. Advertising makes everything conspicuous, public, and a catalyst for envy.

Advertising feeds your dissatisfaction, telling you that you never have enough. Therefore, you want more. There is forever something that "so-and-so" has that you don't have. What *didn't* you get for Christmas?

In this society of conspicuous consumption, we encourage envy by impressing others. We say, in effect, "Look at me! Look how much I own! Look how much more successful *I* am than *you* are! Look how much more *I* have than *you* have! If you envy me, that proves I am successful." Have you seen the Volkswagen Beetle with a bumper sticker that says, "My *other* car is a Porsche"? Or the poster of model Cheryl Tiegs carrying a sign that reads, "Don't you want to look like me?"

Mass media. Advertising is able to have such a force on our emotions because in today's world any image, phrase, or jingle can be made immediately available to just about everybody.

Information about those Joneses we're trying to keep up with appears in every newspaper, magazine, subway, billboard, TV commercial, sitcom, movie house, and, soon, on every computer screen. There are no limits to our desires because we see every possibility right smack in front of us.

There are many causes for our current explosion of envy: expectations of immigrants; the breakdown of class, race, and sex barriers and the increased visibility that brings; our consumer economy; overpreoccupation with ourselves; unrealistic expectations; advertising; and mass media. While these new causes of envy have been developing, our society has also been eliminating the protective devices other cultures employ against envy.

LOSS OF SOCIAL PROTECTIONS AGAINST ENVY

Other cultures have many societal protections against the green-eyed monster. For example, people in other cultures don't compliment freely. They believe in the evil eye, they hide what they have, they don't brag, and they have many ways to share. Let's examine these protections and observe how they operate elsewhere in contrast with America today.

The Compliment

A compliment displays envy. In other cultures, people fear the compliment and protect themselves by limiting its use. They believe that a person will be "brought down," or made to fail, if he or she prospers more than a neighbor. The one who prospers will thus insist his good fortune is a matter of luck, that he does not deserve to be successful, that his success is a matter of fate or God's will—not caused by any personal effort: this is quite the opposite of our society's "you're responsible for everything" philosophy.

Complimenting exposes a person to the dangers of envy. If a Greek shepherd is told his sheep are in fine condition, he feels threatened, afraid something terrible will happen to his flock, fears he will be singled out and attacked by the forces of envy.

Greeks believe that an admirer wants to acquire what he admires, even though the wish may not be conscious. If the admirer cannot acquire what he wants, he will be frustrated and envious—therefore dangerous. In many societies, if you admire something, the person who owns it will give it to you in an attempt to ward off your harmful envy.

In many parts of the globe, people fear praise. In India, Egypt, the Middle East, and southern Asia, for example, a mother would be as unlikely to show her new baby in public as an American mother would be to expose her new baby to a contagious disease. Indian parents do not praise their children for doing well or for offering to work around the house. Servants likewise do not accept praise. And a husband seldom praises his wife's cooking. If you know these patterns, you will avoid praising an Indian too much.

When people compliment you, they may be admitting they would like to have what you have. Have you had the feeling of not knowing how to react when praise comes your way? Do you deny its truth? Do you say "thank you" because it *is* true and adds to your self-esteem? You may be confused as to how to respond because you sense the envy behind the praise. "You look good today," says Max, and Mort replies, "Appearances are deceiving. My health is very weak. Last week I was almost dying."

Americans compliment each other quite freely. In this way, we encourage envy. Your neighbor may say, "Wow, you look great today! That was a terrific meal you cooked! Your house looks so clean; how do you do it? Your child is beautiful, talented, adorable, and oh, those curls!" Your house, your car, your work, your generosity, your home improvements, your waistline—almost everything about you is visible and available for compliments. In fact, Americans seek compliments. If you get dressed up for a party and no one compliments you, you wonder what you did wrong.

Our excess of complimenting suggests that a traditional protection against envy has been lost in our society. In societies where compliments are avoided like the plague, envy is less problematic.

The Evil Eye

Belief in the evil eye and protections against the evil eye are attempts to ward off envy. In many European and Asian cultures, envy is expressed directly through a practice of witchcraft, such as looking with an evil eye. The evil eye is an envious look that actively projects harm onto whatever is most valued. The glance of the person possessing the evil eye has the power to hurt you.

According to researchers, the evil eye creates "loss of crops, wasting of animals, rotting of pork, disease, sterility, abortion, and mental disorders." A hungry person may give an envious look to someone who is eating. The person eating gets a stomach ache, slumps over, and can't eat anymore. The hungry person is then accused of possessing the evil eye.

Perhaps the satisfied eater slumped over because the food was rotten. However, the blame for the stomach ache is usually placed on the envy of the hungry person. In primitive societies, the cause of many disasters is unknown. Believing in the evil eye makes sense of unknown happenings. Envy offers an obvious reason for something going wrong. Thus, anyone who has more than anyone else may fear being envied. And people refrain from expressing envy directly, because they know they may then be suspected of harming the person they envy.

Who is suspected of possessing the evil eye? Women are most often suspected. They are at a physical and social disadvantage and are therefore likely to feel deprived and envious. Barrenness, for example, could make a woman suspect.

Others suspected of possessing the evil eye are strangers, as are people with physical defects or unusual features, such as blue eyes where they are rare or eyebrows that meet above the nose. Beggars are also suspect; that is one reason people give them money—to avoid their envy.

India has a special class of people called untouchables. Born to low status, poor ancestry, and deprivation, untouchables are considered to possess the evil eye. In Ethiopia, the evil eye is cast by similar people, called *Buda*, who are poor, own no land, and inherit low status at birth. Throughout history, the evil eye has most often been imputed to the poor, the unattractive, the landless, the uneducated—in other words, those with the clearest justification to feel and express envy.

Precautions against the evil eye. Societies that fear the evil eye have elaborate ways of guarding against it. In Italy, peasants try to ward off the evil eye by hanging strips of garlic, red chilis, or using red paint at the door entrance. Red is an important color in the prevention of the evil eye. In India, women wear a red spot on their foreheads for protection. Some American-born mothers of

Eastern European descent still use a red ribbon to protect their newborn children from the evil eye.

Wearing charms and amulets is another precaution. In Italian cultures, people wear the horn of a billy goat and a mermaid with a tail of chili. Jewish people wear the Star of David for protection; Christian people wear a cross.

Another way to ward off the evil eye is to make the "feige"—a gesture popular with many Jews and Christians—pressing the right thumb between the middle and first finger. Spitting is another precaution, as is throwing salt over the shoulder. You can sweep your house many times a day or recite various chants to get rid of the evil eye. "Gesundheit" or "God bless you" means you in no way wish ill health on the person sneezing, reassuring the sneezer you are not casting the evil eye.

A Jewish protection against envy is to say, "Kayn aynhoreh," when you compliment. This phrase means "an evil eye shall not befall you" and attempts to assure the person you compliment that you are not envious. In many cultures, the proper response to someone wearing new clothing is "Wear it in good health," in order to protect them from evil that might follow their successful purchase.

For cultures believing in the evil eye, there are almost as many ways to protect yourself from being envied as there are reasons to envy. In America, we don't have enough ways to deal successfully with the fear of envy, and if we used any of the methods mentioned above, we'd probably be laughed at.

People who believe in the evil eye guard carefully what they have, fearful that it will be taken away. They also avoid overtly wanting or wishing for anything that would place them under suspicion of having the evil eye. In contrast, today's aspiring Americans wish for things without restraint. No wonder envy is more prevalent: we are more encouraged to want, and at the same time we have fewer protections against envy.

Bragging

In societies that believe in the evil eye, people do not flaunt what they have. In small towns, for example, villagers opposed using glass windows in their homes, not for fear of burglars, but because people would be able to look inside and envy what they saw.

While Americans retain some remnants of this moral precaution, bragging—showing off what we have—is encouraged. We have big picture windows, drive fancy cars, wear expensive or flashy clothes, eat abundantly in restaurants, entertain in large and beautifully furnished homes, expose sexy bodies, and dress our children in designer clothes. Movies and literature of the 1930s and 1940s demonstrated that ostentation was a serious social error. Now, in the 1980s, there's a license to ostentatiousness.

Many women don't brag about their pregnancy too early in their term. In Mexico, Latin America, and the Mediterranean, for example, women often do not admit they are pregnant until it shows. This fear stems from a superstition that bragging too openly could harm the fetus.

We used to treat pregnancy as an illness, hiding it, confining it. But now pregnant women wear shirts reading "BABY" with an arrow pointing to the abdomen. In other words, "If you've got it, flaunt it."

In other countries, a forty-day quarantine period after a birth protects both mother and baby from envious stares and compliments until both are stronger and more able to deal with envy.

Forced Sharing

In winter, an Eskimo housewife inside her igloo is able to conceal some of the better pieces of meat before the guests arrive. In summer, when most of the cooking is done outside, she has to share whatever she has.

If one Navaho feels he's better off than the rest, he also feels under social obligation to share the wealth, to lavish gifts on others. If he does not share, witchcraft and the whispered voice of envy will make his life miserable.

Many societies have rituals, parties to equalize the wealth. Someone who has achieved more wealth than others, for example, will give a party for the community that puts him in debt and reduces him temporarily to a level below that of his previously poorer neighbors. Most Americans do not feel obligated to share what they have.

Remaining Social Protections Against Envy

Present-day Americans haven't lost all protections against envy, however. We still employ at least one favorite way to protect ourselves: denying what we have. We may pretend that what we have is worthless. For example, if someone says she likes what you just bought and you fear being envied, you may reply, "Really? I'm not sure I like it." In many countries, when someone admires what you are wearing, you might say, "Here, take it. It's yours." This is only symbolic sharing, because the person who is giving the praise rarely accepts the offer of the gift.

Americans ward off envy by saying, "Oh, it's really nothing at all." Such false modesty shows a formal allegiance to American values of equality—it lets you have your croissant and eat it, too.

As a successful American, you might also use the following approach: If you have been successful, say, in a job promotion, and you anticipate being envied, you quickly compliment the other person on how she is doing in her job. But to do this effectively, you have to spot the envier approaching.

Another social protection we use to guard against envy is giving a sop, a token or substitute gift, to help ease the disappointment for someone who has lost a competition or has not been successful. One form of this symbolic sharing is a "booby prize." Another is inviting friends over to drink in celebration of something newly purchased, such as a car. Many traveling Americans bring home presents to their friends and relatives who have stayed at home. During the trip, the traveler worries about choosing the right gift for each person, hoping to avert envy when he or she shows off beautiful snapshots and souvenirs. Fathers give cigars at the birth of a baby. Thanksgiving and Christmas baskets given to poorer families is another example of sharing.

It is sometimes hard to distinguish between the fear of being envied and pure generosity—the two traits are intertwined. For example, the custom of giving little gifts to all the children at a birthday party as a way of keeping them from becoming envious of the loot the birthday child has acquired is also an act of generosity.

Of course, another strong defense against being envied is the Snow White syndrome, holding yourself back and thus remaining unsuccessful. This precaution against being envied occurs across sex, race, and class barriers.

As an American in the 1980s, you are likely to experience more envy in many aspects of your life. Yet you do not have the same rituals and precautions to protect yourself from this increase in envy. Therefore, Americans have fewer ways to avoid, reduce, and conquer envy than other societies have had.

MALE ENVY OF WOMEN

The current explosion of envy in the United States hits everyone to some extent. However, one particular problem arises because we have begun to dismantle the barriers between the privileges of men and those of women. One major dismantling, an example of segregation breaking down, is women's liberation, fueled by women's envy of the power men have traditionally held. But when a person feels threatened, feels that he is likely to lose his position in the world, his response is often one of anger and fear. All social solutions to problems of inequality create a reaction or backlash. As women in this culture gain rights and privileges that have previously belonged to men, there is a backlash, and men may well respond with envy.

We've all read about the subjugation of women. We know that for the past three thousand years women have been segregated, undermined, stereotyped, and been granted few economic and political rights.

But now women are entering the male sphere. We can be lawyers, doctors, plumbers, astronauts, carpenters, architects, economists, contractors, truck drivers, riveters, and Supreme Court justices; we wield power in the male world of decision making and power brokering. We are increasingly listened to and admired, and can aspire to being president of the United States.

Women are questioning previous stereotypes about themselves, while demanding equality in the workplace and still raising children. Men today have more arenas in which to feel envy toward women. An extreme stereotype of the envious male is the man who feels considerable rage at the equality women are gaining.

Male Chauvinism

When we think of extreme stereotypes about women, we think of male chauvinism. The term "chauvinism" comes from Nicolas Chauvin, a soldier of the French Revolution and the Napoleonic Wars. Wounded in battle many times, he received a small pension and became famous for his devotion to Napoleon. Chauvinism came to mean blind patriotism; male chauvinism, in turn, came to mean blind allegiance to male stereotypes—and the corresponding attitude toward women.

The male chauvinist firmly believes in his superiority. He belittles women. Male chauvinism, at a psychological level, is a way to avoid feeling the little boy's dependence on his mother. The male chauvinist dislikes what reminds him of being a little boy: neediness, dependency, tenderness, and weakness. As long as he devalues women, he does not have to envy her strengths. He imagines he, not the mother or the woman, reigns supreme.

Male Envy

During the Stone Age, both men and women worshiped the Great Goddess. Archaeologists and anthropologists have found figures of her, carved in stone throughout Russia, Asia, the Mediterranean, and Western and Central Europe. The Great Goddess is associated with sex, pregnancy, and the earth. She is self-sufficient. She does not need a husband—she is connected with the earth, and children are borne from her, the Earth. The Great Goddess is not a human mother, but she is the mother of all, the *Alma Mater*, the source of all being. She brings wisdom to men and gives spiritual and real food to all.

Breast Envy. The Great Goddess is proud of her breasts; milk and honey flow from them. Most sculptures represented her as presenting and announcing her breasts, holding them, showing off their fullness. In these sculptures, one hand points to her breasts, the other to her genitals—her two great sources of awe and wonder.

Nowadays, the breast represents the human mother, the child's first social connection. Psychoanalysts confirm finding "breast envy" in their male patients. The breast has the power to make the child feel either full and content or hungry and in pain—men envy that power.

Envy and Fear of the Vagina. Woman's genitals are also mysterious; the vagina is hidden, unknown. The male penis is quite visible. From the vagina, blood flows monthly. Men fear a woman's blood; they see her as unclean. According to the Talmud, a menstruating woman kills one of the two men she walks between. To some men, a woman is twice as sinister when she is bleeding. In some primitive tribes, men believe contact with a menstruating woman could be fatal, causing loss of strength and death to pastures and animals.

With fear may come envy of the power that is feared. Psychoanalyst Bruno Bettelheim tells us that in certain cultures, the puberty rites of circumcision—which is a brutal cutting of the penis's foreskin—is actually intended to mimic the female ability to menstruate. He says that the circumcision symbolically reproduces both the menstrual blood and the female vagina, which to the boy resembles a cut or wound. These primitive rites may express the wish to experience the organs and functions the woman has that the little boy does not.

From the female vagina, of course, also comes life itself. Until recently, men have not been allowed to attend childbirth—the greatest mystery of all. But that taboo is beginning to relax.

Man does not know what to make of woman. He considers her "the other." The child comes from "within" her, the male enters "into" her—and may fear being swallowed by her. Certain tribal peoples believe in the *vagina dentata*, teeth inside the vagina.

Fear of Woman Debilitating Man. It comes as no surprise that another destructive image is that of the "castrating" woman. Literally, castration involves cutting off the male testicles. Men may fear that women want to rob them of their manhood and power.

An extension of this castration fear is the belief that the woman can be debilitating to man. Legends tell us of Lorelei and the sirens, who lured men to their destruction. The woman is accused of being insatiable, of having unquenchable sexual thirst. "Can't she ever be satisfied?" This fear, or grudging admiration, is compounded today by the recognition, popularized by Masters and Johnson, that some women are multiorgasmic.

Envy of Woman's Capacity for Conception. Another problem

for a man is that the woman can lie passive, she can just be. Even if she is nonorgasmic, she can conceive a child. And man admires, resents, and envies her for this capacity. He must ejaculate, must perform, in order to create. Furthermore, a woman can be artificially inseminated, needing only sperm, a doctor, and modern technology to help her.

Woman as Destroyer. Along with being the source of creation, woman has been seen as the source of all evil. From the Old Testament, we learn that Eve brought evil into the world after she was born out of Adam's rib. (This is actually the reverse of what happens—man is born from woman.) In Greek mythology, Pandora brought evil, sickness, and death to mankind by opening the box she was told not to open.

Fear and Envy of Woman's Prophetic Powers. Men have also attributed to woman the power of the "positive witch," the prophetess, the predictor of the future. She is the "seer without whom men would have had to brave their fate in ignorance." She is a source of magic: many priests and shamans wear women's clothing to emulate her power, thus resembling the objects of their envy. The priest envies the witch's power less when he is wielding power of his own.

The mystery of woman begins with the mystery of the mother. Freud observed that the female genital is the "place where we have once been," the home men long to return to, the mother. Says psychoanalyst Wolfgang Lederer about woman, "We need her, and depend on her altogether; for she is the shipyard in which we are built, and the harbor that is our base and strength."

Woman is connected with life, death, decay, evil, sexual excess, sexual fears in man, blood, nature, magic, and power. An endless mystery. And what about all that power she has been known to have, power that is "magical and secular, physical and spiritual, personal and institutional"?

Says Dr. Lederer, "Man envies woman her tricks." Even Freud, who was not one to glorify women, wrote about pregnancy envy in men. Psychoanalytic literature yields many examples of male envy of childbearing, childbirth, and child rearing.

Until now, man had his separate sphere, his male-dominated clubs, business lunches, sports, politics, segregated arenas of success. Yet here she comes again, briefcase in hand, into the men's club where man was once in charge, the sphere where he could avoid any envy, where he had comfortably felt superior and, without competition, reigned supreme. No longer.

WOMEN AND ENVY

Women's Envy of Men

Many books have been written about women's envy of men. Feminist literature of the 1960s and 1970s is replete with this information. Pioneers Simone de Beauvoir (*The Second Sex*, 1953) and Betty Friedan (*The Feminine Mystique*, 1963), and more recent popular writers such as Germaine Greer (*The Female Eunuch*, 1970), Phyllis Chesler (*Women and Madness*, 1972), and Colette Dowling (*The Cinderella Complex*, 1981), have written about it. Almost everyone who has written about the predicaments of women in our society has at some point focused on women envying men or has implied that women envy men. Enough said.

What About "Penis Envy"?

What do psychologists focus on most when discussing women and envy? Penis envy. Penis envy was an invention of Sigmund Freud, who believed that women envy what men have that women do not—the penis. The symbol of male power and freedom is the penis. It is now generally accepted that women do not want the literal possession of a penis. What they *do* want is what a penis stands for, namely the status and power generally held by men; the power men have wielded that has been used to exclude women from the man's world.

The famous psychoanalyst Erik Erikson studied playroom activity of preadolescent boys and girls. He thought that if women did have penis envy, they would build towers and tall buildings with their blocks as the boys did. Instead, he found that the little girls built buildings that were inner spaces, spaces that could be opened or closed. Erikson doubts the role of penis envy. He suggests that the girl feels superior because she has an inner space, which is productive; that she does not experience herself as missing an organ.

As Dr. Lederer says, "History, mythology, and anthropology are replete with dominant and ruling women, but not one of them ever bothered to grow a penis."

Women's Envy of Women

We need to explore women's envy of women. The same cultural stresses that have allowed envy to flourish have also led to greater envy among women. Mothers envy their daughters' youth, intellectual and career opportunities, sexual freedom, and fun. Sisters envy each other's attributes in both the marriage and job markets. With the breakdown of the nuclear family, mothers compete more openly with their daughters for men and envy their daughters' capacities to find jobs and men. Daughters envy their mothers' affluence acquired over a longer life span, and some daughters envy that their mothers grew up knowing what they would be—a wife and mother—without having to worry about so many choices. Career women who feel the stress of career and marriage envy the housewife who doesn't feel guilty about staying home with the kids. And housewives envy what they see as the glamour and freedom of the career woman.

Few people want to turn back the clock to a time of tighter social structure, less economic possibility, and more rigid ways of looking at the world. It is unlikely that the movement of our times will slow down, which means that we are bound to face more and more occasions for envy. Our task is not to stop the inevitable, but to live in a changing world more comfortably with the envy that comes our way.

CHAPTER 4

Envy and Mom

> It isn't fair that our mothers' lives should be discredited just because we changed our values.
>
> —SHARON PERCY ROCKEFELLER, 1985

SYLVIA

Sylvia, a twenty-five-year-old patient of mine, is an attractive, lively office manager and mother of two. She is in her mother's living room. Her mother sits in "her" chair, the red one that no one else can use. She has a migraine. The scene is familiar to Sylvia. From age two on, she would come home to find her mother, Nan, in her chair, her arm bent over her forehead, the curtains drawn, lights off, aspirin on the coffee table, in pain.

The two women talk. The mother, who knows Sylvia's visit will be short, at least makes an effort to talk, speaking in a very quiet voice. Sylvia strains to hear the same stories she has heard for the past twenty-three years, stories about her mother's success as a teacher in an elite private school. Even at home, her mother dresses in extraordinary clothes, as if she were going off to teach at that school, although she hasn't taught in twenty-five years. When Sylvia compliments her mother on her clothes, her mother's head hurts more. "You're talking too loudly," she complains.

Sylvia knows the stories well. In fact, she barely has to listen to the words; her eyes roam the room instead. She notices a book her mother has been reading, *How to Suffer Through a Migraine*. She knows her mother has felt real pain, the physical pain of constant headaches, the emotional pain of her husband's early death, and the cold facts of her reality. Sylvia tries to feel empathy for the pain, but as always finds herself annoyed at her mother's inability to let go of the past and of her fantasy version of the present. Her mother, from London, has a carefully cultivated Mayfair accent.

Sylvia remembers how often Nan made her feel bad just for being what Nan was not. But the two were never able to talk about this. Instead Nan would be reassuring: "Sylvia, the only feeling I have for you is love." Nan's comments, however, centered around what was wrong with Sylvia. "You have too much emotion. You're too expressive. Why can't you calm yourself? Your face gets flushed when you're excited." Sylvia's mother envied Sylvia's ability to feel and express herself without constraint.

A less envious mother might have said, "Boy, are we different. I am generally reserved. You are effusive." Even when she didn't have a migraine, flu, cold, or ache, Nan would tell her daughter, "You are to much for me."

In a strange way, Sylvia's mother envied exactly what she criticized: her daughter's lack of femininity and her more masculine body. Nan grew up believing that being feminine, demure, soft-spoken, in the background, and bowing to male authority was the way to win a man, but Sylvia sensed the fragility behind these qualities.

Nan also envied Sylvia's health. Whenever Sylvia went out, her mother would comment plaintively from her red chair, "Oh, you're going? I wish I could go, too, but you know how my head is killing me." Sylvia would suggest numerous pain remedies, but the position of envier is hard to budge. "Do have a good time, luv," was the spoken message. The real message, the one Sylvia took with her, was, "Don't forget to think about me, home alone, suffering."

Sylvia was never certain if her mother felt this way because Sylvia's body was lovely or simply because it was pain free. Once, during a visit home when Sylvia was twenty-four, her mother disrobed abruptly, showed her breasts, and asked, "Don't you think they are still firm?" This came at a time when Sylvia was breast-feeding her second daughter. The comment suggested strongly that her mother envied Sylvia's breasts for their abundance and needed to prove her own were still beautiful and functional. In a sense, she was asking Sylvia to be her magic mirror, asking her daughter to respond, "Yes, dear mother, your breasts are still the firmest in the land."

What Nan envied most, however, were not their differences, but any ambitions Sylvia had that encroached on Nan's own territory. She had been a successful teacher, and Sylvia had no right to try to be one, too. There was room for only one outstanding success in this home.

Sylvia can now look back and see that her mother could not tolerate her going to a prestigious college, for this would have threatened Nan's superiority. Sylvia's personality already had threatened Nan's weak sense of self-worth, just as Snow White threatened her stepmother, the queen.

Nan lives in the world of past dreams and present disappointments. She loves her daughter but she dreads competition from Sylvia in the few spheres she considers her own. Both Nan and Sylvia suffer from Nan's envy.

THE LESS ENVIOUS MOTHER

There are, of course, many mothers who are pleased with the choices they've made and enjoy their lives; for them, envy is a fleeting emotion. Such a mother understands, Of course I envy my little Sylvia. Look at her—she's enviable. But my envy of Sylvia doesn't make me a bad person or make my own life worthless. It doesn't mean that I'm unimportant. It doesn't make me want to curb my daughter. My envy of her is just a passing feeling.

The less envious mother can enjoy her daughter's good fortune and learn from her. She looks at her daughter and thinks, There is my daughter. She has opportunities. Good for her.

The less envious mother is supportive. She observes her differences from her daughter uncritically. She might consider mistakes she made and wish her daughter not repeat them: "My mother wanted to get a social work degree but married my father instead. She's happy with her life but wonders what her life might have been like. She'd tell me, 'You can do what I didn't do.' She didn't undermine me."

A less envious mother may feel envy, but she doesn't need to act on it. Her commitment to her role as mother wins out over envy. She feels a longing for her daughter's youth, what was once a vista before her. Her daughter might sound like this: "I had opportunities my mother never had, like going to college, travel, the option of not fitting into a stereotyped role of wife and mother. My mother didn't have that choice and told me she envied me. It made me uncomfortable because I felt sorry she didn't have what I had. But she had a generous heart, and I inherited that legacy, the capacity to love without strings attached."

This is a compassionate daughter speaking. What helps create that compassion? Her mother talked of envy but did not try to take anything away from her daughter. This mother is able to

- *recognize her own envy,*
- *understand the causes of that envy,*
- *have some compassion for herself and her natural aging process,*

and therefore is less likely to harm her daughter. And the daughter who is able to recognize her mother's envy, understand the causes of that envy, and have compassion for her mother, is less likely to find herself entrapped in the Snow White syndrome.

If Your Mother Is a Housewife

In order to feel compassion for your mother, you need to realize that her role as housewife has been so devalued in our society that it is inherently difficult for her to feel good about herself. Envy is related to the esteem society gives you for what you are doing. If you look at the housewife in an historical context, you can better understand your mother's envy. As Glenna Matthews discusses in her book, *Just a Housewife,* in nineteenth-century society, a mother—in the home—was considered a valued and important part of our society. No longer.

Clergymen, authors and husbands glorified the skills of the housewife in the nineteenth century. During the early 1800s, prosperity brought an abundance of material objects. As both ingredients and utensils became more accessible to less wealthy households, women could proudly exhibit their skills and crafts: cooking, sewing, and cleaning were considered essential functions.

Domesticity provided many of your grandmothers and great-grandmothers with opportunities for high self-esteem. Recipe and quilt contests offered rewards for doing well. People need recognition to feel good about themselves, and these women felt important. Now, with fast foods, cake mixes, TV dinners, food processors, washers, and dryers, a woman needs less skill to be a housewife. Her work has come to seem meaningless.

In the nineteenth century, the home was also the center of religious education. A mother had authority because she taught moral standards. Religious and civic values such as kindness, cooperation, and humanity were fostered in the home, which was seen as a hub radiating into society.

Mothers have now lost much of their authority because television, radio, newspapers, and magazines are filled with advice from experts: what to eat, what to wear, how to cook, how to raise your child, how many hours a day you should exercise, how far you should go sexually, where you should go to college, what to do with your feelings, and, of course, what you should buy. We used to turn to our mothers for advice on all this.

In the nineteenth century and before, Mother was worth listening to. She had wisdom, lore, skill, expertise in the domestic arts. She wasn't bored. As her daughter, you apprenticed yourself to her and other female relatives to learn the sacred mysteries of the womanly arts of recipes and sewing, wisdom valued by the community. You gave sustenance and received sustenance from the home.

Everyone, men and women, in the religious culture of the late nineteenth century, was expected to make sacrifices for the good of the home. *Both* men and women were told they should practice self-denial. The clergy told men to control their sexual appetites and not pollute their pure wives. But by the mid-twentieth century, women, not men, were told to forfeit their sexiness, just to bear children and take care of the home. Men read *Playboy* and *Esquire* and no longer felt that they had to deny their sexual needs. Women, on the other hand, were still expected to deny themselves and sacrifice for their family. "Your husband's career depends on you." "You are a bitch if you make demands on your husband."

In the 1940s, Philip Wylie wrote a bestselling book, *Generation of Vipers,* which heaped scorn on housewives. He wrote, "I have researched the moms, to the beady brains behind their beady eyes and to the stones in the center of their fat hearts." He learned that Mom is "about twenty-five pounds overweight, with no spirit . . . In a thousand of her there is not sex appeal enough to budge a hermit ten paces off a rock ledge. She none the less spends several hundred dollars a year on permanents and trans- formations, pomades, cleansers, rouges, lipsticks, and the like— and fools nobody except herself. If a man kisses her with any earnestness, it is time for mom to feel for her pocketbook . . . In a preliminary test of strength, she got herself the vote and, although politics never interested her (unless she was exception- ally naive, a hairy foghorn, or a size forty scorpion), the damage she forthwith did to society was so enormous and so rapid that even the best men lost track of things."

Housewives in the 1950s received very different messages than their mothers. They were told they should make the home fun, for if they didn't, their children would leave and enjoy themselves elsewhere. Women in the 1800s were not burdened with "making the home fun." The home was not a source of recreation, nor was it trivialized.

No wonder so many of the women I surveyed reported being envied by their mothers. Why shouldn't a mother who feels unimportant, nonsexual and devalued envy her daughter and her daughter's pleasures and possibilities for "fulfillment"? She envies her daughter because she feels bad about her choices in life. She envies her daughter because all that is valued about being feminine—youth, attractiveness, sexuality—is now located in her daughter.

Let's look at how these envious mothers express their under- standably bad feelings about themselves.

THE ENVIOUS MOTHER

Your mother's envy may not be clear cut. Your mother may seem envious at one moment and full of love, concern, and dreams for you the next. You have difficulty comprehending that your mother has such opposing forces in her. The "Snow White" fairy tale needs to separate "mother" into "real mother" and "stepmother" because maternal envy is hard to take! You don't want to feel envy from your mother; when you do, she becomes the bad mother. This is not a cause for blame but for understanding.

You can appreciate a mother who feels envy but overcomes it for the sake of her daughter. But what about the mother who can't overcome her envy? *How do you recognize her?* What triggers her emotion, and how does she demonstrate her envy? How can you live your life free from the destructive power of your mother's envy, free to do what you want in life? How can you learn not to take in your mother's envy and live out that same envy with your own children? *How can you learn to understand her better? How can you feel compassion for your mother, whose disappointment in her own life has led her to be envious of yours?*

Our sense of what is possible is often limited by what we see around us. In your mother's day, daughters were more likely to follow the rules and roles their mothers taught them. Most of our mothers lived lives in keeping with the conception of what a woman's life should be, lives not so different from their mother's. They sacrificed their hopes and desires for their husbands and children. This sacrifice is called *altruistic surrender*.

Altruistic Surrender

"Being 'my daughter's mother' is a major source of identity. That way I know who I am."

How might your mother handle her envy of you? When a mother wants what her daughter has, and thinks she can't have it for herself, she may identify with her daughter. In identifying with her daughter, she feels she *does have* what her daughter has, and in so doing "surrenders" her own needs and aspirations for the "good" of the daughter. Sigmund Freud's daughter, the psycho-analyst Anna Freud, coined the term for this: altruistic surrender.

Here is how it works: Your mother wants to be loved and admired. She sees you being loved and admired or having what you want. She thinks, Ah, I could be like her. And that thought quickly becomes, I am her. She imagines you and she are the same person. It's as if what happens to you, the daughter, automatically happens to your mother. When your life feels uneventful (as many of our mothers' lives did), you are more likely to identify with someone whose life seems more eventful—whether it be a celebrity, movie star, or your own child.

Why does someone use altruistic surrender? Because outright envy toward a daughter feels unacceptable—and identification is more acceptable, a way to avoid feeling envy. With altruistic surrender, a mother feels good will, not ill will, toward her daughter. Unfortunately, altruistic surrender is never truly satisfying. Your mother expects you to live out *her* dreams. Not only does this create a false expectation of what you want for yourself, you will probably fail to live out her dream exactly as she wants you to.

Another problem is that our mothers expected us to live lives similar to theirs. Today, influenced by the sexual revolution, the women's movement, the availability of education and training for work outside the home, the necessity to work, and, often, encouragement from fathers, daughters are presenting their mothers with a new picture of the world. Even mothers who are happy with the choices they made still observe their daughters having more freedom.

Your mother's envy is aimed at two primary targets:

1. Opportunities you have that she did not have
2. Competition over advantages she previously had but no longer has

Opportunities

Sarah and the Envious Mother

Take Sarah, for example. A twenty-nine-year-old patient of mine, Sarah feels bad about herself. She has a high-powered job as a hospital administrator. A year ago, she married an architect who loves her and is good to her, encouraging and proud. She is fun to be with, has many friends, is giving to others. She is knowledgeable about literature. She is pretty and has a lovely, voluptuous body.

Yet to hear her tell it, you would think she is an unattractive, unspontaneous, humorless, dull, overweight loser. These are some of her complaints: "I am not happy. I need to go further in my career, but I don't know how. I want to be more articulate but not sound arrogant. I want to be better at a hobby. I want to have prettier skin. I need a better body, a firmer, flatter stomach. I feel old, like I've always been depressed."

Sarah is critical of almost every part of herself. There is a large discrepancy between how she is seen by others and how she views herself. She cannot accept that other people like her. She needs to distort the reality of who she is. Why?

Sarah has an extremely envious mother. It can be hard for people with envious mothers to like themselves, because if you

1. believe you have good qualities,
2. like yourself,
3. believe that people like you, and
4. act self confident and self-assured,

you risk being envied.

Envy from your mother is the most frightening kind of all, because you need your mother to make you feel safe and loved.

From an envious mother, you learn "Don't feel too good, be too good, look too good, do too well" or you will be envied. This message creates the Snow White syndrome.

Sarah's mother's dissatisfaction with herself is not unusual. She grew up during the Depression, was worried about economic survival and fearful of the electric toaster, cars, airplanes, and life in general. Sarah's mother was embittered and belittled her husband for working in a delicatessen. Many envious mothers pick on their husbands and children.

Sarah's mother's dissatisfaction with her life made her envy her daughter. In envying her daughter, she felt aggressive toward Sarah and expressed her aggression in two ways: she was critical of Sarah, continually chipping away at her daughter's self-esteem; and she tried to make Sarah perfect. Her mother's dissatisfaction with herself laid the foundation for Sarah's lack of self-esteem.

Let's look at how this happened. Sarah's mother longed for more education but didn't have the money to finish high school. Had I been able to ask her, Sarah's mother might have replied, "Sure, I wanted Sarah to have the opportunities I never had, particularly education and music. I want the best for my little baby."

Envious mothers are usually ambivalent about their daughters' success. They want them to fail *and* they want them to succeed at the same time. Instead of achieving for herself, Sarah's mother pushed her daughter to achieve but was critical of her at the same time. If Sarah ever received less than an "A" grade in elementary school, her mother was furious. "Don't you know you're smarter than this?!" she'd say as she waved the report card in Sarah's face. If Sarah received an A: "That's nice, dear," in a bland voice.

Says Sarah, "I was afraid I wouldn't make it through junior high. Isn't that a pathetic worry for a smart twelve-year-old? Even when I was seven years old, my self-esteem was tied up with grades. My entire experience in school, from kindergarten through two master's degrees, has been fraught with anxiety."

Sarah grew up feeling she wasn't smart. Since she has always scored high on scholastic aptitude tests, reality does not confirm her doubts. *When you feel envied, you doubt yourself. You don't want to be the object of envy, so you make yourself less enviable: the Snow White syndrome.*

A mother's envy creates a no-win situation for the daughter. The mother wants her daughter to have what she didn't have. When the daughter achieves what the mother was unable to, the mother is envious. If the daughter does not do well, the daughter gets criticized. If she does do well, she feels the attack of her mother's envy.

Your mother had fewer opportunities than you for a life outside the home. She just assumed her life would be marriage and children. If she went to college and wasn't married by the time she graduated, she might have taken a job until the right man came along. She may have worked outside the home but surely had fewer chances for a satisfying career. If your mother believes her life was lacking, she may feel insecure and unhappy. Thus, she is likely to pick *any* opportunity her daughter has to target her envy. Here are some illustrations:

INDEPENDENCE

Jane, a gardener, reports: "My mother has never been on her own. She envies my independence. She doesn't think about who she is, or who she could be if she tried to be different."

FREEDOM

"I do what I want to do," writes Jo. "My mother did what was expected of her and envies that I did not. She worried about me when I went through college without 'winning a man.' When I went through medical school and still had no husband, she was despondent. For my thirtieth birthday, she gave me the gift of a cemetery plot because she was sure I'd be alone when I died with no one to take care of me."

SEXUAL FREEDOMS

Jo continues, "My mother envied that I had the time and opportunity to go out with different men. That I enjoyed making love. She bought a system of life that she never challenged, a safe but tedious life with my father. She never took risks or was an adventurer as I have been."

FREEDOM NOT TO BE MARRIED

Mary remarked, "My mom envies my living with people in nonmarried, nonsexual situations. She felt she had to get married in order to have a family. I just created a family without having to marry."

FREEDOM TO HAVE MY OWN MONEY

Lynn told me, "I don't have to ask my husband for money for the groceries like my mother did. I buy whatever I want and can afford. I work."

FREEDOM TO BE AWAY FROM HOME

Since many mothers thought their role was to remain at home, they envy their daughters' freedom to be away from home for *their own* reasons and needs. Jenny described it this way: "If my mother calls when I am out, say with a friend for dinner, and my husband or son answers, she'll ask, 'Doesn't Jenny cook dinner for you anymore?' When my mother next talks to me, she'll ask, 'What about your family? Aren't you afraid your husband will want to find someone to stay home and take care of him?' I'll respond, 'The line forms at the right. The new woman can take care of me, too.'"

FREEDOM TO BE MORE "SELFISH"

Kim's mom envies Kim's ability to take care of herself rather than always giving to others. Her mother thinks it is selfish when Kim takes times away from her children for her studies.

CAREER

The lovely actress Julie Harris told me her mother, a housewife with many helpers, once remarked, "You know, I could have been an actress." Julie saw this as an expression of envy. She reassured her mother: "Yes, you could have been a won-derful actress! With all your charm and glamour, you sure could have been." Julie's mother loved people like Gertrude Lawrence and Ina Claire, the sophisticated comediennes. Said Julie, "She could have done that. She had great charm and vivacity, but she didn't let herself be an actress. My mother only felt alive when my father was alive, when she was a reflection of what he gave her."

LESS DEVOTION TO THE HOME

Ellie says, "I'd hear Mom tell people, 'Oh, Ellie can do anything.' But she was dripping with resentment. She felt trapped in the home with cooking and incessant housework. Excelling at housework, such as spring cleaning, fall cleaning, and silver polishing, made her feel like a worthwhile person. When she has free time, she puts it back into cleaning."

FUN

Here's an example from Patty, an eighteen-year-old high school student whose mother envies her having friends. "When my mother was younger, she didn't have many friends, nor did they talk about feelings like we do. One way she shows her envy is when my friends do call, she'll say, 'No one called,' or, 'I'm not sure who it was. I forgot the name.'

"When I was ten years old and had done my chores, I asked if

I could go for a walk with my friend: 'All you kids want to do is have fun, fun, fun! No, Patty, you have chores to do.' She would then dream up another chore for me. The next day I asked, 'Can I go play with Janie today?' Then I found a heap of clothes on my bed waiting to be folded. The next day, it was wash the windows, do the dishes. Once, when I did go to the beach with a friend, my mother appeared. In front of everyone, as we were lying in the sun, she said, 'Patty didn't hang up her bathrobe. She has to come home to do that.'"

JOY

Ann revealed, "My mother remembers how somber it was at our house and envies my family's joy. When I got pregnant, what I felt from her was, 'Now you and John will have to face the music. You will have to suffer as I had to suffer.' She envies that our children don't make us suffer."

ACCOMPLISHMENTS

"My mother envied my musical ability," realized Carrie. "She wanted to play the piano. She took lessons, but complained that every time she sat down to play, my brother would pee on the carpet. She didn't think she had options other than to quit her playing. For me, it's easier. I have a baby-sitter or friend watch the kids when I practice music. It was no surprise that when I started to play recorder my mom stood back, was unsupportive, and never listened."

CREATIVITY

Beth wrote, "My mother thinks she is not creative. She envies my creativity. I took poetry and art after school. She never had lessons. When I showed my mother my poetry, she said, 'Oh, so those are the silly things you do at home.'"

Fear may be behind your mother's envy. If you accomplish more than she has, she's afraid you will no longer recognize and appreciate her importance. Some women remain in the Snow White syndrome so that they won't leave their mothers behind. Guilt at surpassing your mother combines with fear of hurting someone who is supposed to protect you in an unsafe world. If you surpass your mother and invoke her anger, who will be there for you?

If you have an envious mother, focus on her fear rather than her envy. Help her accept that her fear of being left behind is common to all mothers. If you both can acknowledge this fear, your mother is more likely to integrate it as an inevitable though unpleasant part of her life.

Competition

Snow White's stepmother needed to ask her mirror repeatedly, "Who's the fairest in the land?" As long as the answer is, "You are," the queen can rest easy. But as soon as the mirror responds, "Snow White," the queen's envy is unleashed.

You and your mother both consult mirrors. Your mother may once have felt secure about her youth, body, good looks, sexuality, and relationship with her husband. But as you, her daughter, grow up, your mother may feel suddenly in competition with you. She may believe you are taking over what had once been hers.

You can learn from your mother what it's like to grow older in a society that values youth and a particular kind of good looks. You can reflect on the poignancy of losing what she felt she once had. Yesterday, your mother was young and, because of her youth, more valued; today, you are. Tomorrow, you'll be in your mother's shoes. Seeing how ephemeral a firm body and endless possibilities are, it's easier for you to understand your mother's envy.

Debbie, a thirty-eight-year-old housewife and tax consultant, is a patient of mine. Her dream illustrates the power of a mother like Snow White's. Debbie is not as thin or in control of her eating as she would like to be. Her weight reflects an area of conflict with her mother.

Debbie's mother is southern, outwardly polite, vain, and thin. She frequently consults her magic mirror, which tells her:

Here is the score.
Debbie weighs more than you do.
Your body is the better of the two.
But Debbie wins in other ways, outer and inner,
At least you know that you are thinner.

Debbie's mother needs to be the center of attention. She remembers her mirror's assessment and shows off her good figure. Even at Debbie's wedding, her mother wore a dress with such a deep cleavage that Debbie's friends had to joke about it.

Debbie's dream

I was in a car going past horse farms in the South. In the car were women who wore black. We were suddenly in an expensively furnished dining room. A woman came into the room with a red, shining apple. She set it on the table. My sister, also at the table, went to grab the apple. I knew why I was there. I picked up the apple, threw it out the window.

A horse ate the apple. All these people were really shocked when I threw the apple out. They knew it was poison. The horse shrank from being a beautiful thoroughbred into a dog that had rabies. The rabid dog jumped through the window, into the house.

Everyone was afraid the dog would bite them. I picked up a broom and tapped it on the ground. I dealt with the dog. Outside, it was a regular dog. But inside the house it was a monster. It was really scary inside the house and almost took up the whole room.

This dream upset Debbie and reminded her of the Snow White fairy tale. She thinks of the woman with the apple in the dream as her mother, who poisoned Debbie's attitude toward her body— just as the stepmother/witch gave Snow White the poisonous apple.

Before her adolescence, Debbie had felt herself to be more like a thoroughbred horse, lean, quick, alert, and proud. During adolescence Debbie became a threat to her mother. Her mother commented incessantly on how big Debbie's breasts were and often recommended breast-reduction surgery; she talked of how chubby Debbie was, questioned her taste in boys, wondered when she would learn to be a lady. Her mother invaded Debbie's privacy, just as the dog in her dream invaded the house.

Debbie identifies herself with the rabid dog who bit the apple and can't control what it eats. The dog, like Debbie, became huge after eating the apple of envy. In a dream, as in a fairy tale, a symbol takes on many meanings. This dog also has qualities of Debbie's mother and her envy, which looks pleasant enough to the outside world but is monstrous at home.

Debbie is determined to win the battle against her mother's envy. In the dream she has a broom, which she uses to deal with the dog. She feels on an equal footing with the dog, which means she can stand up to her mother's envy now. Within a year after this dream, Debbie lost twenty pounds.

What interests Debbie in the Snow White fairy tale is the similarity between Snow White's naiveté and her own; Snow White was willing to *trust* the witch/stepmother even after repeated attempts on her life. Says Debbie, "I always give my mother another chance. I can't believe she wants to hurt me." Just as the wicked queen disguised herself in different garb, Debbie's mother sneaks in a new way each time. "When we are getting along, my guard is down. And when my guard is down, she sneaks in with a mean remark or put-down. She never gives up."

Why do Debbie, Snow White, and many other women remain incredulous of their mother's envy? Debbie and Snow White can't believe their mother's ill will not only because they need a good and accepting mother, but because they know no other possibility of mothering.

Mothers feel in competition with their daughters for their:

BODIES

Lilly, a forty-year-old word processor/secretary, told me that her mother felt fat and hated her own body. She showed her envy of Lilly by making Lilly uncomfortable about her body. When Lilly was still thin, her mother would tell her, "If you gain any more weight, you'll have to wear chubby sizes." Or, if Lilly's legs looked good, her mother would say, "Your legs aren't that pretty, it's those shoes that make your legs look good."

The concern with weight even extended to Lilly's daughter. Her mother's first comment upon seeing her granddaughter was, "She has such chubby legs!" And this was a newborn baby!

Lilly had always been a good, pleasing, and dependent daughter. When she turned thirty, she realized she was still an extension of her mother and told her mother she didn't want her to comment on her weight ever again. Her mother tried but found it impossible.

Said Lilly, "When my mother was in the hospital, dying of lung cancer, I came to see her. I was wearing something red. As I entered the room her first comment was, 'You shouldn't wear red, you look big in red.'"

YOUTHFUL LOOKS

Sandra: "Mother envies my being younger and therefore, to her, more attractive. She shows her envy in competitiveness. For example, one time we were going to attend the same wedding, and I was anxious about what to wear. I chose silk pants, a rayon blouse, simple jewelry—what would be comfortable, sophisticated, unusual but not out of place. She came to check out what I was wearing and responded, 'Oh, Sandra, what a good idea. I could wear similar pants, but I wouldn't want to upstage you.'"

SEXUALITY

"My mother is incredibly repressed. She is also very saintly and lived under my father's thumb for years. She envies my being able to get out of a bad marriage and find other possibilities. When I was younger she envied my looks. She took me to a woman dermatologist for a foot condition, and the dermatologist suggested helping me get rid of my facial zits. My mother objected: 'No, she's fine the way she is.' My doctor showed the concern I needed, and my mother squashed the doctor's interest in my zits."

Women report that envy is even greater when their mother was without a good relationship with a man. A forty-year-old college professor from Kansas told me, "My father died when I was little, and my mother never dated or remarried.

"Even after I was married, she had trouble with my being sexual. She would freeze out any man I was with, belittle him to me. When my husband and I visited her, we lived under her rules. She put us in a room with a table between twin beds." The table, which they removed, was a buffer zone—more a symbol of the mother's envy than her interior decorating skills. Perhaps sexuality here stands for life—all of life's missed passions, freedoms, joys, and powers of the self.

Youth and Future

"What my mother envied me for was the chance to begin again."

Mothers fear their mortality, they are closer to death than we are, and envy the fact that we have longer to live. Most women feel blamed for getting older, since society tells us there's something inherently bad about aging. As they age, they take a closer look at what they've done with their lives. If they feel regrets, as we all do, they may feel envy.

A Lost Career

"My mother envied my theatrical career," reports Kim; "that envy has colored almost everything I have done. As a child, she encouraged me with one hand and knocked me down with the other. She wanted to be in the theater herself, but she was married with children. My mother discouraged my theatrical efforts, told me I was 'high strung,' 'unpoised.' She suggested that I take fencing lessons so I could learn to become graceful and agile on the stage. As hard as I pursued a degree in theater, she used guerrilla attacks to steer me into education. I'm afraid my mother almost succeeded in convincing me I was inadequate and untalented.

"Even though I received the coveted Drama Award for Excellence in Theater from Oberlin, I believed that to succeed would destroy my mother. I gave up writing plays for a long time. At our last family Christmas get-together, I said I was proud a play I had just written had been presented at a major conference. My mother's voice, dripping with sarcasm, came booming across the room: 'Yes, and I'm sure *you* got all the applause.' I am forty-five, she is approaching sunset. She cannot give up her envy. I can't stand to be around her with it."

DADDY'S GIRL

One of the most striking findings of my research is the number of mothers who envied their daughter's relationship with their father. We have all been taught about the Oedipus (Electra) complex. The little girl envies her mother because the little girl really wants Daddy, and Mommy has him for herself. Wait a minute! Many more women reported being envied by their mother because of their closeness with their father than they reported envying their mother for the mother's close relationship with her husband. Most women saw their mother as having an unsatisfactory relationship with her husband and in no way wanted that for themselves.

Some examples: "My mother had been deprived of a father. She made my father into her father, and then envied me being the daughter."

"My mother envied me for having things she didn't have as a child. She envied that my father gave me everything I wanted, and even things I didn't want."

"My mother envied me and my sister for any time that my father would spend with only us, not her. No matter how small the exchange with my father, timewise or meaningwise, my mother always hated me for it."

Many women report their mothers envied their daughter's relationship with her father, especially when father and daughter had something in common. Mother's envy here is intertwined with jealousy; she feels left out and unimportant. But what she envies is the connection the daughter has with her father, a connection the mother feels is lacking with her own husband.

Such envy makes sense when you realize that many mothers accepted an all-too-familiar bargain: "Give up your dreams for a relationship with a man." The payoff is supposed to be a wife's place at the center of her husband's life. If the mother discovers her own daughter threatening her position, naturally this will cause some strong feelings.

Take Mara's case. Mara's father preferred Mara's company to that of his wife. He preferred Mara's tomboy qualities to his wife's passivity. Father and daughter went fishing, played tennis, basketball, and football. Mara's mother envied their relationship and often warned Mara of the psychological dangers of being too close to one's father. "He is your father and should keep his distance. You'll never get a husband if you are too attached to Daddy. If you are too athletic, you could become a lesbian."

Because the father's role in life is usually more valued than the mother's, father envy may be less. Nevertheless, fathers envy their daughters. One woman mentioned her father envied her because she made a career out of her music while he, because of his business commitments, remained an amateur. A few Hollywood television writers reported that their fathers envy their earning ten times the money their fathers do. "I've taken more risks than my father. He has abdicated. He never asks how much money I make, but my mother always does. I don't answer because I don't want to reinforce his sense of inadequacy. But he would be proud if I were a son. It is more threatening if a daughter makes more money than her father. Your daughter is not supposed to show you up."

THE EFFECT OF OUR MOTHERS' ENVY

When women sense their mothers' envy, a common response is the Snow White syndrome. They

1. doubt themselves,
2. hold themselves back in life,
3. try not to upset or hurt their mother.

Nora, a thirty-nine-year-old patient of mine with curly bright red hair, chose all three responses in dealing with her envious mother. Looking back, Nora discovered how much her life had been influenced by her mother's envy and how disguised that envy had been. *The effect of her mother's envy was such that Nora gave up her only child for adoption.* Therapy helped Nora to discover her mother's envy and liberate herself from it.

Nora's mother *said* all the right things. "Oh, look how beautiful you are, all the men will love you, wait until the right one comes along." But there never was a right one; no man was good enough for Nora's mother. She found flaws with each one. When Nora was thirty-six, her mother told the ladies at her bridge club,

"Nora's not married yet because she is waiting for the right prince to come along, and *we* haven't found him yet."

Nora later learned that her mother didn't want her to marry. Her mother wanted Nora to take care of her. After all, her mother took care of her husband; Nora should therefore take care of her mother. A fair deal.

Every envious mother isn't like the wicked queen in "Snow White." Some take the opposite tack and put their daughters on display, hoping it will make them, the mother, look better. Like daughter, like mother. "I was never a real person," said Nora. "I was a showpiece. I made my mother look good."

When Jordan, a prince sufficiently elegant to live up to her mother's standards, came along, Nora married him. Nora's mother would play up Jordan, go on and on about how lucky Nora was. Remember, the envier often throws a barrage of compliments.

Nora, in turn, played her mother's unspoken game. She would reassure her mother, who was suffering from a bad marriage, that Nora's marriage wasn't doing all that well. *Another effect of her mother's envy was that Nora downplayed her marriage and began to doubt her love for her husband.* Said Nora, "I exaggerated my problems to make her feel better. In order to appear less well off in her eyes, I would fall into the trap of diminishing my marriage, time after time."

Nora's mother also envied Nora's enjoyment of sex. Since this mother never enjoyed sex, she felt her daughter should never enjoy sex, either. Her mother would confide in Nora, "Isn't sex ugly? How could anyone want to do that? It's degrading and awful."

Nora said to her mother, "Yes, Mother, sex is awful. I'm just like you. I could never like it." *Disliking sex was yet another effect of her mother's envy on Nora.* Nora's mother successfully used the envier's technique of spoiling what the envied person could feel good about.

Nora was able to be influenced by her mother because her mother had taught Nora to be weak and unopinionated, convinced her from an early age that she, the mother, had to be the queen bee, the one to be looked up to. "Mother raised me to be subservient, to take care of people, mainly her. Like most women, the caretaker role came naturally."

Psychiatrist Dr. Ruth Moulton calls mothers like Nora's "queen-bee mothers." Queen-bee mothers are competitive with their daughters and can't stand to be surpassed by them in marriage, career, or life. They make their daughters feel guilty if they dare to challenge the mother's cherished position as the one and only.

Queen-bee mothers, says Dr. Moulton, exploit the real dependency the daughter has on her mother. The little girl is initially dependent on her mother both physically and emotionally. Mothers hold baby girls closer than they do boy babies, later provide them less freedom to be physically active, and restrict their exploration of the world outside the home. "Since mothers are the original source of nourishment, sensual gratification, and gender identification," says Dr. Moulton, "girls are more fearful of separating from their mothers than boys are." Allegiance to mother equals protection from mother. But what price allegiance?

For Nora, the biggest price was giving up her own son for adoption. Nora was not married when she had her baby, but believed she would be an excellent mother. However, Nora's mother did not want Nora to become a mother, to usurp her maternal role. She also wanted Nora's full attention. Nora realized, "When I got pregnant, ten years before I met Jordan, my mother thought only about how it would be for her, what her friends would think if I had an illegitimate child." Nora's mother feared her friends would no longer see her as a perfect mother with a perfect daughter. In many cases envy is hard to detect because social mores allow us to hide envious behavior.

Nora described it this way: "It wasn't just having a child, it was anything, any independent thought or action, that my mother couldn't stand. Anytime I didn't coincide with her image of how I should be, she would give me that *look*." Nora had once dreamed that her mother, looking like a kangaroo, was standing in the doorway of my office, blocking Nora from coming to therapy, therapy Nora considered her route to independence. "That *look*" was a kangaroolike, ratlike stare that meant, "Don't you cross *me*. If you do, I will take away all the love I have for you, you will be alone, you will have nothing." As Dr. Moulton says, the daughter fears surpassing her mother because she fears losing her mother's love.

When Nora began therapy, she said she had been "dead inside" ever since she'd given up her baby boy for adoption. "I couldn't stand the pain of feeling like a nothing." "Will the real Nora Simmons please stand up?" she would ask herself, and no one stood up.

How did Nora learn to stand up to her mother's envy? First, she had to identify the envy. Second, she chose a helper and friends for confidence and strength. Third, she had to stand up gently to that "look."

None of it happened overnight. It took three years of therapy before Nora felt safe enough to look at her mother's envy and enjoy the little victories of no longer buckling under to her mother's every wish. Each success gave her more confidence.

Nora's mother had needed to be in charge at any cost. Giving up her baby had cost Nora a great deal, and after our discussing it for four years, Nora decided to take her *own* needs seriously, to find her son. She did so in an extremely careful way, maintaining consideration for the adoptive parents, who understood and accepted Nora's quest. Now, both Nora and Jordan and the adoptive parents are friendly, and the son, at college, writes home to two sets of parents.

The only one who is displeased is Nora's mother. "How could you do this to me?" she wailed. "What will your husband say? Are you sure you talked to Bess [for some reason she could never pronounce my name correctly], your therapist, about this?"

"She never asked about the search," Nora told me. "When I did find my son, after looking for six years, my mother was very quiet, and said these exact words, 'Oh, is that right? I have to go now.'"

Not surprisingly, Mother's Day became a nightmare for Nora as she grew older. Because her mother needed to be the queen bee, Nora had to fete her mother from dawn to dusk on Mother's Day, entertain her in ways so unique that her mother could then tell her friends and arouse their envy for what a devoted child she had.

The Mother's Day after finding her son was the worst. Her mother called and said, "You will begin my Mother's Day with a pancake breakfast." Nora objected, "But I'm a mother, too. This is what I want to do. I'll come over later in the day and make you dinner." But her mother wouldn't quit. "Of course you're a mother, but I'm a grandmother." In other words, "I am the grand mother, the only mother, the queen. We will do it my way."

Why would a daughter behave the way Nora did, submerge her sexuality and give away her child in order to make her mother comfortable? Besides fearing the loss of mother's love, Nora saw her mother's life as impoverished and needy. Her mother had told her, "You feel like it's your world. I've never felt that way."

Nora felt she had to make her mother's life better even if it meant hurting herself. Consequently, she was caught in a web of blame until she could identify the reality behind her mother's envy: her mother felt powerless; she didn't want to destroy her daughter. Once Nora was able to see her mother's envy in a large context, she was more able to separate herself from and show compassion for her mother.

HOW MOTHERS SHOW THEIR ENVY

There are four principal ways mothers show their envy:

1. As we have seen with Sylvia, Debbie, Sarah, and others, mothers' envy can have damaging consequences. *A mother will offer unhelpful criticisms and cut her daughter down.* No matter what you do, she can find fault with you or your feelings; you are never good enough. When you have an envious mother and are not able to identify her behavior as "envy," you might wonder, "What did I do wrong?"

Envy may be evident not only from what your mother says, but from how she acts: cold, withdrawn, preoccupied, giving subtle looks or putting a certain something in her voice. "It was nothing she ever said. I could just hear it in the edges of her voice."

2. *A mother may have great difficulty letting her daughter surpass her or separate from her.* Here's how Dr. Ruth Moulton describes what I call the Snow White syndrome: "If the mother does not encourage and reinforce her daughter for fear that she herself may be surpassed and feel superfluous, the resulting discouragement can undermine the daughter and result in extreme anxiety and a tendency to fail. The fear of failure is usually conscious. The fear of success is apt to be unconscious. A daughter can become fearful of the competition with other women, afraid of their disapproval, and as a consequence, sabotage her own development."

3. *A mother may not want her daughter to show her happiness.* She feels that your joy or success depletes the possibilities of her own joy and success. If you have it, she can't have it. So you hide your good feelings because you don't want to make her feel bad.

4. *A mother may try to live vicariously through her daughter.* As we saw when we discussed altruistic surrender, a mother often forfeits her own desires and wishes to further those of her daughter. In making this unspoken bargain, a mother believes she is living her life for you, receiving your success and rewards for herself. The bargain assumes that you will be successful for your mother and she will be proud and joyful for you.

Women mentioned that the following problems arose when their mothers tried to live vicariously through them:

1. When the daughter becomes something the mother can't claim as her own, the bargain will be broken. For example, Elizabeth's mother, a very bright woman, felt cheated being a housewife; she felt that she had missed something. After her third child left home, Elizabeth's mother commented sadly about her life: "The recipe went all wrong. Is that all there is?" She had pinned her hopes for success on her daughter.

Elizabeth's big moment came when, as an archeology professor at age 32, she got her own office. Her parents came to visit Elizabeth's charmed room. "My father loved the office. He was proud. My mom was matter of fact, 'Oh, yes, this is your office. Mmm, hmm . . .' and then she changed the subject."

Elizabeth came to understand that her mother's response didn't honor their agreement, an unspoken bargain that her mother would enjoy the success she pushed Elizabeth to achieve. Because Elizabeth had achieved what her mother had not, her mother could not identify with this part of Elizabeth's life. *A mother can live vicariously through her daughter only to a point. Then the mother must feel the separate worlds.*—"that world, the new office and career, belong to my daughter, it doesn't belong to me." Elizabeth fulfilled her end of the bargain, and by that success, her mother realized Elizabeth had become something she, the mother, could never be.

2. "My mother wanted me to be perfect. Her hope was that a perfect daughter would create a perfect mother. *Of course I failed her.*"

Mothers who use altruistic surrender take credit not only for the success of their child, but for their child's failures as well. You must succeed in the area your mother wants you to or you fail. Your failure then becomes your mother's failure.

"I'm mother's creation. If I am happy, she is happy. There is a lot of sabotage in that sort of relationship. *I can never show her my problems or ask for help.* She won't listen to my problems because she needs me to 'have it all together.' If I ever need her, she becomes incompetent."

3. "My mother had dreams of glory for me, pushed me to have the opportunities she never had. In living through me, she wanted to be included in my life as much as possible. If included, she thought she, too, could have the same success I have. That was the silent deal she made. I push you, and you include me. *Since I never include her enough, I upset her.*"

4. *"My mother was selfless,"* admitted Betty. "She could give only to me, not to herself. When I was college age, my mother paid for me to have a series of facials. I asked my mother all the time to use one of the facials for herself. She wouldn't. I sure didn't need all of them." Betty's mother died of cancer two years ago. When her mother was dying, Betty asked her, "If you could do anything differently with your life, what would you do?" She replied, "Not much. Hmm, I would have had a few more facials."

Does being a selfless mother work? When there's a genuine choice, when the mother truly enjoys her role, selflessness can work. When the mother forfeits her own development to be a mother and wife, and then resents that choice, being selfless does not work.

5. Sure, mothers relive their own joy when their daughters fall in love, marry, have children—as though it's happening to the mother for the first time. But when the mother lives vicariously through her daughter too much of the time, it may feel unsettling to the daughter, as if something's "off." Many women complain about their mothers' *lack of authenticity;* that Mom sees only Mom's version of her daughter's life: "She's not seeing me, but who she wants to see."

6. "Before Mom married, she was independent. She expects me to live out that independence for her. I do, through my political action and my fight for social justice. She, too, is concerned about poverty and misery in the world but doesn't do anything about it. Whenever I go off to work in a poverty area, *she tells me how to act and tries to undermine me.*" The vicarious mother can be a controlling mother. She implies, "Do it my way because that's the way I didn't get to do it."

7. *The mother who lives vicariously through her daughter often takes credit for her daughter's success.* A well-known woman runner appeared on the cover of a sports magazine. Her mother told her, "You wouldn't believe how many people said you looked just like me." Her mother showed the magazine to the cab driver, the parking lot attendant, sent seventy-five copies to people she knew. Her mother kept repeating what a good job she had done as a mother. Said the runner, "My mother would create distorted fantasies of what she thought was my mega-success. She brought copies of the magazine with her to cocktail parties and could talk of nothing else. Her gushing over me was becoming too much. Her identifying with me was embarrassing."

8. *When a mother substitutes vicarious living for direct living of her own, she identifies with her daughter's rewards rather than seeking those rewards somehow for herself.* Given society's emphasis on youth and beauty, finding her own rewards can be hard.

Take Denise, a highly visible, successful fashion model in New York City. She has a mother who tries to live vicariously through her.

Denise remembers, "My mother panicked over asking my father for money so she could go to the bank and cover the check she had just written. He shut the door because he didn't have the money. I saw her as a victim.

"My success was my mother's vicarious ticket out of the inner city of Cleveland where we lived. She wanted to live in Shaker Heights. 'My friends got out. Denise got out. Why isn't it happening to me?' my mother wondered. When she talks to me now, I can feel her taking notes on the other end of the phone so she can call her friends. She couldn't believe in herself or in my father, so she pins her hopes on me."

Denise pays a price for her accomplishments: she feels her mother's hidden anger. "My mother's life was so connected to my success that when she talked to me, it wasn't as a mother, but a fan. I felt discounted. Also, when you dissect someone in terms of their looks, as my mother does, you miss the whole person.

"I knew I was digging at my mother with every success. It's hard for me to look up to her. I chose other women as mentors, but she wanted me to choose her. That hurt her. My mother's theme was, 'There should be more. We should be more and live up to the Joneses.' But when I became more, she resented me for it.

"On the first moment of our meeting at the airport when I come to visit, there is the expectation that I must be the gorgeous daughter she has just been telling everyone about. If I do look gorgeous, she's envious. If I don't, she's disappointed."

COMPASSION FOR MOM

Seventy percent of the women surveyed reported they did *not* envy their mothers' lives. Their mothers were *not* role models. No wonder the women's movement emerged. These women felt sorry for their mothers, saw their lives as trapped and limited; as these women found more choices for themselves, their mothers' envy increased.

Why show compassion? Because people need to feel understood. The person who feels compassion has the enriching experience of feeling someone else's heart. Compassion is a gift to both the giver and the recipient. Empathy and compassion lead to forgiveness. Forgiveness leads to freedom. *With compassion, you open yourself to growth. Compassion is a key to freeing yourself from the trap of the Snow White syndrome.*

In feeling compassion, you can respond to new situations more clearly, as they are now, without seeing them through the filter of the past and your previous ways of dealing with your mother.

If you can look at your mother's life, see her disappointments, understand her reasons for envy, and feel the effect her envy has had on your own life, you can more easily let go of all of this. If you hold on to anger and resentment about your mother's envy, if you blame your mother, you are continually reacting to her, still governed by her needs. In extending compassion to your mother, you no longer agree to be limited by her envy, a victim of the Snow White syndrome.

These women understand the importance of compassion:

"My mother needed security. The only way she knew how to get it was by closing off a large part of herself when she got married. She resents it now and envies me. Why wouldn't she envy me? She tried to be the typical American housewife. She had to give up many dreams."

"Yes, my mother envied much about me. She criticized me a lot. But my mother raised us kids on her own, and I never felt I was the child of a single parent. She had such little time for herself. For fifteen minutes every evening, she would sit down, drink a glass of wine, and listen to the news on the radio. That was her only time for herself."

"My mother envied all my relationships with people," says Judith. "Once, at a dinner party, a male admirer of hers held my hand and called me 'sweet one.' My mother later told me, 'He used to call me that.'" Suddenly Judith saw how much her mother grieved for what she was no longer getting—and Judith felt more kindly toward her. "My mother wasn't trying to hurt me. She was just hurting herself."

One way to understand the envious mother is to sympathize with her lack of outlets for expression. When a mother does feel envy for her daughter, it's a social taboo, the last thing in the world any mother *wants* to feel for her daughter, completely unacceptable with the ideal image of Mom. Consequently, envy makes her feel she is lacking in her one area of importance—motherhood. She had better rid herself immediately of the feeling, certainly never mention such a dreadful thought.

Regina, whose mother couldn't talk about her envy, described their home life as resembling the TV commercial of a happy American family and its dog: "When I was growing up, no one was honest with each other. We were saccharine, polite. We internalized our feelings. No one expressed hurt, pain, sorrow, or disappointment. Everyone pretended we were perfectly wonderful." Instead of acknowledging her envy, Regina's mother would feel worse about herself or try to make Regina feel bad for causing her mother a painful emotion.

Many women reported feeling compassion for their mother at her deathbed. That was when Trudy, a forty-year-old owner of a public relations firm, finally understood what her mother's envy was all about. Trudy's mother never went to a dance or musical production Trudy had been in, and Trudy never knew why. Just before she died, Trudy's mother said, "You have always intimidated me." Trudy: "I was flabbergasted. I asked her, 'Do you mean even when I was a little thing?' She repeated, 'You have *always* intimidated me.'"

"I think that if I had done worse in school, had fewer friends, been unable to dance or make a joke, then we could have been closer. She saw herself as insecure and joyless. She would criticize my accomplishments and point out the worst things that could happen if I went to Europe, took a new job, had friends, got married, communicated with my father, or bought a goldfish, let alone a new house.

"I thought my mother wanted me to achieve, but now I see that being an overachiever was the worst thing I could have done because it only 'intimidated' her more. I saw my mother's weakness behind that critical face, and I felt love for her for the first time I could remember."

Remember that underneath envy lies fear. Fear that you won't have enough. Fear that you aren't good enough.

Compassion for your mother's predicaments is possible only after you're secure in and know your own feelings. Most daughters with envious mothers are always worried about their mother's feelings and consequently have not had enough room for their own.

FROM THE MOTHER'S POINT OF VIEW

Trying to see things from your mother's point of view is one way to become compassionate.

Nadia, the mother of a sixteen-year-old daughter, has a career, is in school and not "stuck" at home with 2.5 kids, yet she *still* envies. She mourns the fact that her daughter is moving out into the world.

"My daughter is at the beginning, she's starting out, while my life is going by too fast. She will make her own mistakes, but she is at the beginning, and it feels like I'm being left behind. It's like leaving me for another person, but her 'other person' seems to be the whole wide world of possibilities. I envy that. After giving so much to her, she's now taking what I gave her and creating her own life.

"I want to be acknowledged and appreciated more. If she did the dishes, cleaned the house more, maybe then I would feel she was repaying me for what I've given her. I wish I could go out as much as she does, be able to buy clothes without thinking about where the money comes from, be taken care of, live with fewer adult responsibilities. I also envy her inner feeling of security that allows her to make decisions on her own, to be comfortable with almost everything she does. She can do so much more on her own than I could at her age.

"But I remind myself that all that's really happening is that she's going off, separate from me, not hampered by my unresolved relationship with my mother. She is leaving me to deal with what's lacking in my life on my own. As it should be—but it's hard.

"It's a dilemma because there is not a specific person to vent my anger on. You can't get mad at the world for taking away your child. And you can't get angry at your child for doing what she is supposed to. I am left with my own frustrations."

Recognizing the envy, whether it's your mother's or your own, is an essential first step. Realizing that mothers envy your opportunities, that you have what they feel they've lost, is necessary if you do not want to be limited by your mother's envy. If you accept the unspoken message of her envy, if you fall into the Snow White syndrome, you pay a heavy price. Once you recognize and understand the envy, you're freer to feel compassion. And beyond compassion lies love. "Getting mad at the world," as Nadia puts it, keeps us tied to envy. What we want is to loosen envy's grip.

CHAPTER 5

Envy in the Home

A mother takes her two daughters shopping for skirts. She chooses two skirts, a red one and a blue one. The mother asks the older sister, "Which color do you want? Red or blue?" The older sister is certain. "I don't care. I just want the one she gets."

—GEORGE P. ELLIOTT

"My husband encouraged me to go back to school. When I did and was enjoying it, he told me to quit. I think it was envy because both messages were given—'this is good, go for it; stop doing it!'"

—ANONYMOUS, St. Louis, Missouri, 1985

Expect to find envy in the home. Your first experience of envy is at home, with your parents and siblings. And as you grow, the rivalry you felt when you were in your parents' home can leak out with your mate. Your siblings and mates are the people you're the closest to, the ones you see in a more personal way. Most likely, you wear fewer masks with people in your family. The less you hide who you really are, the more intensely you experience your feelings.

SIBLING ENVY

Your first experience of envy is as a child, at home. How you learn to deal with sibling rivalry, with envy in the home, may set the stage for how you handle envy later in life. How was envy expressed between you and your sibling?

There are certain givens in your sibling relationship that universally create envy. Either you are a boy or a girl, younger or older. Even the middle child gets envied for not having the same problems as the youngest or oldest! It just depends on what side of the fence you're on. There is an absurdity to the stories I heard siblings tell. What seemed most clear is that your birth position makes little difference in the envy level. Let's look at how nutty it can get:

Being the oldest has certain advantages. "Let's face it," says one woman, "as the oldest, your siblings envy you for being in on everything, for your power and independence. You get to do it all first, be there first. I was envied for being the first to move out of the house, to marry, travel to Europe, to have a child. It's natural."

Let's hear from a youngest sibling. "I was envied because I was the youngest of ten kids, I got more attention and had fewer responsibilities. There were ten years between myself and the next oldest. My parents loosened up as we got older, and they also moved up financially." Parents are not static. They change as they grow older, and their economic position and attitudes toward child raising may also change, affecting how they raise children of different ages.

And now from the middle: "My brother, five years younger, envies me for being older. He'd try to act like the big brother. With a painful pinch to the cheek, a loud voice, and too tight a hug, he'd call me 'little sis.' My older brother envies me because Mom gave me special attention. She ironed my sheets, gave me embroidered pillowcases, and told me, 'You're my special little gift.' She didn't do that for him."

Your position in the family determines much about your person-ality. If you are the oldest, you are often supposed to be (or you just are) the most competent. A forty-year-old woman in advertising told me, "Because I was five years older than my sister, there were certain things I could do better, and it seemed I could do everything better. It set up a situation where my parents expected me to be better, and then I expected myself to be better. Since I thought I should be better than my sister, I became competitive with her, so I could keep winning. She envied that I was winning, and, liking to win, I kept the game going."

Another given in a family of brothers and sisters is that someone is the boy and someone is the girl. One woman said she envied her brother because he was the little king. He got to do things with her father, like hunt and fish, that she wasn't permitted to do. "I couldn't change that—I *am* a girl. I became an architect, what my father wanted my brother to be, and it made no difference. He treats us as he always did; my brother is still the little king." But this "little king" brother saw his sister as "pampered" because she was sent to art school. He let her know "You are such a princess, you don't even use self-service gas pumps." Looks like this family had a little king and a princess, so the royal children were heirs to envy.

One woman remembers, "My mother had different standards for boys and girls, requiring that boys do the harder things. We lived for many years in northern Montana in a one-room house with no indoor plumbing. My brother now reminds me how he hated emptying that potty. But I envied him because he was allowed to go outdoors on a cold day and chop wood."

Many women reported being envied because they were the favorite of their opposite-sex parent. Alice, a forty-four-year-old writer, put it this way: "My mother favored my brother; my father favored me. My brother envied me for getting more of my father's attention, and I envied him for getting more of my mother's."

Envy depends on your own perception of your situation, rather than on objective reality. Except in extreme situations like poverty, lack of health, or real physical, financial, racial, emotional limitations, your own particular point of view creates your reality.

OPPORTUNITIES FOR ENVY

Even though birth position and gender universally arouse sibling envy, all you need to feel envious is your own, perhaps distorted, perception of who's got it best—who's got the most of what. You've seen that any difference between two people can be used as fuel to feed envy's fire. Here are some of the arenas in which these fires burn.

LOOKS

"My sister envies me for being petite. She was six feet tall when she was twelve years old. She's good at sports, and almost looks like a halfback. I'm a dancer. She envies me because I don't have acne and she does. I do have plantar warts, but they don't show."

"My sister envies me for being thinner. She would always sneak into my closet and take my clothes, especially my favorite sweaters, then sneak back to her room and squeeze her body into them. I would find them in my closet the next day, thoroughly stretched out."

HAIR

Envy among siblings is often mutual: "My sister envied me for my straight hair. I envied her for her curly hair."

Aren't we in the realm of the absurd here? Whatever your sibling has is what you think is "it"—that's what you want. Whatever you have is "not it"—but it may be what your sibling thinks is "it." Siblings wish, "Why couldn't we just trade _____[hair, legs, arms, eyes, noses, you fill in the blank]?"

MONEY

"My brother envies me for making more money than he does. Would you believe he charged me two dollars for a phone call I made at his house, after I had just taken his whole family out for an expensive dinner! Out of guilt, I end up sharing my income with them. Now I am always short."

"I envy my sisters because their husbands make more money than mine does. They both have diamond rings; I don't. They have no idea I envy them. My sisters say to me, 'Wish I were like you, and never worried about a diamond.'"

Here we see that siblings envy for having, for not having, for the joy of not having, and for the contentment of having, for the having of not, and the not of having.

PERSONALITY

"My sister, twenty months younger, envied me for being outgoing and exuberant. She complained that if she stood next to me in a room, she'd disappear. Maybe that's because I kept forgetting my sister's name."

"I envied my sister for her more overt sexuality, for the fact that men responded to her. When she told me, 'I've made love in the backseat of fourteen cars this year,' I felt like a fool for having been envious of her."

"I envied my sister, two years older, when we were teenagers. When I hit puberty, I was overweight, unpopular, and awkward. She was graceful, beautiful, the all-American girl. I envied her ability to flirt with my father. So did my mother."

"My siblings envied me for being the one who defied our mother. They couldn't do that."

LUCK

"My sister envied that I had a gorgeous hunk of a husband. I was lucky. But he lost his hair and developed a beer belly. She doesn't envy me anymore."

"Luck" is a big one on the envy list. When you have things working out for you, when things "just go your way," expect to be envied. If you're a person with good luck, you may seem like the preferred child, that fortune, the good mother, is on your side. The envious person imagines that life prefers those who seem to have everything working out for them.

ACHIEVEMENTS AND ABILITIES

"My sister envies my ability to get things done and also my housekeeping. She says, 'Oh, you're so lucky.' As if some fairy godmother came in, and bibbity-bobbity-boo—a clean house. I show her my wrinkled, chapped hands and explain that her house could look the same."

"My sister envies my athletic ability. I'm a tetherball champion."

"My brother envies me because I publish books and he doesn't publish his writings. When I sent him a book I published and asked him his opinion on it, he asked, 'What book?' "

"My brother envies me my success (I'm a teacher). He shows it by refusing to see me when he visits New Jersey. I live in Pennsylvania."

A friend of mine is a successful research psychologist, wife, and mother. When she presented her research to three hundred people, her sister came to the conference. After the presentation, the sister came up to my friend, the "star," and said, "It was a great talk, but I have to be going. I have an appointment with Dr. Chellis." "Who?" asked my friend. "Chellis," replied the sister. "You know, it rhymes with jealous."

LIFE-STYLE

"My sister is an unmarried bartender, neurotic, lonely, and six years older. She envies that I am married and have children, what she considers the good life. She shows her envy by acting like she is taking over my life. She sends lavish gifts every week. On one level it's the sweetest thing, but on the other level it's too much. I am bombarded; it makes me the bitch again. I can't have a sincere response. The excess makes it a parody, a caricature. There is a lot of hate and envy behind all that giving."

RISK TAKING

Eleanor Roosevelt once said, "You must do the thing you think you cannot do."

"My sister envies me for my risk taking. For years I'd been an adventurer while she lived the safe life of a homebody. She would rather be envious than take risks. What changed that? My second husband got cancer, divorced me, and took everything I had. The week he died, the man I'd been going out with decided he didn't want to commit himself *and* my cat died. My sister was there to help out. She saw that I refused to be beaten, saw me bring myself out of the mess. She decided she didn't have to play it safe, that she could live more like I do. Before, I had to downplay the good things in my life. I don't have to do that anymore."

Criticism is one way siblings show their envy. "My sister envies everything about me—my marriage, children, sports, artwork. She shows it by criticizing my children, the way I bring them up, who their friends are, what their grades are, their jobs. It's worse than having a mother."

In Chicago, I interviewed a fifty-five-year-old powerful businesswoman, the vice-president of a major catalog company with a subscription of four million people. Her sister, fifty-eight, divorced, and unemployed, envies her and shows it with criticism.

"You'd be amazed," said this vice-president. "When my sister comes to my house, she will complain if there is a slippery spot on the sidewalk, or the step is too high, or her bedroom is too cold, criticizing me for not having enough covers, even when there are many.

"Some people find good things to say about you. My sister finds the opposite. I wore contacts for quite a while, starting when I was forty. The first time she saw me wearing contacts, her comment was, 'That's one thing about wearing glasses, they hide the bags under your eyes.' "

Trying to convince a sibling to become more like oneself is another ploy. "Be like me, sis. Take a more conservative approach to life. Don't rock the boat, don't take risks, take your place in society, fulfill the role for which you were born and raised. Stop gallivanting all over the country, don't expect great things, rein in your spirit, don't be so public."

Having to make everything equal is a third tactic. "My sister envies me. I am twenty-two, she is seventeen. Whenever either of us gets something new, the other runs out and finds the same thing, whether it be a new blouse, jeans, pierced ears, boyfriends, or friends. We've done this all our lives."

"My sister envies me for leaving the home environment, despite my family's dire predictions about what would happen to me if I did. My husband is handsome, I have a good job, three beautiful kids. My sister went to bed with my husband, and I believe it was a direct result of envy. This was her way of feeling equal."

What Is Sibling Rivalry?

The word "rival" comes from the Latin *rivalis:* an inhabitant of a river or stream bank who competes with his or her neighbors for access to the river or stream. A competitor, a rival, is in pursuit of the same object as another.

In the phrase "sibling rivalry," the word "rivalry" is used loosely. Siblings compete for the "river," the supply of water needed for survival. This supply is the parent's ability to satisfy the child's needs, particularly love and affection. The child *rivals* his sibling for "exclusive access to the source" of love. Envy results from the reality, even the fantasy, that your sibling has more of the parental love supply than you do. But, what child feels he or she *is* getting enough of the attention supply?

WHAT FEEDS ENVY BETWEEN SIBLINGS?

Siblings are like inhabitants of a river bank, wanting to claim ownership for this river of parental love. Parents play a large hand in determining how nourished or deprived each child feels. Parents create, encourage, and inflame envy between their children by

1. not paying extra attention to one child when a new sibling is born;
2. overtly favoring one child over another;
3. stereotyping and pigeonholing children;
4. making unnecessary comparisons among children;
5. trying to avoid envy by pretending children are all the same;
6. pretending sibling rivalry doesn't exist or being insensitive to it; merely telling children not to fight;
7. being capricious or arbitrary when helping children solve their fights;

8. giving special privileges to one child and not the other;
9. not reassuring the rivalrous child that he or she will be all right in the long run.

Even if you avoid all of the above, sibling rivalry will still exist. Maybe you think you can lick the problem by having only one child. Forget it. Your child could develop "cousin rivalry" or envy your work or anything that takes your attention away from him or her. All siblings at some time in their lives consider themselves to be low on the totem pole and "hopelessly outclassed." Since every child sometimes feels small, stupid, and inadequate in relation to the complex world of adults, each child will compare himself or herself with someone who seems, for the moment, better off. And when your child feels outclassed, inadequate, or fearful of losing parental love, the ingredients for envy are present.

How Parents Feed Sibling Rivalry

SHOWING INSENSITIVITY TO A BIG CHANGE IN THE CHILD'S WORLD

Anything that changes the river's supply, that actually takes away the parents' love and attention, can create sibling rivalry. In a happy family, the first child feels good about herself, secure in her parents' love. That river is flowing all for her. The first change in the river's supply comes when another baby is born.

"I was the queen child, the first grandchild," remembers a friend. "No one told me I was going to get a baby sister." When you're not prepared for the disruption in your life, you can resent the birth of your sibling even more. Researchers report, "The birth of the first sibling is a complicated task for the older sister. She must cheerfully accept this 'gift' of a baby sister for whom she never bargained, while suppressing her angry feelings about being swept from the maternal nest." Try not to force the older child to be the caretaker for the new baby brother or sister.

A parent who remarries also creates a change in the river's supply and must be prepared for sibling envy over who's getting more of what. Anna, a twenty-two-year-old student from South Carolina, said her stepsister envied her because her father sent her to a private school. Even though he paid for her stepsister's two weddings, he required that she attend a state school. Anna wondered out loud whether she, too, should go to a state school, since the private one was so expensive. Her stepsister heard her and replied, "Oh, don't worry, Father would sell his grandmother to send you to any school you want."

FAVORITISM

Every child at some time wants to feel he's the "best." No matter how much the parent tries to treat each child fairly, most children have moments of feeling second best. "Achieving a feeling of overall fairness is the best a parent can hope for."

Favoritism exists in all families. But Stephen Bank and Michael Kahn, who researched siblings for eight years, discovered that in the healthiest families children are favored for different reasons. Balancing who is the favorite helps lessen envy. Favoring one child one day and another the next (or at a different period of the child's life), so that no child is clearly favorite or dominant, is what works. When one child is favored over another, the favored child develops an identity of being privileged, entitled, superior, overly powerful. In larger families, there is less tendency to favor one child because there is less parental attention to go around: there's a "we're in this together" attitude.

There are negative sides to being favored. First, you carry an expectation of special treatment into the classroom, into the world. You try to arouse envy from others, to assure yourself that you are still the favorite. This behavior often turns off other children, so that you have trouble making friends.

Second, you can feel guilty about being the favorite, especially if you see your sibling suffering because of it. A patient of mine, June, was clearly favored over her younger, less studious sister. She remembers how one Christmas after her family had finished opening presents, her sister said, "It's not everybody who can hold all her presents in one hand." June told me, "The realization came over me that I had gotten a lot more presents, especially from my mother, and I felt terrible."

June carries this burden with her into the job world, where she longs for success and works hard to get it. But when she does well at a meeting, she feels guilty for getting more attention than others, even though she prepared diligently for the meeting. She

imagines that those receiving less attention resent her for being the
favorite, like her sister did. Being the favorite may burden a
person with a lifelong fear of arousing envy.

STEREOTYPING

Stereotyping children, pigeonholing them, can limit their abilities.
"You are the smart one, you are the pretty one." Stereotyping can
create sibling rivalry and is also a way to *deal* with envy. You are
supposed to succeed only in your area of expertise. Parents hope
that if their children believe they have little in common, or if each
is in his particular niche, there will be less competition and
hostility.

One woman told me her mother decided which area each child
was supposed to do well in: "There wasn't room in our family for
more than one of us to succeed in the same area. I was the musical
one; another sister, the artist; another, the domestic. I wasn't
allowed to do anything that leaked into their skills. I told my
mother about some flowers I planted. 'You don't know anything
about gardening,' she replied. 'That's your sister's area.'" Why
not allow your children to develop areas of competence according
to their natural abilities and temperaments? Clearly, the child's
personality and role in the family is not fixed at birth but is flexible
and can change as the child grows older.

Researchers inform us that brothers and sisters compete in three
main areas—achievement, sexuality, and social relations. Rarely
does one sibling dominate all three areas. "Usually siblings realize
that a brother or sister 'controls' one, or perhaps two, of these
areas; thus the other sibling may feel compelled to seek distinction
and superiority in the remaining area." A thirty-year-old housewife reported, "I was smart, and my sister was pretty. I'd go out
with brilliant men, and my sister would go out with the handsome
ones. We envied each other."

Here's an example of Marcy and her younger sister, Renny, that
shows the direct connection between a mother's stereotyping of
her children and sibling rivalry. "Mom used to introduce us to
family, friends, and perfect strangers as the 'brainy one' (me) and
the 'beautiful one' (Renny). According to Mom, Renny is skilled
in all the 'womanly' duties—better housekeeper and cook than I
am. My husband has never complained about my cooking or
cleaning, so I must be doing something right. Whenever Mom

comes over, she gives my house the once-over. Her comments then usually begin with the word 'Renny.' 'Renny has a better job, Renny has an office job. Renny's husband is better looking, Renny's kids are adorable, Renny this, Renny that.' I've tried hard to get rid of my envious feelings, but my mother keeps rubbing it in my face every chance she gets. If I didn't have the support of my husband, I think I'd go insane."

COMPARISONS

Envy increases when parents compare, asking, "Why can't you be more like your sister?" Parents can avoid comparisons, but here's an example of what happens when they don't.

Here is a case of a parent both overly comparing and showing favoritism. "My mother set up envy between me and my sister. She talked about my sister's little head and rosebud mouth. I had the big head and the 'sunflower' mouth. My sister was also well developed, and my mother would tell me what a perfect figure my sister had. My sister was a star in everything, sports, student council. I was shy and retiring. My mother petted my sister all the time, made her special dresses for the prom and graduation. Not me. It's the little things that hurt." This mother associates one daughter with the ideal of herself and the other with her negative side. She then plays the daughters off against each other as a way to deal with what is essentially her own mixed feelings and conflicts about herself.

Another woman reports, "I was envied by my sister because my parents thought I was smarter. Even though I was two years younger, my parents ordered me to help her with her homework, and she hated me for that."

Even if parents don't set up comparisons and competition between siblings, the outside world will. The oldest of two girls reported a minimum of envy in her home but added, "When my younger sister came to school, everyone gave her the 'Oh, so you're Sophie's younger sister' routine, and she told me she envied me for being there first."

TRYING TO AVOID SIBLING RIVALRY

As a parent, expect to do the wrong thing. One mother tried to discourage rivalry among her children by making everything equal—even so, the older daughter *still* envied her younger brother. "I was the oldest but didn't get any special privileges. We always had the same allowance. I hated being equal." This parent was making two people equal who are not, denying the privileges that naturally would come to the older child; a good way to instill envy.

Another parent lumps all the "kids" together. "We are the parents, they are 'the kids,'" or "the girls" or "the boys," as if there were no real differences among them. This "lumping" process, an attempt to lessen envy, actually creates it because the child, when not given a unique sense of self, will lack self-esteem.

A child in this type of family may often be blamed for something he or she didn't do, since the parent may not take the time to figure out which child misbehaved; all the children are punished and reprimanded identically. These parents may say they are avoiding "playing favorites," that they are hoping to lessen their children's arguing and competition, but in so doing they may actually create more competition. The child can become confused about who he or she really is; he or she may try to imitate, wanting *exactly* what the brother or sister has. Once again, we have the seeds for envy.

Healthier families have found ways to lessen sibling rivalry. They set limits on how destructive the envy is. They have learned to accept sibling envy and explain the concept to their children. They do not tell their children how simply marvelous it is to have brothers and sisters. They pay attention to how the children really feel about their siblings. When a parent's attitude is, "My children all get along and love each other," it's a relief for the siblings to grow up and talk with one another about what it was really like to be rivals, competing at the stream.

Limited Good

Playing favorites, stereotyping children, or giving special treatment to one child and not another are all influenced by an attitude of "limited good," the feeling that there is not enough water in the river, not enough "good things" to go around. Envy is created by both the concept of and the reality of limited good.

The concept of limited good. Thinking of love as limited creates love's limitations. Love is not like a cake that is divided among eight people and then used up. Love re-creates itself; there need not be a fixed and limited amount.

The child may believe there is a limited good. He or she is convinced that there is not enough of the parent's attention, love, and appreciation to satisfy all the siblings. There won't be enough left for me, thinks the brother or sister who experiences this sense of limited good. If she has it, I can't.

Siblings don't compete only for parental attention and love. For some, possessions equal love. A seventy-two-year-old housewife in Minnesota told me, "My sister, Sue, envied that I was prettier. She was far better off financially, but that didn't matter because she believed I had what I wanted.

"After our brother died, we found a sterling-silver flatware set among his valuables. I mentioned I would put the set in my car. I never had a set before. Sue replied, 'If you don't mind, I only have two sets, and I need a third set for when I entertain.'

"I reiterated, 'But Sue, I don't have a set.'

"Sue said, 'Yes, but you have all the rest of the good things in life.'"

The assumption that there's not enough for everyone leads to the feeling that you don't have something *because* someone else has it. This leads to division and rivalry in the family and to competition for the "limited goods" available.

A thirty-five-year-old nurse from Montana writes about envy among her siblings:

"I was the youngest and was sent to boarding school as a teenager. My sisters resented this and thought I was a spoiled child who got everything I wanted. But I envied their being adults, married, making their own decisions, their closeness as a family group. No one shoved them out of the way."

Her mother's engagement ring was the "good" that was limited. "When my mother died, my father didn't know what to do with her engagement ring. He checked the hands of his five daughters and also those of his four daughters-in-law. I was the only one without an engagement ring, so he gave me my mother's ring. It was worth less than fifty dollars.

"He was trying to be impartial, but my sisters and brothers took exception, saying I didn't deserve anything since I always got everything. I said I didn't want the ring, it was causing too much trouble. My father insisted I take it.

"I was hurt by their reaction. I felt like a bad person for evoking those kinds of reactions from my own family. I am unable to get pregnant and to have children. I thought that if I had what they had, nice homes and children, I'd never act like them.

"How do I handle being envied? Talking about it hasn't worked. I tell myself that 'family' is not a magic word. 'Family' does not make you have to associate with one another. 'Family' is just a group of ordinary people with problems."

The sense of limited good is universal. We find it even among animals. A friend told me the following story: "I have two dogs. If I give each of them a bone, each dog wants the other dog's bone. Each dog gives me a look that implies if I really loved *him*, I would never have given the *other dog* a bone, that I would give the one dog both bones, not split things equally. To show my love for the one dog, I'd have to put the other dog out in the cold, hungry." Most people believe, in their bones, that love is limited, that there is not enough to go around.

Sometimes the available goods actually are limited. In the above example, there was only one engagement ring. One way to create less rivalry when there is a real limitation of available goods is to discuss the problem with your children. Point out that if one child gets a unique gift, another child might get something equally good.

If the goods are actually limited, parents should not rub it in when one child gets special privileges and the other doesn't. "My brother envied that I got a bedroom while he had to sleep on the living room couch." Who's got the best bed here? Bed envy and living space envy, who has to share a room and with whom, are high on the envy list for siblings. No matter how crowded the

Sigmund Freud household was, Sigmund was always allotted the largest bedroom for himself, while his five sisters and one brother had to share the smaller ones. Sigmund, the oldest, was treated like the favorite, expected to be admired by his siblings, and considered himself superior to his sisters. In his autobiography, he doesn't even mention that he has brothers and sisters. I would imagine they envied him.

When the goods are limited, when parents are inadequate or unavailable, there is greater competition for parental attention. "My sister envies everything successful about me, and vice versa, and it goes back to the inadequacy of the available parenting we had. There is always a certain baseline deprivation that we feel."

A Turning Point

Sometimes the supply of what you want is not as limited as you think. As with the dog bone, one sibling getting parental love does *not* mean the other sibling can't get it.

One woman, who had borne the weight of her sister's envy her whole life, woke up to the fallacy of the "limited good" view of the world. "When I visited home the last time, my father bought a new car—a really powerful, big car. He told me, 'You can drive it.' My mother said, 'Your sister and I can never drive it,' implying that I wouldn't be able to, either, that we women weren't up to a car like this. Because I had just arrived and wasn't yet back into the reality there, I burst out with, 'Then I guess I'm not you or my sister.'

"The turning point came a few days later when I recognized my sister's envy. She and I were arguing, and she screamed, 'You're smarter; you're thinner!' This is the typical number my family laid out—what was ostensibly positive was said with tremendous anger. Like something that should be a cause for happiness always coincided with hurt and anger. That's envy.

"I didn't get mad at my sister because she can get so upset. I told her that I wasn't smarter than she was, told her about her good qualities, but I finally got sick of what my mother and sister were doing. Their behavior had led to my incredible guilt. *When I had something or did something that should be a cause of joy, they implied that by virtue of my having it, I was denying it to them.* They also implied that if I had something they didn't have, I had to make it up to them in other ways.

"Now I don't tell them of my success or achievements, at least not right away. I know their response will deprive me of my pleasure at that moment. I wait until I am more solid in what I've done, so their envy doesn't rob me of my success."

WHAT YOU LEARN FROM SIBLING RIVALRY

Like most psychological behavior, sibling rivalry has its pluses and minuses. We have focused on the negative side, but there is a positive side. Rivalry encourages a natural aggression in siblings. When you and your sibling act aggressively toward one another, you know you are alive, you are noticed; there is contact and warmth, which are the bases for human survival. You can learn how to manage and resolve conflict, how to be a good sport, how to win without humiliating your opponent, how to lose without feeling like a failure. You learn healthy competition, the desire to excel, and how to defend yourself. In vying for your parents' love, you can learn how to share love, especially in situations where your claim is not exclusive, as with a friend or a mate. This serves you well later, when you and your mate share the love of your children. You learn to be more thick-skinned, not to treat every disappointment and lack of attention as the end of the world.

Through understanding your rivalry with your siblings, you gain insight into your shortcomings as an adult. As Anne Isaak, New York restaurant owner, admits, "I find myself forgetting to admire what's good in other people, a trait I learned from rivalry with my siblings. When I withhold praise, it reminds me of my siblings gloating, "Nia-na-na-na-na. This is mine," or, "I did this," or "You can't do that." I never wanted my siblings to be too full of themselves, and I ignored them when they did show rivalry in that way. Because of defenses built up through sibling rivalry, when I am asked to give attention or praise, I have an instinctive reaction against giving it. When I remember my sibling rivalry, and how I hated it when my brothers and sisters got more than me, I stop myself and keep from acting as if my co-workers were my siblings."

You can also learn to be more sensitive to people who have less than you have. If you're the sibling who gets the most attention, does better in life, or is most envied, you can feel empathy for the person who seemingly has less than you do.

Healing

Envy between siblings is a primitive envy. It's there from the start. But you can move away from sibling envy later in life, and many people expect to.

To heal the envy between you and your sibling, you need to remind yourself that you have a shared history, similar early experiences. If you're close in age, not separated by more than eight to ten years, you've shared the same home, schools, friends, parties, and parents. Your siblings are the only people in the world who know what it was like to have been brought up the way you were. You might show your sibling more about yourself than you show your parents, confide certain secrets you'd rather die with than tell your parents. You can fight differently with your siblings than with anyone else. You and your siblings often form a group against your parents, need each other to better understand your parents. You help each other take care of aging parents. There is a nitty-gritty quality to the sibling connection. You have formed who you are in close proximity to one another. Since you have a deep connection to begin with, mutually exploring envy may flow more naturally than it would in other situations.

Envy among siblings is also intense because, having the same genes as your parents, you could so easily have had what your sibling has. "Just a slight ripple in the gene pool, and that could have been mine," a sibling muses unconsciously. Since what you have could have gone either way, you and your sibling can joke about the direction the gene pool took.

When you look beneath the superficiality of envy, you and your sibling may find ways to help one another. A twenty-five-year-old Manhattan law student writes, "I was in modeling school when I was fourteen. My sister constantly wore an old, beat-up ugly army jacket to hide her fat. She was put on diets and castigated frequently by my mother for her weight and appearance. I got attention because I was tweezing my eyebrows, learning how to tie scarves, to walk down a runway, to open and close doors in a feminine way, to wait in a ladylike fashion for the bus.

"The way my sister showed her envy was by utter despair and by eating more. She was envious of my being with boys, even though before I knew what a sexual experience was, my mother was calling me a 'whore.' My sister decided to hit the books, become an excellent student, and gain my mother's respect.

"Then I began to envy her intellectual life and the attention she was receiving. This envy made us miserable. She felt herself to be a social outcast and wanted to become a nun. I came to think of myself as stupid, emotionally frail, incompetent, a 'doll' for men; and I played the role well, too.

"Over the last year, I've made a great effort to close the gap between us that envy caused, and to move into a caring, close relationship. Whereas my sister has always thought of herself as ugly, with my encouragement she is seeing herself differently; I take her shopping, her style has changed, and she no longer gives as much credit to what my mother tells her. And were it not for her constant, unflagging encouragement and confidence in me, I wouldn't have begun working to resume college for my law degree."

In reminding ourselves of the depth of the sibling bond, we find that sibling envy, while not eradicated, can be healed, especially when siblings focus on the positive aspects of sibling rivalry. If siblings face rivalry and envy head on, the rawness and intensity of that experience can enable them to explore the depths of envy, seeds of which exist in all the other relationships in their lives. Siblings have the potential to understand each other in a way that friends, co-workers, bosses, and mates cannot.

MATE ENVY

When you marry for better or for worse, do you expect to find envy beneath the sheets? When you have a boyfriend, a lover, you no doubt think of the chase, romance, a partner, someone to have meals with and depend on—but do you think of envy entering your love affair? Jealousy, sure. But envy? Not from your mate, the person you respect and rely on.

While husband envy is less expected than sibling envy, 70

percent of the women interviewed reported envy from their mates. Whenever anyone feels an emptiness inside, that person can envy whatever he or she imagines will fill it. That is a constant. What varies is how the envy is expressed.

Mates envy the same goodies that mothers, co-workers, bosses, friends, and siblings envy: youth, upbringing, personality, friendships, accomplishments, career, and good fortune.

YOUTH

One husband, uncomfortable with his own aging, asked his younger wife as she put on her nightly restorative cream, "Do you really think you can be helped?"

MONEY

"My husband, from a working-class background, envied that I was part of the social strata he wanted to be in. Marrying me was an entrée; I was an acquisition."

PERSONALITY

A lesbian woman reported, "My shy lover envies that people are more open with me than they are with her—even in elevators. At a social event, she'll act like it's torture for her to be with me, as if I gobble up all the attention on purpose. She'll say, 'My friends looked at you more than me,' or, 'Glad to see *you're* having so much fun.'"

FRIENDSHIP

"He envies that I have richer connections with women than he has with men. It's not just jealousy—that he's afraid of losing me. It's envy—he wants the same security for himself that I get from my friends. He shows his envy by downgrading the particular friend I'm with: 'When you're around her all you do is eat, talk, and waste time.' Or: 'You don't realize it, but she's using you.'" A good reply for this woman would be: "Well, then I'm using her, too, because I enjoy her company."

ACCOMPLISHMENTS

Mates envy a variety of accomplishments: being disciplined, well organized, well read with a large vocabulary, practical with money, able to make quick decisions, and able to remember people's names, to list just a few.

Here's another: "My husband envied my knowledge, what I knew that he didn't know. He would argue with me, get angry if I was right. Very often he sounded off the wall, like he was stretching the facts just so he could sound right. It was hard for me because I wanted the man I was with to know at least as much as I did. I didn't want to be the one who knew more. Maybe I wanted to envy him." Women were taught to look up to their men, and when their mates envy them, it's surprising and disturbing.

CAREERS

Many men encourage their mate to succeed in a career outside the home. They want their wife to be fulfilled, to earn money; but as soon as she finds too much gratification or earns more than he does . . . envy may follow.

"My husband envied how I love my work. He didn't like the work he did and didn't know what to do instead. He tried to distract me from my professional life. When I finally got my Ph.D. he told me I'd never earn as much money as he earns. That's true. He also suggested it would be cheaper for me to stay home and clean my own house than to join the work force and hire a cleaning person."

Envy is hard to bypass in two-career marriages, yet in most families these days both partners must work.

MOTHERHOOD

The marriage bond also provides particular items to envy. One is motherhood, the closeness a mother might share with her child. Another is pregnancy. A friend's husband was clear about his envy: once, when his wife was 4½ months pregnant and they were taking a drive, he pulled the car over to the curb. "Okay, the pregnancy is officially half over," he announced. "Give me the baby for the second half." Of course, he wanted to put the baby back right before the birth.

"FREE TIME"

Men have traditionally borne the brunt of breadwinning. If the family's income is not enough, they blame themselves. Many husbands, with good reason, envy wives who don't have the same pressure of earning money. They also envy their wives' "free time," the freedom from a structured life.

Says one woman, "My husband envies that I don't have the responsibility of making as much money as he does, that I have time to take ballet and art classes. He keeps up the old joke that all I do is watch soap operas. Or, especially in groups of people, he'll say something sarcastic like, "Monique works, but she spends more time on her art than cooking dinner, and tonight, once again, we're having takeout Chinese."

THE QUALITY OF MATE ENVY

What's special about mate envy? What makes it different from other envies? We bring to our marriages and relationships with boyfriends unresolved envy from our relationships with siblings and parents. Often we use our mates to work through envy toward and from our siblings.

DEPENDENCY

So many of our emotional needs (especially the wish to be taken care of) are supposed to be met by our mate that this becomes the most dependent relationship in our adult lives. And because dependency can make you uncomfortable, you may envy your partner (or he may envy you) for putting you in this uncomfortable position. Your mate may envy that you have the ability, the power, either to hurt him or to make him happy. You envy the people you depend on for closeness, security, and self-worth more than you envy anyone else.

This dependency is not only emotional, of course. You and your mate share a home, children, money, and possessions. This sharing, in addition to bringing pleasure, can bring an increase of vulnerability and dependence.

In a love relationship you're often drawn to someone because you want that person's qualities for yourself: please be my "better half." But you realize those qualities remain in your partner, that you don't gain them by osmosis. Thus you envy and resent your partner for having what you had hoped for. That hope comes from a deep place, a magical and primitive level—you have shared your bodies and maybe your soul. Why not each other's qualities, too?

LOVE AND HATE

In the closest of relationships, your feelings, especially love and hate, are strong. Your mate may want the best for you and, at the same time, feel threatened by your success. *"I've always felt my first husband loved me and hated me for the same things.* He loved and envied my ability to be close to people. He hated that I was close to anyone other than him. He saw my strengths as something he didn't have and wanted to take them from me."

Your mate may encourage and discourage you, almost at the same time. This particular kind of envy, a mixture of pride and resentment, was reported by many women. "My husband gave me money to open my own office. He was initially supportive until my work began to gain recognition. Then his envy came out strong and he wondered why he'd given me the money in the first place!"

Why this ambivalence? You've read about the current explosion of male envy: now, besides all the traditional reasons a man envies a woman, he has an additional reason to envy her—she has entered his world and is beginning to usurp areas that previously belonged to him.

The wife earns money, has an important career, travels for sometimes long periods of time, may come home from work later than her husband, wears pants, and sometimes coaches Little League. The husband is proud of his wife, pleased about and dependent on the extra money and status. Yet, men and women are often taught that "real men" earn more money and are more successful than their wives. A man's virility may be threatened when his wife gets a job promotion that makes her more "successful" than him. When resentment outweighs pride, envy becomes destructive. According to Nancy Friday, "the envious person will hem the beloved in, guard her, watch her; will erect ever higher barriers against her ever being exposed to real or imaginary joys without him . . ."

This woman describes the worst side of envy: "I was in a two-year graduate school program. We'd had a summer break. When I went back to register in the fall, saw my friends again and started to get all excited about school, I was very high. When I came home and told my husband how happy I was, I could physically see him get depressed. I finally realized, after many such experiences, that every time I felt good, he got depressed. Every ounce of self-growth I had, he held against me."

Nancy Friday observed that "as women do become as powerful in the marketplace as their mates, studies show the relationships darken, sour. The man's identity has been threatened. Also, his defenses against envy of women's power have been destroyed. She already had too much power, and now she has his, too: 'New marriages where the wife is ambitious are less stable. . . . Among married couples who have broken up, we find that the more ambitious the wife, the more likely that the husband wanted the relationship to end.'"

JEALOUSY

Of course, envy and jealousy are especially intertwined in the marriage bond. Your mate is likely not only to want your success or personality for himself—envy—but also to fear that your success or personality will lead you away from him—jealousy.

SUCCESS

Envy comes up more often *when you both start out at the same place,* and you succeed at something and your mate does not.

"I was excited about opening a gourmet cooking school, and my husband wanted to join me in the venture. I had eight more years' experience than he had. We actually learned cooking at the same time, but I went forward with it, encouraged him to come along, although he mostly dabbled. But he saw how much pleasure I was receiving. He envied the money I was making: 'How much are you going to make at your next demonstration? Oh, God; oh, no, you'll be making more than me!'

"He'll show his envy by coming to assist me at a demonstration and then making competitive cracks in the class, like 'Can this marriage be saved?' I'd refer to something in the room as 'my table' or 'my bowl,' and he would respond, '*My* bowl,' making it sound like a joke, but it would have a knifelike quality. He would make jokes that took the attention away from the food I was presenting, beautifully timed comments in order to pull the attention to himself."

When a man marries a woman who is already successful and established in her career, he has an idea of what to expect: lack of availability, late-night meetings, trips out of town, endless phone calls, rushing here and there, pressure. But if there's a change, and your focus moves from your mate to your work, sometimes even slightly, be prepared for envy.

"My boyfriend lives in Los Angeles, struggling to make it big. He kept encouraging me to move there, to try to make it, too. He introduced me to a woman to discuss a screenplay I was writing, and she was very interested in promoting my project. My boyfriend freaked out: 'I can't stand it, I've been here five years, and you breeze into town and you're off the ground. It takes time, you haven't paid your dues, you don't understand how things work here, you can't become an overnight success, no one does.'"

Is the best way to handle being envied by your mate to avoid being in the same career? "My husband and I were both in journalism, and one of my articles made the front page of the *Washington Post*. People began asking him if it bothered him. It did, and I quit because I didn't want my husband to envy me. If I went back to work, I'd choose a different path. I won't compete head on with my husband. Even though I love journalism, I can do other things well. I hate fights! Marriage is hard enough without letting envy enter in."

But is quitting your career the best way to avoid envy between mates? You need to be sensitive about your mate's reaction to your possible career success; you need to talk it out, find compromises, see what you can do for each other, explore envy's mutuality, focus on what you love in each other—all this works, but you can't eliminate mate envy. It's not easy for either party these days.

WELL-KNOWN WOMEN AND THEIR STRUGGLES WITH MATE ENVY

Television and movie critic Rona Barrett tells me that in the early days of her career, men envied her aggression and ability to function well on her own. They showed envy with "silly, stupid, catty remarks like 'How's my little star doing today?'"

In 1967, Muriel Siebert became the first woman to purchase a seat on the New York Stock Exchange. Since 1969, she has owned her own Manhattan discount brokerage firm and for a time was the only woman to head a NYSE-member brokerage firm. She was the first woman superintendent of the New York State Banking Department and is credited with "saving the banks." Men envy her. She is dynamic, high-powered, philanthropic. "I've been envied for the publicity I get. It takes a very secure man to walk into a room with me.

"Envy shows itself in all kinds of ways. Men will say to me, 'If you didn't work so hard, you'd have time to go to the beauty shop.' When one man picked me up at the airport, he commented dryly, 'Here comes Tilly the Toiler.' When I became head of the Boy Scouts for greater New York, all five boroughs, seventy thousand scouts, one guy told me I got the job because they needed a woman for the position. He could have said, 'I'm proud of you.'"

Rona Jaffe, the well-known novelist who has written twelve books in the past twenty-seven years, including *The Best of Everything, Family Secrets, Class Reunion,* and *After the Reunion,* described some difficulties in being a successful woman in a relationship with a less successful man. She is now with an ambitious and accomplished man, but in past relationships men have showed their envy by complaining she was too absorbed in her work, not available enough for them.

"When you're a creative person, your work is who you are," says Rona. "If your work takes over your life totally, and the person who loves you says, 'Give that up for me,' that's envy." His wish for you to give up your creative work for him seems like envy because you feel his attempt to thwart your spirit, to spoil your joy.

"The more successful you are and the less successful your boyfriend or husband is," Rona continues, "the more you have to wash his damn laundry. Some men would show their envy by being hostile; I think it's worse when you're in the same field. If I'm involved with another writer, and my book becomes a best-seller and he can't sell his screenplay, I'll have to clean, cook, wait on him hand and foot to make up for it. I've seen this kind of resentment in couples when the woman pays the bills. The man won't put his dishes in the dishwasher; I mean you end up being their servant to make up for your success, waiting on them to prove you love them."

Attractive, humorous Ann Fraser, the popular San Francisco talk show hostess, had an envious husband. The marriage didn't work out. Ann was trained as a singer and a dancer; she had sung with a big band and was part of the first theatrical group in history to perform at the White House. Her husband told her, "Now that we're married, you don't sing in public anymore." Ann told me, "I should have known right then that he envied my performing."

Envy and fear are sometimes indistinguishable. Carolyn Kizer, the 1985 Pulitzer Prize winner for poetry, author of *Mermaids in the Basement* and *Yin*, and first director of literary programs for the National Endowment for the Arts, was married to a man who was more jealous than envious. He was jealous of any connection she had with intelligent men because he felt insecure about his own intelligence. "In fact," remembers Carolyn, "when Dylan Thomas came to town, my husband forbade me to see him. What amazes my friends is that I agreed to this! My attitude with this husband was, 'Yes, dear,' which makes my friends now roar with laughter."

Carolyn's husband was afraid of losing her. After she had three babies in four years, he said, "Now I've got you. No one will ever want you again!" "Of course he was wrong," said Carolyn. "The way I 'dealt' with this was by getting a divorce."

Divorce is one response to a husband whose envy is serious and destructive rather than fleeting. Fifteen years ago, Barbara Corday found herself in a situation familiar to many women who become extremely successful after marriage. Barbara Corday is the first woman president of a major Hollywood television company, Columbia Pictures Television, and coauthor of the original *Cagney and Lacey* TV movie. She talked to me about her ex-husband:

"From the day we were married, for the two years that we were together, I went steadily up, he stayed the same, and it completely changed the balance of our relationship. He was unhappy. So was I, desperately unhappy. I couldn't walk in the door at night feeling upbeat or pleased for myself, couldn't expect an atmosphere where we could talk or be excited about the day.

"Two things made me realize that the marriage wouldn't last. First, because I couldn't look too happy to him, I had to calm myself down on the front steps before I could open the door. Second, at a New Year's Eve party, he wouldn't shake hands with my business associates. I would introduce them to my husband, they would reach out a hand to shake, and he would just stand there. He was hostile. On the way home from that party we talked, and it was clear he didn't want to deal with the problem. He wouldn't admit there even was a problem."

I asked Barbara if *that* husband was mean to her in other ways. "He was actually a very gentle, intelligent person, but he was mean in that he would stop speaking to me or be sullen. I could never, ever take him places where there were people I was working with, people I was having a good time or laughing with. Of course now I know that he was terribly threatened and unhappy."

Barbara put it this way: "When you marry someone who is already a movie star, like Janet Leigh, for example, then you know what you are getting. When you marry a woman at the same level, and one of you—especially the woman—takes off and the other doesn't, it's 'How dare you get going and not me!' There's something unfair in that situation. My last husband, a very sweet, nice man, at his young age of twenty-six was not capable of dealing with his own envy. I couldn't, either. My present husband is very comfortable with my success."

If you can't admit you're envious, you can't say you're sorry. If Barbara's husband couldn't admit what seemed so obvious to her, how could they even talk about the problem?

Julie Harris is another successful woman whose husband became envious when the balance in their relationship shifted. She is one of our greatest actresses. She and her husband had started out in school together when they were young. After not seeing each other for a long time, they got back together when they were in their fifties. He told her bluntly, "You're successful and I'm not." Neither of them could change. At the beginning of their marriage, she spent less time working, but as time went on, she realized, "I couldn't not work. I knew he was envious, I could feel it." Julie confided in me that it was because of her husband's envy, and her inability to deal with it, that they were not able to resolve their problems.

It Ain't Me, Babe: The Fascination/ Intimidation Factor

Underlying envy of all successful women is what Peggy Hora calls the fascination/intimidation factor. When Peggy Hora, age forty, was running for judgeship in Southern Alameda County Municipal Court, she herself walked over one hundred precincts and worked twenty-hour days in order to reach over seven thousand households. Her efforts were not in vain. She became the first woman judge in that court, winning by more votes than any man running. She gave me insight into the problems men have with successful women.

When she was married, in 1964, she knew no women working outside the home. "My ex-husband now is very proud of what I'm doing, but he didn't want me doing it while I was married to him. That was too threatening. He has traditional views of what a marriage should be."

Peggy has only met one man who didn't try to change her, "tame me, if you will." "I am a fine-looking woman," she continues, "but I don't break mirrors. So, usually men who are attracted to me are fascinated by how they became attracted in the first place. I think men are fascinated because I don't fit the role they're used to. Like Chief Justice Rose Bird said in an interview a couple of years ago, 'Hey, when you're a justice of the California Supreme Court, it's hard to get a date on Saturday night.'

"As much as the guy is fascinated by me, he's also intimidated. People are intimidated when they don't know what to make of you. The part that has been the most fascinating, the part they least understand or know what to do with, is the part they want to make go away, to blanket, to tone down. Self-assuredness, power, the extroverted personality, the fact that almost anywhere I go I'm recognized. I know people—that's threatening."

Peggy tells me about Peter Beagle's book, *The Last Unicorn*.

"When the unicorn first gets out of the forest, she's lost her horn.
It has become invisible. There's this crass guy who tries to lasso
her, catch her. She can't be caught because she has a golden horn.
She's magic. She finally throws off the lasso and continues up the
road being a unicorn. The guy falls into the mud, totally defeated.
The unicorn says, 'I can't understand what he would have done
with me if he would have caught me, anyway.' That's what I feel
like. Men have been fascinated by me, and then once they have
me, they don't know what to do with me, so they try to change
me. Then it ain't me."

HEALING

These are certain qualities women reported that can keep a mate's
envy from harming a relationship, which make you a pleasure to
be envious *with:*

1. *Accept basic differences.* As my son has told me since he was
four years old, "I am not you. I don't think like you. Just because
you like spinach does not mean I have to like it." Some mates
have trouble accepting the inevitable differences and inequalities
that occur between two people.

A twenty-year-old mother and nurse from Kansas writes that
her husband *doesn't* feel threatened by their differences. "I have
more formal education than he does. He freely admits he knows
nothing of my field, and I freely admit I know nothing of his. He's
a car mechanic. I'm a nurse. I like to read almost anything. He
only reads technical and car magazines."

2. *Don't let your self-worth depend on being more successful
than your wife.*

My friend's husband is a high school principal. She is a
corporate executive and earns three times what he earns. He
realizes that society rewards his wife's work more than his. He
understands that the disparity in their salaries is not a reflection of
his actual worth.

3. *Realize the mutuality of envy.*

The mother and nurse from Kansas continues, "Sometimes my
husband gets upset when our twenty-two-month-old daughter
behaves more like me than like him, but I get upset when she
behaves more like him than like me. That, I think, is a natural part

of being a parent." Here, being envious of each other is an acceptable part of the relationship.

4. *Talk about your feelings.*

A fifty-year-old housewife from South Dakota told me, "My husband used to tell me I looked terrible whenever I went out to meet my friends for dinner. I'd leave feeling like a schlump. One night I asked him, 'How come the only time you tell me I look awful is when I go out with my friends? I know I've looked a lot worse in the mornings.' He admitted, 'I wish I had as many friends as you do.' This openness made me understand his feelings and I didn't take it personally the next time he criticized me before I went out to eat with the girls."

5. *Change what's not working in your life.*

A thirty-eight-year-old nutritionist writes from North Carolina, "My husband envied me because I had more education. He was afraid I'd decide he wasn't good enough, that I'd leave him. He became sulky or suspicious if I had long conversations on the phone or talked too much about people at work. Just telling him I wasn't going to leave or giving him extra attention made no difference, didn't diminish his envy. He felt it as pity.

"I was frustrated and worried that his anxiety and insecurity would break us up. It wasn't fair for him not to believe me. I found that joking about his envy helped. I offered him one of my degrees. I told him anecdotes and let him meet a few overeducated ninny-hammers. All was finally resolved when we decided he could go back to school while I supported the family. An adviser at the local university told him if he had that kind of time, money, and backup from a wife, heck with school, start a business. No trouble with envy since."

6. *Have a generosity of spirit.*

When one husband spilled coffee over a report his wife had just written, she felt he was envious of her drive and ambition. She didn't want him to be and decided to give up her ambition: "I realized, though, I couldn't do it, that I couldn't give up writing lengthy reports for work. And to his credit, he realized it, too. He told me and meant it, 'Do what you have to do.'"

7. *Work hard at being a team. There are enough good things in life for both of you. If your mate wins at something, it doesn't mean you lose.*

A woman reported that her husband took her out for a special dinner after she received a raise. They discussed how they would both spend her windfall.

8. *Become a supportive part of your mate's success.*

When I gave a talk at a conference, my husband tape-recorded it. In so doing, he felt a part of my accomplishment.

9. *Be inspired by someone else.*

A friend, who is a successful therapist, has a husband who is just starting school to become a therapist. He feels awe at how much she enjoys her work and realizes that his goal is to use his envy of his wife to further his own development.

10. *Laugh at your own envy.*

Richard Blum, husband of San Francisco mayor Diane Feinstein, introduced himself during a trip to Israel as "Mr. Diane Feinstein."

CHAPTER 6

Envy in the Workplace

Lynn, an envied worker, wore a mohair dress to an office party. Her envious boss introduced Lynn, saying: "Oh, Lynn is from Anchorage, that's why she wears blankets." Lynn's friends call this boss a "True Pluperfect Bitch Boss."

EXPLORING ENVY IN THE WORKPLACE

Why is there so much envy in the workplace? It was reported by 84 percent of women surveyed—in fact, respondents reported more negative envy in the workplace than anywhere else. We do spend a large chunk of our time at work, but is there something particular about the workplace that makes it a setting ripe for envy?

Business is a calculated game, a game with rules based on competition and comparison. In most work situations, the stated goal is to get a job done. Unfortunately, the job often gets done by "besting" your co-worker rather than by working together as a team. Many workers believe that success at work is determined by who comes out on top: Who is earning more money? Who's getting promoted faster? Who's doing better work? Who has a higher position? Who does the boss like best? The comparisons underlying these questions lead to dissatisfaction, and where dissatisfactions abound, envy grows.

In the workplace, envy takes a number of forms, sometimes outrageous, sometimes benign. Some women are victims of envy, some evoke it. However, there are possible ways to deal with the envy you feel at work.

What Are Women Envied For at Work?

Women gave these answers: for being younger and more skillful, younger and more carefree, younger and more ambitious, younger and prettier, older and attractive. For getting more attention. For special treatment by a boss, for a good relationship with her supervisor, for not being intimidated by her supervisor, for her assertiveness with co-workers.

For being a waitress preferred by customers; a nurse more liked by patients; a poet more popular with the public; an artist who demonstrates more creativity. For being the boss's daughter. For having more patients than another psychiatrist. For job contacts, for landing the largest contract an architectural firm ever had. For working her way through college, for not having to work her way through college. For financial comfort, for her husband. For being the one in charge, for being able to give orders, for not having to do her own typing. For her sudden success in writing a published article. For self-confidence, spunk, for loving life, for having a strong personality, for taking things in stride.

For catching on quickly to the task at hand, for doing a good job with the boss's work when he was on vacation. For landing a job that another worker wanted. For a foreign accent. For getting ahead in her career; for being hardworking and taking fewer breaks; for not being hardworking and being able to take time off. For being able to get changes made, for competence, for skills, for praise from others. For being good at office politics. For working full time, for working part time. For popularity and high spirits. For a husband who sends flowers. For her wardrobe, for her possessions. For not kowtowing to people, for stamina and organizational ability. For a husband who shares the child care and housework, for having "the perfect life," for "having it made," for "having made it." And throughout all these examples, the whimpering wonder of "why you and not me?"

Privileges

"Privilege" means having a right or advantage not enjoyed by another. As women talked about what they are envied for at work, I heard that one's skills or ability to do a job are not envied nearly as much as one's privileges.

Sometimes these privileges are real. Helene, a teacher in Los Angeles, has the advantage of inherited wealth; she teaches in a public school but lives in a palatial home. A fellow teacher refuses to come to her house for school meetings, because, as she says, she needs to meet on neutral territory.

Helene admits, "I don't like being envied. It's an unfriendly feeling. It's not that people like you because you have more than they do. They don't like you. I would rather be liked than envied.

"When I'm envied, I feel embarrassed. I laugh it off, but that doesn't work. I wish I could just say something direct and honest, like 'I live in this house because I can afford it. My father died and left me this money to buy it. That's the way it is. Period.' "

Being envied for privilege comes as a surprise when you don't feel privileged. A woman told me her co-workers see her as privileged because she has good relationships with her supervisors, and others consult her. At a staff meeting recently, she made a comment to which one of her co-workers retorted, "How would you know? You eat off china." The woman had no idea at the time what the co-worker was talking about, but a friend later explained, "She meant you are privileged."

A thirty-five-year-old purchasing agent for a Washington hospital writes that co-workers envy her because they think her life is too easy. She disagrees. "They see only that I cope easily with problems. They aren't aware of my private feelings of frustration, loneliness, fear, and depression. They prefer to see the appearance of my life because it justifies their position. They could be in my position if they worked as hard as I do. Being envied should mean I am successful—but it makes me feel misunderstood, angry, and frustrated." Any woman who does a good job can be seen as privileged by her co-workers. And she will have to deal with the envy the real or imagined privilege arouses.

Owning your own business and having employees. What happens when you are in charge of your own business and have people working for you? Patricia owns her own massage studio and has four envious employees.

One shows her envy by trying to do Patricia's job for her. Because she envies Patricia's being in charge, she acts as though *she* were in charge. Another employee tries to change the rules without Patricia's approval; she gives orders to her co-workers, says *she* won't see this or that type of client.

A third employee shows her envy by being critical, complaining that there isn't an adequate supply of sheets or that the studio fails to serve enough kinds of tea (there are already twelve varieties being offered). She openly criticizes Patricia anytime Patricia doesn't agree with her.

A fourth employee disguises her envy with a mask of gooey affection: "Oh, Patty-poo, aren't you the sweetest thing, my peach tart!" Her display embarrasses Patricia and is experienced as hostility rather than caring.

Working in a family-owned business. Sally works for her father's company. Her co-workers believe she has special privileges at work, but actually she doesn't. They are sarcastic and ask probing questions about her life. Once Sally was called upstairs to the manager and told that people were complaining, "You have body odor." Sally thought it was funny. "This is the way I smell." Just to make sure, she checked it out with her cleanest friends, who all agreed she didn't have body odor.

Being preferred by the boss. Being in a privileged position in a company, as we all well know, creates even more privileges. Paula is a stockbroker who earns more money than the other stockbrokers; they see her as having management in the "palm of her hand."

Two groups of people envy Paula. The rejecting group shows its envy by snubbing her or never asking her questions. Those in the overly accepting group want to be friends with her not because they like her, but because of her position in the company. They are like co-workers who suddenly become your buddy just because you have been made a supervisor. They are friendly, but you keep wondering why.

Paula knows that management has created some of the envy because it made her the fair-haired child. Management doesn't care about fairness, it just wants Paula to keep bringing in the bucks. She is treated with special favors, has more people working for her, her expenses are paid for, she gets to travel, and she is exempted from rules that apply to others. You might receive similar envy if you, like Paula, are in favor with your management.

In addition to her privileged position at work, Paula is also cute, blond, athletic, and thirty-one: the perfect target. Paula lists the ways in which she tries to limit the envy coming her way.

- She acts like a "mother type." She likes people to tell her their problems, and she is helpful.
- She quietly encourages people to get to know her and her problems.
- She goes out of her way to befriend any co-worker she feels is potentially envious. She makes herself accessible.

Paula believes these actions are a necessary part of her job, and this pays off, so to speak.

Promotions and salary increases. Nora, the thirty-nine-year-old bank consultant with the curly red hair and the envious mother, has been envied for getting a pay raise, and rising up in the company—a situation that always creates envy.

"I am highly envied now because I am a consultant and I make twice as much money as my managers. Some say it straight out: 'You're lucky to earn so much money. You can make your own hours, you don't have to put up with all the politics.'"

Nora is envied because she has regularly been promoted. She worked as a secretary at the bank for six years—worked hard—and was promoted to supervisor of the secretaries. Other secretaries struggled to understand her promotions; they would band together, and ask personnel "How could Nora be promoted? We are older." But Nora, unlike the other secretaries, had gone to night school and earned a B.A. in business.

When Nora wanted to become a paid consultant, she continued her schooling and received an MBA. Some associates asked, "What magic wand is changing you from a secretary to consultant? Lucky girl, you have all the breaks." Nora would simply respond, "There weren't any breaks. I don't have a rich father. I studied. I went back to school. I worked hard."

People often assume your success is handed to you on a silver platter. Or they believe it's because of what you look like, whom you slept with, whom you know, or what you ate for breakfast, rather than your perseverance or skill.

Nora continues, "My previous manager is now thirty-three, a very bright woman. When I chose to become a consultant and got a raise, she was dismayed. 'I can't believe *you* did that.' She offered me a full-time job as employee instead of hired consultant. If I'd accepted, I would have gotten half the pay for twice the work. That is how she showed her envy."

Nora told her manager, "I'm really sorry that you have difficulty with my raise. I don't blame you. But I deserve to make what a consultant makes." Nora knew her manager was upset because of envy, she was patient with her, and soon her manager changed her attitude.

Being on the move. You don't have to be a wealthy teacher, stockbroker, or banker to be envied. Every waitress I interviewed reported envy at the job. As a career waitress, you might envy younger, livelier, more cheerful women who move in on your territory. When waitressing has been your lifework and you treasure your skills and your particular relationships with customers, when you've worked hard, you may feel the young new waitresses are upstarts and intruders. These "intruders" are often able to find another job if waitressing doesn't work out. Some women reported being envied because for them, waitressing was a stepping-stone to something else.

One new waitress is also envied because she naturally smiles all the time and the customers like her. Customers request her table, and with her they talk, talk, talk. She told me, "The waitress who particularly envied me had been at the restaurant a long time, had made a career out of the job, and wasn't a happy person. She herself had trouble smiling and being cheerful, and ended up not even speaking to me. I was the new waitress. I got great tips. Not only was I an intruder, but I am a happy person."

Another woman, who was not a career waitress, reports that her boss envied her ability to leave the job behind. "My boss bitched constantly, rode me horribly. She would always side with the unsatisfied customer against me, saying that I was an 'asshole' and the customer was right. It was my fault even when it obviously wasn't my fault. She would give me the worst schedule, nights with the least customers, and on those nights would give me the worst tables. I was insecure at first, afraid I couldn't find another job, but I did, and ended up earning three times as much as I had as a waitress."

On the other hand, younger waitresses might envy the older waitresses' skills. You know, the waitress who can carry fifteen plates at shoulder level and remain unriled while her customers bang their spoons for service.

Waitresses, those free to come and go and those whose antennae pick up the threat of young blood approaching, need to recognize they share a situation full of potential envy. They must address the problem from both sides of the coffeeshop counter.

Standing One's Ground

Envy plays in a higher octave when the person who envies you has power over you, your job, and your life. Many women told me they are envied for not being afraid of their bosses or supervisors, for being able to stand up to them.

Melinda, a forty-two-year-old architect in Manhattan, describes her last job. Her immediate supervisor was incredibly obsequious to his superiors and envious of Melinda's ability not to "kiss ass." He treated Melinda sweetly in front of their mutual boss, but when the two of them were alone, he dropped his façade.

Her supervisor gave her the dirty work, trying to sidetrack her from design, the work she loved and was hired to do, work that made him feel inferior. If Melinda came up with a good idea, her envious supervisor would try to undercut it. Finally—and this is a common ploy—he would try to prevent her getting access to information she needed to get the job done. He "forgot" to leave her messages when people called her. "He had a direct line with the clients, would do all the communicating with them, and would misinform me of what they said. I found that I would design something based on the wrong premise, so then to make sure, I would call the clients directly and they would put me on the right track. They liked me; we had good rapport, and that left my supervisor feeling worse."

Mary, thirty-eight, works for an executive search firm. Her supervisor, Jim, worries that Mary will move in on his relationship with Barry, Jim's boss and vice-president of the company. Jim envies Mary's self-assurance and self-confidence.

Mary realized that Jim was envious of her. "I was working diligently and hurriedly toward a deadline on a consulting assignment. Barry walked by my door and, as usual, declared, 'We have to have a meeting immediately.' He never scheduled meetings; he had them only when he wanted to, on his timetable, like King Tut.

"Two hours earlier he had told me to work hard and get the project done. I was hot, on the phone long distance with a candidate, taking notes, doing important work for the company, when he came in and demanded a meeting. I replied, 'Not now, Barry. I'm busy.' He backed off meekly. 'Oh, I'm sorry.' "

That evening Mary worked late and went for drinks with her supervisor, Jim, and two other workers. When they were at the bar, Jim asked, "Do you guys want to hear what Mary said to Barry? She said, 'Not now, Barry.' " It was a joke to the three of them, and they teased, "Can you believe she said that to Barry Carter? 'Not now'?"

Mary had the nerve, the guts, to speak up to Barry. Jim, her supervisor, was scared stiff of Barry. Jim envied Mary because Barry respected her enough to apologize and jump back.

"Jim became more actively worried about my taking control. He would try to subvert me, lie about my performance. He was afraid I'd do a bang-up job. I wondered, How could he be envious of me? He and Barry were buddies. What could he have to worry about? He was a man—and higher up in the company."

As long as you are in the winning or losing mode, you will, like Jim, likely feel envy.

Having Whatever Your Boss Wishes He or She Had

Roberta, in a Ph.D. program in anthropology, is envied by her teacher, Cheryl, the head of her Ph.D. dissertation committee. Says Roberta of Cheryl, her own wicked queen boss, "I could kill her. I wouldn't kill her, but I sure do hate her."

When Cheryl first taught Roberta, she found her to be one of the brightest students in the department. When Roberta initially entered the Ph.D. program, she was married but had no kids. She appeared to have a great career ahead of her. Cheryl had one child, a nine-year-old boy, whom she had placed in full-time child care when he was two months old. Cheryl works full time, is now tenured, and her son is still in full-time child care, before and after school.

At first, Cheryl and Roberta worked well together. But Roberta recalls, "After I had my first child and refused to put him in full-time child care, and our differences became apparent, my relationship with Cheryl totally changed. Although I didn't know it at the time, envy invaded our closeness. I had thought that my professional and personal lives were separate: I was naive.

"Cheryl envied my ability to make time to take care of my own child." Roberta didn't know that her attitude about child raising would put Cheryl into an envious frenzy from which she could not exit.

The first sign of envy came when Cheryl invited Roberta to begin work on a doctoral thesis and suggested the topic of "The Role of the Mother in Transmitting Language in Comparative Cultures."

All Roberta knew was that "after I didn't put Danny in full-time child care, and then, two years later, when I didn't put my new baby girl in full-time child care, either, every communication with Cheryl engendered vituperation. For example, she wrote me a note about scheduling. When I called her back she launched into a tirade: 'You haven't finished your dissertation. You are letting down the whole research team. Because of you, no one else has published any work, and no one will get a grant. You are holding everyone back. And because of you, no other women graduate students will be admitted to the anthropology department.'"

The envied person often feels guilty for being envied. Roberta had chosen her topic so that she would *not* be on a team and was doing research in areas where she could not possibly hold up anyone else. But she still felt guilty. "Cheryl implied I should feel guilty, and I did. She accused me of spoiling everyone else's effort, and I thought how terrible it was of *me* to have two babies."

Six weeks after her daughter was born, Roberta reported on her recent research at a seminar during which Cheryl repeatedly asked the same question about an analysis Roberta hadn't done yet. Another graduate student came to Roberta's rescue. "Look, Cheryl, Roberta said she is going to do that question next. So don't keep asking her about it." Cheryl replied, "Roberta doesn't ever do what she says she is going to do. She says she's going to do things, but all she does is keep having babies."

Cheryl's criticism was not true. "The fact that I was six weeks postpartum and had gotten together this talk, a good one that was well received, was amazing. Furthermore, I always follow through on time. I'm compulsive that way. Cheryl went so far as to suggest, 'If you were more serious about your work, you would ask your husband to take a six-month absence from his job so you could finish your dissertation.'"

After a series of humiliating confrontations, "she stopped talking to me. I went home one day and burst into an hysterical fit of tears and told David, my husband, 'She will never sign my dissertation. She is behaving irrationally, and I don't know how to handle her. She is emotionally disturbed.'"

Again, a big problem exists when the person who envies you has power and authority over you, and you need something from him or her. She can use your dependency on her to make you suffer. You feel you have to give in to her wishes to get what you want. It was a real fight for Roberta not to simply give up, but she knew that if she stayed calm and produced work of scientific merit, Cheryl would be vetoed by the other dissertation committee members.

Two weeks later, the department secretary called Roberta at nine A.M. "Cheryl asked me to invite you to a seminar today at two P.M." Cheryl, who knew that Roberta had limited baby-sitting, planned the seminar weeks earlier and had just that morning asked the secretary to invite Roberta. Roberta asked, "What is the title of the seminar?" When the secretary told her, it sounded like the topic of Roberta's dissertation!

At the seminar Cheryl came as close to plagiarizing Roberta's work as she could. "She didn't cite my work. Instead, she used it, rewrote it independently without my consent. Bad business. Since she had had my research proposal for the past 2½ years, she was hardly ignorant of what she was doing. It was psychological warfare. She was trying to force me out."

The faculty at the seminar made it clear to Cheryl that she was clearly out of bounds. But envious people can be very clever. Cheryl sandwiched in another graduate student and made her the primary author of the work presented at the seminar. Roberta went into a panic and realized she had to write up her work as soon as possible. Quickly she finished chapter one. Cheryl was hostile. "Okay, if you're so close to being done, it is now October and I want a complete draft by Thanksgiving." Since Roberta had written only one chapter, the other committee members thought this an impossible deadline.

Roberta bit the bullet and accepted the challenge. "I went right to it. I stayed up every night until three A.M. My husband did all the child care. I did all the typing."

She surprised everyone and met the deadline.

After Roberta gave Cheryl the completed dissertation, she heard nothing for months. Cheryl wouldn't even answer Roberta's phone calls, so Roberta enlisted the help of her major adviser, demanding to receive Cheryl's comments on her work. The adviser reported that Cheryl had insisted on giving her comments only to him, not to Roberta. He sent the material to Roberta anyway, but only the first of ten chapters had been reviewed!

Roberta demanded that her major adviser get the comments on the other nine chapters or, she told him, she would quit. "Cheryl's plan was to pretend I didn't exist and maybe I would go away. That must have been her wish—to snuff me out. You can't do that, hold on to a student's work for five months and never comment on all of it."

The major adviser, who avoids conflicts, told Roberta that he had no control over Cheryl. Roberta was furious. "Well, then I'm going to the dean." By announcing that she would inform the dean, Roberta demonstrated she would not give in to Cheryl's envy.

On the same night Cheryl agreed she would sign the dissertation, she came to Roberta's house with a bottle of wine and congratulations. "Is that nerve? I never drank it. I knew it was poison. I just knew she would come over that night, I just knew." Snow White should have known the apple her stepmother offered was poison, but Snow White longed for maternal kindness more than Roberta needed Cheryl's well-wishes or approval.

Because Roberta developed a growing awareness of Cheryl's envy, and because she had a strong wish to succeed and do fine work, she refused to let Cheryl's envy destroy her. But it wasn't easy. It never is. Said Roberta, "I suffered. My family suffered, my psychological health and spirit suffered. Cheryl almost destroyed me."

Surprisingly, Roberta never tried to get back at Cheryl but just worked with the lessons she was learning on her own.

- Identify the envy.
- Talk to others about the envy.
- Expect to be criticized and undermined.
- Bypass the envy.
- Realize the attempt at sabotage and find alternative ways to protect yourself, especially when the envier has power over you.
- Forge ahead.

Evoking Envy in the Workplace

Few women know that the negative behavior coming their way stems from envy until this behavior becomes a tremendous force. Some women certainly don't feel that they do anything to provoke or create it; they say they don't flaunt their skills, money, beauty, ambition, clothes, spunk, or individuality. They "can't help" being envied—they think they're "just being themselves."

At work or anywhere, you want to make the most of what you've got. There's a fine line, though, between "just being yourself" and subtly seeking out the attention and envy of others. Although not everyone tries consciously to be envied, most of us want to be recognized, appreciated, accepted, liked. We play up our gifts with an awareness that it feels good to be noticed. But when we are not sensitive to how our success affects others, we may evoke envy.

Remember Sarah, whose envious mother pushed her toward good grades? Her co-workers were bothered by her cheery manner and seductive body. These qualities did not cause much envy during her first six years at the job, years during which she complained of an unhappy marriage and then a painful divorce. By the seventh year, however, Sarah was in love and about to marry. It is no coincidence that her co-workers and supervisor chose this time to exhibit their envy.

Sarah is an open, talkative, enthusiastic young woman who does not always think about the consequences of what she's about to say. As her wedding approached she was bubbling with excitement, using her office in the hospital administration department to make many of her wedding plans. She used the hospital phone to call about the flowers, the catering, and her gown. She talked about the wedding, discussed the gifts she and her fiancé were getting, and described the fun they had had the night before.

She invited her co-workers and supervisors to the wedding, and all seemed to have gone well. Everyone laughed and drank champagne and appeared to be sharing in the wedding joy and merriment. But when Sarah returned from her honeymoon at a Jamaican resort, all hell broke loose for her at work. She was due for her biannual progress review, at which the staff meets to inform the employee of her progress, with an emphasis on her capabilities. It is commonly agreed that all criticism be constructive; no one is ever trashed at these meetings.

Sarah was not prepared for the onslaught she encountered, because her past reviews had been replete with praise and positive regard. This time her supervisors, who presided over the meeting, presented a long list of Sarah's problems. Sarah had been

- acting anxious, and this made her co-workers anxious;
- curt when patients would call with problems;
- angry;
- falling behind on the literature in hospital administration;
- late to work;
- out sick.

The list went on and on. Nothing was said about Sarah's wedding plans or that her mind was not on the job; nothing about her strengths or that she was actually doing good work. When Sarah tried to defend herself, to say that she didn't think she had been angry, the response was, "You're being defensive."

This is an old and familiar trick used by people who use psychological jargon. If you are attacked verbally, you want—and have the right—to defend yourself. But if you defend yourself, you are often labeled as "defensive," which is a put-down. Then, if you defend against *that,* you are criticized again for being defensive. When you are put down for being defensive, you could say, "Yes, I am being defensive. I feel I am being attacked." This puts the other person on the spot.

Sarah continued to defend herself but never put the others on the spot: "You have been talking for one hundred minutes, and you haven't said anything positive." One supervisor replied, "There is nothing positive to say."

Sarah took this pretty hard. She and I talked about envy and its implications. Weddings, in all cultures, create envy. If Sarah had been aware that her wedding and her joy would create envy in those who felt they didn't have the same fullness in their lives, she might have acted differently. She might have been more careful about broadcasting her wedding plans at work; she could have lowered her enthusiasm, not altogether, but maybe an octave. She might have anticipated some negativity at her peer review meeting.

Sarah was supposed to have been given constructive criticism.

Instead, out came the big guns telling her how bad she was. The intensity of the attack should have made Sarah suspicious that something else was going on.

She could have reassured herself, "They are upset with me for getting married, for showing off about it. However, I am still a good worker." In maintaining a sense of her own worth, Sarah could have listened better to their criticism, deciding for herself what was valid and what wasn't. In becoming upset at their response, Sarah gave her co-workers something real to criticize: she became so anxious to please *after* her review that she subsequently performed worse than before.

Sarah could not deal adequately with this situation because she had not learned to handle envy from her past, her mother's envy in particular. Only hindsight provided her with answers. "Now it all seems familiar. My mother felt the same way about me. I let my mother win. And I let my supervisors win by doing worse at work. Not next time!"

As usual, her bosses had the final word. They encouraged her to leave her job by threatening to demote her. Sarah felt better about herself after we were able to identify their envy and her fear of their envy. She decided to find a new job and made a number of resolutions:

- To be more aware of envy the next go-around.
- To do less to evoke envy, and to be sensitive to the effect her joy could have on others.
- Not to take the envy of her bosses or co-workers as a true statement about herself, and to see envy as a statement, in part, about them and what they feel they are lacking.
- To maintain her good feelings about herself in the face of someone else's envious assault.

How Your Envy Hurts You

It's clear that all these women have been hurt by the envy of others. But women who envy also hurt themselves.

Diana teaches at a southern university. She co-teaches with a woman who is an effective, popular teacher. In one class, Diana happens to be especially funny. When Diana teaches this class there is a mood of congenial repartee that isn't there when it's her colleague's turn to teach. Diana is "on" in the best sense, catching the flow, quick on the uptake.

The co-teacher wants what Diana has and becomes more and more envious. She grows hostile to Diana, with whom she has previously gotten along. The more envious she becomes, the more her appeal with the class diminishes, the more the class enjoys Diana, and the funnier Diana becomes. Diana told me, "I knew I wasn't better. I knew we taught differently. She has her own strengths. We never talked about it. The more my co-teacher compares herself to me, the more she turns the hostility she feels toward me against herself, and the more envious and less effective she becomes."

What can you learn here? Different does not mean better or worse; it just means different, *not alike*. For example, the co-teacher is intellectual and knows more than Diana about theory and publications in their field. Her students liked her in the past. The co-teacher needs to reestablish herself as a separate person with her own style and values, her own standard of excellence.

HANDLING ENVY IN THE WORKPLACE

Sexism, Racism, and Envy in the Workplace

When we deal with sexism and racism in the workplace, we are also dealing with envy. Racism, sexism, and envy are ways of separating one group of people from another. Each is based on the assumption that the number of rewards in the workplace is limited; on the fear that if someone takes a small piece of the pie, your piece will be in jeopardy.

In the following examples, racism, sexism, and envy play a role: a black woman in a white-dominated workplace, a white woman in a male-dominated workplace, and a Chicana woman in a Chicano male-dominated workplace all are effective in dealing with the racism, sexism, and envy they encounter.

JENNIFER

Jennifer, a black attorney, joined a prestigious law firm directly out of law school. The 140 attorneys in the firm included only 4 black men and 2 women. Jennifer tells us, "I was hired because I was qualified, but also because of what they called my 'visibility.' People were uncomfortable with me, and I felt I had to spend all my time making others feel good in order to avoid that look of 'Why are you here, this is *my* place.'

"They acted surprised when I actually came up with something from all the shit work they gave me to do. They didn't expect good work out of a black woman. Like 'My God! You can do that!' when it was exactly what I was hired for."

For minority women, envy and racism are rarely distinguishable from one another; Jennifer felt she was envied, yet her story has the familiar ring of racism. Many people, she explained, go overboard with, "You dress so well." She can never be sure how much is racism, how much is envy, and how much is a simple statement about her dress.

RUTH

Ruth Gordon, fifty-eight, is the first woman registered as a structural engineer in the state of California. She has been married to a supportive husband for thirty-six years and is the mother of three children, all doing well. She is gracious, popular, high-spirited, and a dedicated feminist.

Considering Ruth's strength as a person, it's no wonder she has met envy head on throughout her career. When she went to Stanford in 1943, only men in the engineering department had access to the files of old exams and tests, passing them on to one another and refusing to share them with women in the class. This discrimination worked to Ruth's advantage when a professor occasionally used a different test from that which was expected. Only those who had really studied were able to pass the test. Ruth passed.

After she received her master's degree, Ruth applied for an instructor's position at a local college. She received an enthusiastic reply to her letter, which she had signed using only her initials. When she walked into the job interview, she was told, "We don't hire women." She went to work elsewhere, for a man who was interested in her abilities, not her sex, and began designing hospitals.

In 1953, she applied for membership in the Structural Engineers Association of Northern California. Because she was the first woman to apply, her application had to go through several months of disruptive board meetings, but finally she was admitted. "When I showed up at the engineers' club for my first lunchtime committee meeting, I was told that women were not allowed to lunch there."

Ruth worked for the state of California, mostly in earthquake safety, for twenty-nine years. Basically, she is a hard hat, but besides the hat, she wears a T-shirt inscribed, "The right man for the job may be a woman."

Ruth is presently opening her own private consultation firm. "The reasons I left the state have entirely to do with envy. Here are a few:

"Item one: I was number two on the list for promotions, and they skipped over me and chose number six on the list. They chose a WASP male. I was completely blocked.

"Item two: One day there was a clipping in my box with the headline, THE IRS WILL NOW ALLOW YOU TO DEDUCT A FACELIFT FROM YOUR INCOME TAX.

"Item three: Another time I returned to my desk and found two fortune cookies with the messages, 'The great fault in women is the desire to be like men' and 'You are almost there.' "

Ruth does not go down for the count easily. There had been a directive from the state saying that not only was it illegal to make sexual and racial innuendos on the job or to discriminate on the basis of race or sex, it was also illegal not to report such incidents. So Ruth stormed into her boss's office and told him, "We have to report all this." When her boss refused, Ruth went to Sacramento, the incidents were investigated, and her boss was told he had to circulate a directive outlawing sexual discrimination. Finally he acquiesced, but he included a disclaimer, announcing he was doing so only because he had been ordered to.

In starting her own firm, Ruth is determined both not to let envy get her down and to help other women with similar problems. "There is not one male or female who has achieved something entirely alone. There is always someone or some group that has been supportive or paved the way.

"One of my pet peeves," she continues, "is the queen bee attitude of successful women who refuse to acknowledge their debt to the feminists who pushed for sex to be included in the civil rights and equality laws.

"Being 'the first,' or 'just one of a few,' is a great responsibility. We should take every opportunity to act as role models for young women and girls." Therefore, we should not let our envy of the success of others hurt them, for we need to rely on each other for help.

Most working women agree that we must move away from the weakness of envy warfare toward the strength of women's natural tendency toward intimacy, relationship, and sensitivity. For example, in her book *Feminine Leadership*, Marilyn Loden finds that women who hold positions of power in business use that power differently from men. Loden describes a more cooperative operating style, a team-oriented organization, an increased concern with quality, and a reliance on emotional as well as rational data. She believes women tend to be more careful with the impact of their behavior on their co-workers and more able to give power to their employees. This is one alternative to the stereotypical office politics that many women find so demoralizing.

DOLORES HUERTA

Dolores Huerta is first vice-president and co-founder of the United Farm Workers, a union headed by Cesar Chavez that represents one and a half million farm workers and laborers in our country. She is married to Cesar Chavez's brother, Richard Chavez. Dolores deals mostly with Mexican-American men, at the organizational level of the union.

She is a troubleshooter for the union, a fund-raiser, and a public speaker. She built and directed the first grape boycott in the East and in northern California in 1968, and the lettuce, grapes, and Gallo wine boycott in 1974–1975. She wrote and negotiated all the original farm labor contracts between the growers and the union, and does political work and lobbying in Sacramento and Washington, D.C. She was one of the first to include toilets, medical benefits, and pension plans for farm workers in the United Farm Workers contracts.

Dolores hopes to strengthen the participation of women in the union. She was at the founding convention of the Coalition of Labor Union Women organization (CLUW), which has over 25,000 women as members. At the last CLUW convention, half the delegates were black and brown, half were white. "I have not seen that kind of participation of minority women at any other women's convention."

When I asked Dolores what it meant to her to be successful, she was quick to respond, "To help the greatest number of people possible and make social changes." She is on her way. And as if her work weren't enough, she has eleven children, four since she turned forty. She is fifty-five, looks thirty-five, and has the energy of twenty-five.

She was thrilled to be able to talk about envy, because it is something she has to deal with every day. She believes that male chauvinism has envy at its base.

Dolores has been vice-president of the union since it began in the sixties. Often when a new man joins the leadership group, her position and prestige are challenged. She'll tell one of the new union officials, "I have had to put up with male chauvinism in general, and I've had to put up with Richard's [Chavez] chauvinism because he is my 'old man,' but I don't have to put up with yours." Eventually, as she gained confidence in herself, she realized that she didn't have to put up with her husband's chauvinism, either.

How is envy expressed toward her? Dolores stresses it is mostly men, aspiring to leadership positions, who envy her. Some men envy her job contacts and the fact that she can work easily with different people. She is comfortable with farm workers, middle-class people, professionals, politicians, labor people, and with the famous and the wealthy, who help her with fund-raising. Some men undermine her, take credit for her projects, or make decisions about her work without involving her.

One time she worked on a communications project for months and eventually turned the project around. But she was taken off that assignment and never told why. She assumed that some of the envious men were worried that if she continued with the communications project, she might become too powerful.

What does Dolores do when she is envied? She calls the envier on it. "Hey, wait a minute! A decision is being made here that involves me. Why am I not being included?"

Dolores is able to take credit for her work because she is not afraid of being envied. "Men don't give you credit for work done. I used to think it was the work of the group alone that mattered. I wouldn't single myself out. But I found that men in the union, out of their envy for me, took credit for my work, such as contracts, slogans, boycotts. I wanted people to know I had done it.

"By taking credit for my own work, I embarrassed one of our vice-presidents. He made a speech at a public gathering and gave Richard, my husband, credit for the grape boycott in New York City. I replied to his speech, 'I want to correct you on one thing. Your speech was very fine, but I was the one who organized the work in New York, not Richard Chavez, but I, Dolores Huerta.'

"Afterward, he was furious. 'How could you do that? You embarrassed me, and it was my first speech as an officer!' "

Dolores was cool. "You embarrassed me," she told him.

Dolores makes sure other women get credit for their accomplishments, too. For example, a man reported on all the gains the union had made in Texas. Dolores stood up and announced, "You forgot to mention Rebecca Flores Harrington. She did *all* of the work."

The man who made the mistake commented, "Oh, well, it's a man's world," as if it were a big joke.

Dolores takes the offensive when she hears what she considers to be disguised envy in sexist jokes. "By the way," she told the man who made the "joke," "I cannot cover the meetings for you that I was going to. You will have to do them yourself." He got the message. "When men make a sexist statement, I call them on it immediately. Women have to. We don't allow jokes about a black person, an Hispanic, or a Jew, so why do we allow sexist remarks?

"I try to get the envy turned into respect. Men respect you when they don't know what to expect, when they see you moving, doing, scurrying about, being effective. If you take the offensive against envy, they have to pull back and respect you, if they need you at all."

In part, Dolores deals with envy well because as a young child, her mother taught Dolores not to take it personally when other girls showed envy of Dolores's popularity. "Don't worry about it," her mother explained, "they're just envious of you." As a teenager, Dolores learned that envy could flare up through no fault of her own. Her mother's mandate was "Be yourself," which also helped Dolores with her own envy toward other people.

Even though Dolores feels hurt when she is envied, *she doesn't let the fear of being envied lessen her self-assertion.* "If I do feel hurt, I try not to give in to their envy. I try to turn it into something positive. Maybe it means I did something good, so maybe it's a plus, not a minus." She is aware that the more visible you become, the more envy you get.

For Delores the worst response to being envied is depression, which she knows from experience can last for months. As a leader, she has been depressed and immobilized even though people expected her to remain active. She becomes upset as she and I talk about this depression. At first she tries to joke about it: "Maybe we should make a slogan out of it, like 'Guys Envy Us—Isn't That Nice?' or 'Guys Envy Us—Too Bad for Them.'" But to her it's not really funny, and the nonjoke falls flat.

"I don't have all the answers," she says more quietly than usual. "Just one: Women don't have to become less to make someone else more."

How Envy Is Expressed in the Workplace

In Helping Professions

Envy hits every kind of workplace, even where the stated goal is helping each other: labor unions, schools, clinics, hospitals, and psychotherapy offices.

Warning: Your therapist's envy may be dangerous to your health. Are you in therapy? Are you considering therapy? Check out the package first. Is your therapist low or high in envy?

As a psychotherapist who has dealt with hundreds of patients over the past sixteen years, I am aware of how envy invades the helping relationship. What's usually written about and discussed is the patient's envy of the therapist; little is written about the therapist's envy of the patient. Yet fifty-seven percent of the women interviewed were aware of being envied by their helpers. And therapists, teachers, doctors, and coaches—people in positions of power and authority—reported envying the people they help.

I will tell my story, but it *stands for and exemplifies* the stories of many other helpers, those who acknowledge their envy and those who don't.

There are many reasons I, or another helper, might envy the person being helped. I am not the patient; the patient gets the help, the concern, the attention. During therapy appointments where

I've been particularly effective, I've thought, wouldn't it be lovely to have someone as comforting and maternal as I am being to listen to *me* now. No one is without her own wishes to be taken care of.

The therapy relationship is a unique one, a vicarious one. I sit in my chair, in a calm, good mood one day and in an agitated, bad mood the next. But I sit: the patient comes and goes. We talk of her exploits, adventures, feelings, and thoughts. I am being paid to hide some of who I am. I envy her ability to reveal all of who she is.

Every person has something enviable. I might envy a patient who is more creative, intellectually quicker, more eloquent, more political, less political, more imaginative, funnier. She might be younger, better-looking, more appealing. She might be more organized while my files are a mess. She might be an artist pursuing what matters to her, not attending to other people's needs. She might be spiritual and have no questions about the Lord's goodness and presence in her life. Whether she is a musician, housewife, or political activist, she might be fulfilling my own secret dreams.

I envy the patient who talks about her trust fund when I just received a pile of "past due" bills that morning. I envy the patient who talks with joy and delight of her recent two-month trip to Europe while I spent her vacation working eight hours a day, receiving crisis phone calls in the evening. I have helped women leave unfulfilling jobs; they now live on unemployment and savings as they take the necessary time to explore a more satisfying career.

Many helpers are driven to excel. Their schedules are consistently full. They envy their patients' capacity to "take it easy." As a working mother, I cannot find enough time to play tennis. I have had a patient, living on unemployment and savings, who awakens when she wants to, call to change tomorrow's appointment because she has an important tennis engagement.

Another moment of envy: I am rushing to my office for a patient at eight A.M. In the car, I try to remember my dream of the night before. The patient is waiting when I arrive. Immediately she begins talking, enthusiastically telling me of two dreams she just had; my attention turns to her. My own dream is lost.

THERAPIST ENVY OF BARBARA

If people in the helping professions aren't aware of their envious feelings, they are more likely to actually hurt the people they are supposed to be helping. Of course their envy is worse on the days they're feeling less successful or fulfilled.

Here's a case where I had to battle envy's nature. Barbara, age thirty, is a funny, perky, self-critical teacher. Athletic and energetic, she recently divorced after three years of feeling rejected by her husband. He preferred women with "more meat on them—something I can grab on to." She has been in therapy for the past year complaining about being lonely, depressed, "over the hill."

Barbara had many dates but was convinced she would never find a man that meets her standards. In order to understand Barbara, we need to know about the patient in the Snow White syndrome. Patients already have a tendency not to get better in therapy because they fear their therapist's envy. Patients view their therapist as a parent figure. Just as children want to avoid their parents' envy, patients want to avoid their therapist's envy. I've seen patients who restrain themselves from getting better because they're afraid that in leaving therapy, they will hurt the therapist's feelings, self-esteem, schedule, or pocketbook.

I know Barbara's complaints are temporary; I know they are, in part, an unconscious attempt to keep me from envying her and her newfound freedom. She has many possibilities for the future. She views me as older, married, not as free to make a fresh start.

Off Barbara bounced one week to Club Med in Mexico. She came back glowing, relaxed, in love: the honeymoon phase. She could talk of nothing other than romance, sex, and the new man, David.

Here comes Barbara: "We made love five times Sunday. It was fabulous. Nothing like it. What do you think, Betsy? Don't you think that's too much? That we're not really getting to know each other? Do you think sex is an escape? That we should be seeing more people than just each other? Maybe we should take it slower."

There sits Betsy, the envious therapist. I feel like saying, "You sound so happy. Shouldn't you prepare yourself for when the sexual excitement wears off?" Or, "Enjoy it while it lasts."

Instead, I check my envy and respond, "Sounds pretty great to me."

Barbara tries again. "I'm sure I'm going to get a vaginal infection from making love so much. Don't you think I could be hurting myself? Maybe I'm masochistic?" she asks, beaming.

Betsy, thinking to herself, Sure, she could get an infection, but Barbara knows how to take care of her body. She's afraid I'm envious of her. "Come on," I tease her a bit. "You call that masochistic? Who are you kidding? I've never seen you happier."

Barbara, trying for a third time to get me to burst her balloon: "I sure am. It's never been like this before. But I'm exhausted. I'm losing sleep. We're up all night, touching, telling each other how beautiful we are, sharing past secrets. It's heaven. Look at me, don't I look like a tired wreck? Bags under the eyes? Hair limp? I think I'm going to get sick if I don't start sleeping soon."

Betsy, sinking back into her chair but trying to look pleased: "I think you're afraid I'm going to say, 'Yes, dear, you should get your rest. Why not tell him not to come over this weekend? Then you could have what you need, eight hours of solid sleep.' Right? Listen, Barbara, I'm not convinced that it's sleep you need right now. You need to know it's okay to be happy."

Barbara agrees, "That's right, and I'm afraid it's not okay."

Patients pick up on their therapist's envy. Whether they wish to talk about it is another matter. Patients don't want to believe their therapists envy them. They want to trust their helper, to feel that their therapist *only* wants to help, that *she'll* never let them down. Most patients would be afraid to ask their therapist or teacher or coach, "Do you envy me?"

I tell Barbara, "You and I have to struggle with your fear of my envy of you. We've talked about your envious mother, and we know how highly tuned you are to being envied."

Barbara went on, "Before I was married, I couldn't tell my last therapist about the dates I had. She looked so sad and alone. You're not quite as bad, but I'm still afraid to upset you."

She knows she doesn't want to upset me, but that doesn't keep her from trying to get me to be like her mother, critical of her. When Barbara told her mother she had "met someone," her mother responded, "I don't want to know the details. Let's talk about him in four months. Maybe it will be over by then, and we won't have to waste this conversation."

Barbara to Betsy: "David is low-key, funny, good-looking, likes to cook. He's smart, but he doesn't earn enough money.

Don't you think that could be a real problem, especially if I earn more than he does? I think I want someone who can take better care of me financially."

Betsy, to herself: Wow! Low key, easygoing, and he likes to cook. She is really lucky. To Barbara: "I'm sorry. What did you say the problem was?"

Barbara continues: "Even with getting an infection, not seeing my friends enough, being so exhausted, you think it's fine?" She looks for my smile of approval. "Good."

She's off the couch, out the door, ready for another enviable weekend, which I'm sure I'll hear about next week. I steel myself, give myself a pep talk: "I am helping her. It's hard work. I could have the same excitement if that were a top priority for me. I've had nights like those myself, years ago. Barbara deserves to be in love." Quietly I list what I do have. I remind myself that a goal of therapy (or teaching or coaching) is to help your patients surpass you, know as much as you—if not more—then leave you for their own life, taking their future with them, just like the parent has to struggle with letting her child go into the world. I think of how much reassurance Barbara needs, how much pain she has had, and I feel sympathetic to her. I must keep my envy at bay. I must allow the patient's needs to dominate the therapy. The work of a helper, and a parent, involves turning envy into love, a most difficult task.

Envy in Other Workplaces

Understanding how envy operates even in helping professions allows you to see that envy is a natural phenomenon in all workplaces.

A fifty-five-year-old woman from Massachusetts says it well. "Envy is hostility, the withholding of friendship, hate stares, snubs, ridicule, cattiness, whispering, troublemaking, calumny, sulking, silence, acting injured, as if someone actually did something to hurt you. It's uncalled-for temper tantrums, like slamming things down, walking very fast with heels banging on the floor (very common, like the woman who huffs and puffs, 'Well!' very dramatically), and sneaking around stealthily. When co-workers act friendly on the surface, and still interrupt you constantly and take your turn to talk, pretending not to hear you when you know they do—that's envy. When co-workers try to steal your thunder and deprive you of your originality, sometimes using your mannerisms and witticisms—that's envy. Envy causes disloyalty, backstabbing, and accusation. When something goes wrong, envy turns all eyes in your direction."

Ways of Dealing with Being Envied in the Workplace

Once you have detected the envy coming at you you must find ways to deal with it. But bear in mind there are no perfect solutions to dealing with a human emotion. Here are some possibilities.

1. *The Snow White Syndrome*—Linda. One way to "handle" being envied in the workplace is not to let yourself become envied in the first place—to hold yourself back and make sure you don't succeed when you really want to. In other words, you get caught in the Snow White syndrome. Linda Blackstone, a drug and alcohol counselor, talks openly about her dilemma; since she is aware of the trap, she has a good chance of escaping.

"I work very hard at not being envied. That is the real theme of my life. In competitive situations, I back out, not wanting to be in the position of having more than others. If taking what's mine means making someone else uncomfortable, I would rather sell myself short. I now see that as patronizing to others, and not fair to me.

"There is a certain self-righteousness at work when I hold myself back from taking on responsibilities that would mean more money. I have a martyr mentality. Being a martyr is doing something that might be destructive to myself but good for someone else. The part that makes it not clean is that there is power in being a martyr. It is grandiose; you actually think you are better than others. It's a sure way to try to make the other person feel guilty about having more than I have."

When caught in the Snow White syndrome, ask yourself the following questions:

- What's the worst thing that could happen if I lived up to my potential?
- Whom do I help, anyway, by holding myself back?

- Is this what I really want, given that I have only one life to live?

2. *Quit.* Leave one job where there are envious people and go on to another, hoping you won't find envy waiting for you there. But, if you are a person who evokes envy, trying to get away from it will not work.

3. *Perceive the envy quickly and accurately.* Many people report that they don't recognize envy coming their way until they are out of the situation. After all, most people wonder, "Why in the world would anyone want to envy *me?*"

4. *Don't take envy personally when it arises from a specific situation.* Since envy is usually expressed as a personal attack, it's easy to believe you are at fault. It is difficult to distinguish between objective criticism based on cool evaluation and negative behavior stemming from envy. Examine the envier's observations. Are they accurate? You need to separate what is being said about you from the emotion that prompts it.

You are also taking envy personally when you react to the person attacking you by saying negative things in return. The more involved you are with what is wrong with the envier, the less able you are to be clear about the situation.

5. *Focus on and encourage others.* Demeaning yourself, lessening your own value, is the most common way to handle being envied. "At work," writes a forty-seven-year-old secretary, "the other secretaries envy me because of my clothes. They don't realize how many luxuries I forgo to buy these clothes. Or maybe that is irrelevant and they would envy me anyway. I deal with their little comments by trying to make them feel good, complimenting them on their appearance, acknowledging their intelligence and their positive qualities. This helps form a bridge between us."

6. *Be calm in the face of envy.* Jackie manages a St. Vincent de Paul home, which cooks for and feeds the very poor. "The people I work with envy my ability not to pass judgment on others and to have a good time. They also envy my ability not to be swayed by their envy of me."

Jackie's job is hard work. At the home, people defecate on the floor and vomit in the soup bowls. Throughout the day, Jackie meanders from group to group, chatting with an "up" spirit. Her co-workers will say, "You just think work's a party," as though she shouldn't feel carefree about working in such a rathole. She responds to them by calmly replying, "Sure."

Jackie explained, "I don't try to talk them out of their feelings or demean what I do. I just take it for granted that I have to work, and this is what I choose to do."

7. *Create a common goal.* A woman in authority needs to learn to be envied in a way that doesn't encourage more envy. A woman who owns a large facial studio told me that she tries to create as little favoritism with her employees as possible. As the boss, she strives to create a common goal, the work product. "We're in this together. If I do well, you do well." This way she creates an atmosphere in which her employees are valued, wanted, appreciated.

If you're in a competitive office situation, you might try to help the envious person see that you are not the enemy, that the two of you are in this together, that the work situation, our culture, and our society are set up for envy. In the corporate world, the co-worker should not be the source of your envy and competition; rather, think about besting the companies with which you are competing.

Creating a common goal is not easy for an authority when a major part of her job is to say "no." Hilda, a dean of academic and professional affairs, has authority over many students. They envy her for having power over them, power to deny their requests.

Some of the students demean Hilda by calling her names like "the Snow Queen." Hilda muses, "When a woman doesn't give completely, she gets terms like 'Snow Queen,' which is the opposite of 'Big Tit.' When men aren't giving, they are not giving. When women aren't giving, they are failing an expectation of being the nurturing one."

8. *Attempt to explain who you really are*—Gloria Steinem. Gloria Steinem seems to have mastered the art of being a woman in authority. She focuses on and encourages others. She is calm. She shares the leadership of *Ms.* magazine. She is determined to create a common goal.

To describe being envied, Gloria uses words like "distance," "barrier," "gulf." "I experience envy," Gloria observes, "as a barrier between me and other women, women I want to reach. I feel lonely, like someone has set me apart. It's frustrating because I don't feel it's really me that they envy. I feel misunderstood. It certainly does not feel good."

Even with all her success, Gloria Steinem envies people with enough money to afford luxury services, such as having someone take her clothes to the cleaners. If she had more money, she could spend less time fund-raising for political causes and more time on meaningful work, such as writing about unknown women who are helping society. Gloria would actually rather envy than be envied. She believes people can control their envy of others but not their being envied by others. She has control over, and doesn't dwell on, her envy.

As a leader and fundamental chronicler of the women's movement, a writer, founder of a successful magazine, a beautiful woman with flawless skin, a woman with serenity, inner calm, and little need to show off, Gloria Steinem is envied.

And what is she envied for the most? Being thin.

A friend who attended a Smith College reunion with Gloria told me that women were more interested in the size of Gloria's jeans, the shape of her legs, or the lack of flab on her arms than in her politics or feminist consciousness.

Gloria uses a familiar method in dealing with being envied: the "attempt to explain 'who you really are'" approach: "Since I feel being envied is a barrier, I need to cross that barrier and explain what my *real* experience is. And it certainly is not what people think it is. I believe that my *being envied is based more on image than reality*, so I try to explain my reality as best I can, trying to find a shared experience.

"I tell people I am indeed your junk-food junkie, that there are not five minutes a day that I am not thinking about food, that my whole family is greatly overweight. People with food addictions are like sober alcoholics.

"You see," Gloria continues, "I envy people who are not tempted by food. I work with a woman who can't even remember to eat. Can you imagine that? She'll order a sandwich and eat half of it. And guess who eats the rest? Me. I just wish I didn't have this food addiction."

The "explain yourself" approach works for Gloria. She believes it helps people. "People want to be the same as others. They don't want to be different, and I show them how we are the same." Gloria also advocates the "if I can do it, so can you" philosophy.

Explaining yourself is different from apologizing about who you are. Gloria realizes she has a large dose of "this familiar cultural disease of wanting to be loved, to be liked. I used to withhold something I actually knew about when I was talking. You know, the sentences that begin with an apology, 'I am not sure, but . . .' Thank goodness I don't do that anymore."

Gloria believes she is envied, in order of frequency, for being thin, being well known, being free, being able to do work she enjoys, or being able to work at all.

A serious and thoughtful woman, Gloria carefully evaluates all this envy coming at her. In terms of "being free," Gloria used to fear that not having children would be a barrier between herself and other women with whom she is trying to connect. "It is such an odd choice in our society that many woman are sort of proud of me for being different."

As for being well known, Gloria does not think she is better than anyone else; she believes it is because she chose to be in journalism, in the public eye, in the first place. "Who is well known and who isn't is not proportional to your contribution; it clearly depends on what field you're in, what the times are, and accidents of many sorts. Who is to say that somebody who lives a less well-known life is any less important as a person?"

She continues, "Sure, I've made a contribution. I work hard. I have a combination of this and that kind of talent and this and that kind of nontalent. Each person is a unique combination. If I were a research biologist at Sloan-Kettering Institute for Cancer Research, I would certainly be doing something as important. Being well known is simply not a measure of accomplishment." Gloria questions the importance of being famous. "Celebrity for its own sake is not terribly difficult to come by. But what does it mean? It doesn't mean anything."

Success for Gloria means that women become more self-confident and not envious. In her work and in her workplace, Gloria has a unique way of helping women become more successful and less envious. She uses many of the approaches described above. In her work as a writer and reporter, Gloria *focuses on others.* As a writer of national importance, she is in a powerful position and tries to use that power to help others. She admires women who are courageous, yet are obscure and have little support. "Being well known, I think my task is to write about people who aren't."

Gloria does not like to hog the show. In her workplace, the headquarters of *Ms.* magazine, she uses techniques to reduce workplace envy. Besides *focusing on others,* she *encourages others, creates a common goal,* and *shares apparent privileges.*

When *Ms.* magazine first started, Gloria was better known than the other women on her staff. "Since I was more politically active, older, whatever, I knew I was in danger of being envied." At other magazines Gloria had worked on, editorial meetings had only one structure: The magazine editor sat at the head of the table, and all the employees directed questions at him. In creating a "woman's" magazine, Gloria did not want to replicate what she felt were mistakes in male-run magazines.

"For the first eight or nine years of the magazine," Gloria reveals, "I never sat at the head of the table. In fact, I didn't sit at the conference table at all. I sat to the side, away from the group. A large portion of the group couldn't look at me, because they were looking at each other. It wasn't unbalanced as in the corporate structure approach, where everyone depends on one leader's opinion. Sitting in the background of these editorial meetings encouraged diverse opinion and a variety of leadership. If you are always at the 'head of the table,' you might as well be by yourself, for you will be making all the decisions."

Gloria encourages her co-workers, especially younger women with less experience in journalism who have a hard time speaking up at meetings. She will speak with them in small groups before the larger meeting begins. These less experienced women then feel free to develop their own stories, to ask Gloria what she thought, to feel they had accomplished something.

Gloria Steinem is not a superwoman. She has innovative ways of managing a magazine, but she also realizes that these attempts at dealing with being envied depend on the state of mind and accessibility of the person who's doing the envying. In private moments, being envied has created conflicts for her. The most debilitating experience is being hated and envied for something she feels she has worked hard for and done right. Like Dolores Huerta, Gloria reminds herself that the worst way to handle being envied is the familiar standby approach: depression.

Gloria seemed pleased to have an opportunity to talk about envy: "If you just name something," she said, "it helps people know they are not crazy."

Many women feel they're going crazy when they aren't aware that it's envy coming their way. You are now better informed and know how easily envy can be triggered in an environment of competition and comparison. In such an environment, almost any quality, skill, or attribute is likely to be envied by someone. You've seen the forms this kind of envy can take, and you've also seen some possibilities for responding to it.

Clearly there is no perfect solution for dealing with envy at work. When you're on the receiving end of envy, one power you do have is to notice the negative behavior directed at you. Look calmly to see what might be justified in this behavior and what simply makes no sense.

When it's your own envy you have to look at, ask yourself if you are accepting the ethic of competition and comparison. Often women are in a hurry to rise to the top of the corporate ladder because they have so much catching up to do. Are you trying to do the best you can, or are you trying to "best" your co-worker? Can you look at the larger picture? What is the purpose of the work itself? What is the goal you and your co-workers are trying to meet? Is it possible to see yourself as part of a whole and find pleasure from doing your part? Is there some way you can personally change the rules of your office politics? If so, you're helping to lessen the level of envy in your workplace.

CHAPTER 7

Envy in Friendship

The grass may be greener on the other side of the fence, but it's just as hard to weed.

—GALE BAILEY, Minneapolis/Berkeley, 1986, friend for 30 years

"Envy is, of course, the most serious obstacle to friendship and bonding. In its worst form, it ignores, denies the existence of the other."

MADONNA KOLBENSCHLAG, *Kiss Sleeping Beauty Goodbye*

My best friend and I talk at a coffee house. I know I have to bring up one of the hardest subjects of all to discuss, one we've never talked about. There is no way around it; time is running out. I am about to write the chapter on envy in friendship. To do so, I need to risk talking to my best friend about envy. "Take a deep breath. Jump in," I command my fears.

BETSY: Do you envy anything about me?

KATHY: Are you kidding? Let me count the ways. When you told me you got your contract to write the book that's been your fantasy for so long, I wanted the same chance. I've always dreamed of fame. The older I get, the smaller the chance of seeing my name in lights. My instant reaction was tremendous envy. I hated you right then. But because you matter to me, I forced myself to transfer that envy into admiration.

BETSY (*defending herself because she doesn't want to make her best friend feel bad*): I won't necessarily have fame.

KATHY: But you *will* have a published book.

BETSY (*still making excuses and defending herself*): If I don't go nuts. If I finish it. If they like it. If this. If that. Besides, I may be writing a book, but you of all people know how shaky my life is now. You can't envy that.

KATHY (*needing to tell Betsy about her envy because Betsy keeps trying to deflect it*): No, but when I feel envious, I don't think about your problems. I envy that you have a son. I work too hard to have children. And when I *really* get into this mood, I become envious of your drive, your energy.

BETSY (*sincerely surprised about being envied for something she doesn't experience in herself*): Me? *You* have the highest energy of anyone I know. Everyone agrees.

KATHY (*putting herself down and trying to make her point*): But my energy is different. I don't take risks.

BETSY (*still trying to avoid the envy, to downgrade herself, and to build up Kathy*): Come on! Kathy, when we go out for dinner, I'm usually about to drop off to sleep, unless I've had a *caffè latte* and three cups of tea.

KATHY (*still trying to make her point*): I don't mean energy like being able to stay up all night. I mean you go after what you want. I'd like to take a course in video filmmaking, but I stop myself. When would I have the time? You make time. I also envy your open expression of feelings.

BETSY: This is getting embarrassing. No wonder when I ask people what they're envied for, they usually add, "I hope I'm not sounding conceited."

KATHY: You're not conceited. You *are* all the things I say.

BETSY (*diminishing herself and then changing the subject, deflecting Kathy's envy and moving toward her own envy of Kathy*): Well, my "open expression of feelings" puts off everyone in my family. As for the video course, of course you *don't* have time. You go to aerobics every day. I envy that.

KATHY (*defending herself against Betsy's envy*): I *have* to go to aerobics every day. I'm driven.

BETSY (*turning the tables*): You don't have to. You're naturally beautiful. People stop on the street to notice you.

KATHY: No, they don't.

BETSY: Yes, they do. I see their heads turn. Most of all, I envy your body. You don't have to be embarrassed. I saw a *Cathy* comic strip where Cathy tells her friend, "In the summer when I lie in the sun to get tan, the backs of my legs get more red than the front." Cathy's friend asks, "How is that, since the sun shines on the front of them?" Cathy replies, "Because the backs of my legs are more embarrassed." That's me. People stare at your legs and at my legs, but at my legs for the wrong reasons. I hate it.

BETSY (*feeling the discomfort of her envy of Kathy and needing to put Kathy down*): Kathy, remember how you were with that cute bus driver we met? Full of questions about his life, as though you were actually interested. I wish I could act like that, be phony.

KATHY (*wincing*): I *am* interested in other people. I don't fake it. . . . Boy, Bets, listen to us go on and on! You know, all the things I envy in you, I also admire. I don't *want* to take anything away from you. In fact, since you're my best friend, you're like a part of me. I feel a vicarious pride.

BETSY: Same with me. When I brag to people about you, that you're my best friend, I secretly hope that knowing you will make people like me more.

KATHY (*uncomfortable at being envied and stressing the less accomplished parts of her life*): Don't count on it. The things you envy in me come from my being so uptight.

BETSY (*still needing to have her envy heard by Kathy*): Well, it looks to me like your life's in order.

KATHY: But it's scary—a tenuous and artificial order. I know I appear to others as laid back. But that's just an image. I'm afraid if I were disorganized, I would fall apart.

BETSY (*to herself, disturbed by Kathy's envy and fearful that her envy might upset her friend*): This is making me squirm. (*Out loud, while hugging Kathy*) Thanks for the talk. I'll call you tomorrow, but I have to go to work now.

Kathy and I have been best friends for over twelve years, and you are listening in on our *first* discussion of what we envy in each other. Why is that? Because envy is hard to talk about even with best friends. Envy is taboo. Admitting your envy admits a failing in your self-esteem. Admitting your envy scares you, and it scares your friend. "Even your best friend won't tell you. . . ." No wonder I never suspected Kathy envied me; I only knew of my envy for her.

This conversation reveals the typical moves friends make in the face of envy: if you and your friend discuss envy, you might

- be surprised, flattered, *and* disturbed.
- defend yourself against each other's envy.
- try not to make each other feel bad.
- deny your successes, downgrade yourselves, make excuses for your accomplishments.
- try to talk each other out of the envy.
- build each other up and put each other down while still actively envying one another.

What is it in the nature of friendship that makes envy likely to arise *and* gives you a ready-made opportunity to work your way out of envy's grasp?

WHAT IS A FRIEND?

In her study on friendship, *Just Friends*, Lillian Rubin found these qualities most often describe friendship: "trust, honesty, respect, commitment, safety, support, generosity, loyalty, mutuality, constancy, understanding, acceptance." Friends are people with whom you can whine, make mistakes, and still trust everything will be okay.

A job description for a friend might list:

1. Able to give you support and appreciation for who you are.
2. Able to reflect who you are.
3. Able to help you learn to move away from the confining aspects of your family. Offer support as you create new rules and ways of being for yourself.
4. Able to heal wounds you inadvertently receive from family, marital, or love relationships: "My friend enables me to like myself better."
5. Able to challenge you to take risks and support you when this risk taking is scary.

6. Able to weather through problems in the friendship that will inevitably arise.

Women have more friendships than men, and women's friendships are characterized by more "shared intimacies, self-revelation, nurturance, and emotional support." In Dr. Rubin's study of over three hundred people, three-quarters of the women could identify a best friend; however, two-thirds of the men could not. Even as early as the fifth grade, girls travel in pairs, boys travel in bunches.

Envy is inevitable in friendship. Since envy feels like a betrayal of friendship, and is difficult to discuss, envy is a problem for women in friendships. Therefore, a friend committed to enduring conflict is especially important.

Who Is a Friend?

The people you pick as friends are usually people you admire, learn from, and wish to emulate, or people who reflect an image of who you think you are. You become friends with people who offer you a quality, a sense of excitement in their presence, a new perception of the world, a feeling that you can be the best person you can be. You may be attracted to your friend because you're "just like twins" or because you see her as having what you feel is missing in yourself.

"I get attracted to what I want for myself," a woman told me. An overflowing, extroverted, unrestrained, impulsive woman might seek a friend who is quiet, restrained, whose still waters run deep. And vice versa. As the cliché goes, opposites attract.

Occasionally, though, you choose a friend for other reasons. A forty-year-old attorney writes: "I think there are times I have unconsciously chosen certain friends to have 'deep' conversations with because, in helping them out, I felt superior. We would have long conversations focusing on *their* inadequacies with men and jobs. I would expound uplifting perspectives. The truth was, much of the time we talked, I wasn't feeling too good, either, but I never told them because I wanted to appear better off than they were. I bolstered my shaky ego." This attorney actually chose friends who would envy her so that she could feel better about herself. She chose what Dr. Rubin describes as "just" friends, acquaintances you consider to be friends.

What Is a Best Friend?

What is the difference between "just" a friend and a best friend? These could be descriptions of your best friend, descriptions that may vary throughout your life:

- The friend with whom you are most intimate and open; with whom you have the fewest secrets.
- The friend for whom you are most likely to change your plan when she needs you.
- The friend you would miss the most.
- The friend who is the most challenging.
- The friend from whom you receive the most "family" type of trust and support.

Whichever definition you choose to describe your best friend, there is the underlying feeling that you and she see the world in the same way. Your best friend offers you hope, "the promise of mutual love, concern, protection, understanding, and stability" in a relationship.

With your best friend, there is intensity; moments of the most pleasure and the most disappointment.

ENTER . . . ENVY

Friendships can break up for many reasons—distance, changing interests, new mates on the scene, and envy. Some mothers warn their daughters about intense friendships: "It won't last." What part does envy play in this assumption? Why does envy help some friendships and wreck others?

Envy is one of the biggest disappointments friends experience. Envy can creep in between best friends, just friends, friends who are similar or different, friends who admire each other, friends who feel equal or unequal. What rings loud and clear from the women I surveyed is that envy can accompany and threaten any friendship.

You envy because you compare, and when you compare you find differences. You are more likely to compare yourself with someone who has something in common with you than someone who is socially out of reach, someone you could never imagine being like. You might hold these people in awe, but it's easier to be able to accept the distance (social, financial, geographic) between you.

Why do you need to compare? You are taught to compare. Your parents compared you with others, with siblings, friends, cousins, society's ideal standards, with themselves. The media compares you with others, forever requesting you to add up who has the most. Schools, teachers, standardized tests, sports all compare you with others. Life is full of comparisons.

Your self-worth in part comes from how you compare yourself with others and from how others see you. If others accept you, if you compare highly with someone else, you may like yourself better. If you are somewhat insecure, as most of us are, you will compare yourself with others in order to get a sense of how you are doing in the world.

Only the enlightened never compare. And never envy.

How is envy in friendship different from envy with your mother, or co-workers?

Envy from a friend feels more acceptable than from a mother. Mothers are never supposed to envy; they are supposed to be selfless and wish only the best for their child.

Envy in friendship also differs from envy in the workplace because in friendship, there is more emphasis on emotions and compatibility. In the workplace, comparisons and judgments are usually based on external, objective standards. In the workplace, you are supposed to deny your feelings if they get in the way of the task at hand. The point of the workplace is to get the job done, not to feel good or envy-free.

Envy is harder to bypass in friendship because friendship is based on feeling. You might wonder, "How do I feel when I am with this friend? How does she feel with me?" You might wonder if she will hate you for envying her, reject you if you do better than she does. You might wonder if her envy or your envy will keep her from "being there" when you need her.

You may have picked your friend hoping she will flatter and enhance you, not judge you as a parent or boss does. In fact, you might choose a "Yes Man" as your best friend, someone who is completely accepting. Her envy interferes with that hope.

Then comes the inevitable moment when one of you realizes you are different, one of you has something desirable the other doesn't have. Enter . . . envy. The wish for oneness, the hope for a haven away from judgment, is shattered.

Envy can enhance, interfere with, or destroy a friendship. Envy is present in all friendships but it won't ruin a friendship when you feel you have your share of the qualities you define as valuable, or when you have a sufficient amount of whatever you envy in your friend.

You can view envy as an opportunity for realistic assessment of who has what. Rather than "I should have what she had," why not accept that what you both have is desirable? In my friendship with Kathy, we envy each other mutually. We both have qualities the other wants. Kathy wishes she had a son, was writing a book, had more focused energy. I wish I had Kathy's body, smile, lack of intense feelings, organizational ability, and financial earning capacity. Friends need to inspire one another.

Friends should expect to envy each other since no two people are identical. There would be no envy if everyone were the same.

Close Friend/Distant Friend

Whom do you envy more, your close friend or the woman you chat with once or twice a month? The closer you are to your friend, the more you know her, the more you see her complete story, her problems as well as her joys. Does this mean you will envy her less? You would think so. But the women surveyed reported *as much* envy for their closest, their best, friends as they did for their acquaintances. Envy for close and for distant friends is felt and experienced differently.

When you don't know a person well, you are more able to make assumptions about that person's life. You can imagine all sorts of pleasures in her life, and this leaves the door wide open for envy.

You fancy this person has what is lacking in your own life, and then you suffer even more from thinking someone else has everything you have ever wanted; your view of her is not modified by reality. Said one woman, "I could only envy someone I don't know well."

This type of envy can be a self-torment. It's as if you create an image of someone in order to envy her, as a way to feel bad about yourself. Since you don't know this person well enough to find out what she is really like, the envy is hard to discourage.

Envy for a close friend can appear when you least expect it.

Have you ever had the experience of being especially loving toward a friend, helping her through a time of sadness, then suddenly find yourself envying her for receiving the very help you are giving her? Or perhaps as you support a friend who is making a major change in her life, you notice that behind your words of encouragement is a sinking feeling that her life is moving at a faster, more exciting pace than your own. Maybe she doesn't need you as much as before, and you envy her that independence. After all, you need her as much as you always did.

Or you may find yourself envying your friend for the very reason you were attracted to her in the first place! For example, an extroverted woman finds she can't become like her quiet friend, their personalities are simply too different.

You may choose your close and best friends to complete a part of yourself that you feel is lacking. A twenty-five-year-old secretary from New York City writes, "Women, not seeing themselves as whole, autonomous, independent people are drawn to friends who, they hope, will somehow 'complete' them. They need to live out their hopes and dreams vicariously through their close friends, since they feel inadequate, unwhole, 'not good enough' in the first place."

With a distant friend, the pain of envy comes from imagining differences that may not be real. With a close friend, envy arises from differences that really exist. With a close friend, you can't tell yourself that "maybe it isn't so, maybe her life isn't all that wonderful."

Look at the word "close." Close means no space between, two (or more) objects right up against each other. If you and your friend are close, this means you're going to feel her almost as a part of yourself. Since a close friendship is based on perceived equality, envy imposes a threat: If you're no longer equals, can the friendship survive?

However, with a best friend, as strong and as threatening as the envy is, it can be overthrown. Since the envy is about real, not imagined differences, it can be easier to penetrate. You can engage in discussion, grapple with your differences, as Kathy and

I were able to do. Quantitative differences, differences that will change throughout the course of a friendship, can enhance your friendship.

You're in This Together

If you have a good friendship, you can speak about your differences in an environment of mutual support. One woman told me, "My best friend envies me. What makes it such a good friendship is that I envy her right back." Another description of a friend is someone with whom you are able to look at your mutual envy.

For example, a thirty-four-year-old mother of two explains, "I envied my single friends' freedom to travel. I complained to them about being tied down. They replied they envied me my spouse and two daughters. We realized we were each lucky in our own way."

Carlene tells me she envies Jill, who used to live with Carlene's current lover. "Jill had been with him, and now I am. She had a closed relationship with him. I have an open one. *We traded envies*. She's amazed at my ability for an open relationship, that I could share him. I am astounded at her capacity to be monogamous and not get bored."

Jane, now thirty-eight, also has a story to tell about mutual envy. "When we were younger, my friend Bonnie lived alone with her mother, who was almost crazy. Bonnie envied my family, that I had both a father and a mother in the same house all those years. I couldn't believe it because I hated my family and knew how little that nuclear structure really meant, that it was a facade.

"I, on the other hand, envied a freedom that Bonnie had. She could stay up all hours, live her own life. My mother made us all be home by four-thirty in the afternoon, no matter what we were doing. Dinner was always at five P.M. Even if we were going somewhere else for dinner, my mother would make us eat dinner at home at five first. And Bonnie envied me?"

The grown-up Jane can see the absurdity in the envy between her and Bonnie. She and Bonnie each assumed the other had a guarantee of happiness. The grown-up Jane can see how our assumptions about someone else's life are not usually accurate.

Diane Watson, a fifty-year-old teacher, mother, and student of

Japanese, also learned the truth about making assumptions about another's life. She envied her friend Thelma, age thirty-two, who started her own business a few years ago. "Thelma is single, tall, and athletic, which I am not. I perceived her to be living the good life, owning her own home and business, free to do as she pleased. I envied her independence, determination, tough-mindedness. She is also an artist. I thought how great it would be if I could draw a picture that was recognized as art, not just a doodle. I envied her talents."

Diane was working part time and had a comfortable but lack-luster marriage. She and her family had become apartment dwellers with no yard to putter in. "I was in the doldrums, and by contrast Thelma's life seemed exciting. I suddenly felt clumsy and, somehow, old. I felt the parade was passing me by." Who is the parade for, anyway?

The more Diane got to know Thelma, though, the less she envied Thelma's life. Diane had thought Thelma to be "completely happy" until Thelma spoke of financial problems: awake at six A.M., to bed at midnight, days of stocking toilet paper and paper towels in the restroom, standing in line to make bank deposits, staying up late with bookkeeping and report sheets.

"Being boss of a one-woman business means wearing many hats," Diane came to understand, "and they are heavy. My perception of Thelma's glamour was beginning to dim."

As Diane's envy lessened, Thelma was freer to talk about her *own* envy. Diane realized her envy was unwarranted. "It was Thelma who envied *me* for being a wife and mother."

Diane remembered her own life at thirty-three—feeling desperate as a homeowner, with no one to share her home. "Since I, too, had felt that kind of loneliness, I knew how she must feel, single, no real prospects, and her childbearing years limited. My heart went out to her."

"The grass may be greener on the other side of the fence but it's just as hard to weed," said my close friend, Gale. The grass is *not* always greener on the other side, and it was important for Diane to see whether her envy was based on the reality or fantasy of Thelma's life.

And the beat goes on. . . . Mutual envies exchanged back and forth, forth and back. Hurts, sadnesses, losses. Why can't we see that we are all women, all wanting similar things in life, all losers and all winners? You have some of what I want, I have some of what you want. Isn't that enough? I guess not. My closest friend has a better body and more money. I've written a book and have a son. So what?

My patient Nora is a prime example of one who has marched to the beat of envy. She tells me about her best friend, Holly, from Napa Valley: "Holly talks about her life, her fabulous career being in charge of sales promotion at a major winery. Holly gets to travel, hires lots of people, sets up offices across the United States. *Plus* she reads the best-selling American novels and knows about important authors. *Plus* she is doing volunteer work, fund-raising for public broadcasting television, and gets to be *on TV.*"

That is more than enough for Nora to accept, but because Holly also has the best *sex life* in the whole world, all of Nora's green meanies come marching out. She feels she is nothing: "All I do is work, go to aerobics, and cook dinner. I also go to the movies and work on my computer. Big deal! After I talked to Holly, I felt like a real slug.

"And to make matters worse, Holly's boyfriend is her other best friend. Holly is thirty pounds overweight, and he loves her body. I am in shape, and my husband drinks in front of the TV every night. What a gyp!"

Like Nora, Joyce, a thirty-nine-year-old personnel manager at a Manhattan bank, has a friend who "has it all." Said Joyce, "One of my best friends, Laura, has about 90 percent of what's possible to have in the world, and about 99 percent of what I want. She has lots of money, a tenured faculty position, a house, glamour, style, she's married, and she and her husband both want kids. They went to the Bahamas at Christmas, and now they're going to the Champagne district in France. I mean they each bought new cars, their apartment is fantastic, and they can still afford to go to France.

"I feel deprived. I start to imagine she thinks she is a big shot and that I am boring and a nothing. I start to feel distant from her. I become less open. She has everything. I have nothing."

Therapists call this viewing a situation in extreme terms "polarizing." Joyce sees herself and her friend at opposite poles. You "polarize" a situation when you see it as stark white and black, all or nothing. It's easy, especially when you are depressed or feeling you've not achieved something you want, to idealize a friend whose life looks more satisfying.

Sometimes you might need to idealize a friend rather than face what is really lacking in you and actually do something about it or "come to terms with it." Or you might need to feel bad about yourself for whatever reason right then. Ironically enough, some people need to envy.

It's also easy these days to have a friend who, on the surface, seems to have it all. There are so many choices for women and much to compare ourselves with. With the superwoman image receiving full media attention, many women reported being self-critical about not doing as much or feeling as "capable" as their high-powered friends.

But we need to remind ourselves, as Diane learned to do, that things aren't always what they appear. As Diane got to know Thelma better, she saw the reality instead of the ideal. Nora also polarized her experience of Holly's worth and her own.

In fact, use this concept of polarizing as a clue. If you find yourself feeling that your friend has everything while you have nothing, you're probably making assumptions based on only one piece of a whole picture—on how you need to see your friend rather than what her life is actually like. What can you do to put the picture back into proper perspective? Let's look at Joyce and Laura. Here are some questions Joyce might ask to enable herself to move out of "she has everything, I have nothing" envy. Ask yourself the same questions when you get the "all or nothing envy blues."

1. Is there anything Laura envies about Joyce? Given the fact that envy in friendship is 96 percent mutual, you can guess the answer to this one.
2. What is good about this long-term friendship? What do the two friends enjoy about each other? They need to remind themselves why they became friends in the first place.
3. How does Joyce's envy make Laura feel? Joyce is so caught up in her own envy that she has little compassion for how her distance might affect Laura. Does it bother Laura when Joyce acts weird around her?

When I interviewed Laura, I was not surprised to find that she hates being envied. "When I am not seen for myself, when my success, who I am, gets attributed to one factor, like money, brains, looks, whatever, but not to my whole person—that is vicious envy. A friend might imagine that *if* she has something of mine, *then* she would be like me. That isn't true.

"When I came back from the Bahamas, I was worried about seeing Joyce. Joyce was feeling financially pinched, and I felt guilty about the vacation. I see life as a balance sheet, that whenever anything good happens, I expect something bad to follow. So I was anxious about telling Joyce I had a good trip. I acted cautious and less open. I have my vulnerabilities, too. But Joyce's envy of me made it difficult to talk to her about my envy. I'm envious of Joyce's spunk, her capacity for pleasure, her sexual freedoms. And Joyce has more fun with people than I do."

Both Joyce and Laura acted distant. But since they are good friends, and usually talk about their conflicts, neither needed to act so reserved. Laura observed, "My fear of Joyce's envy got in the way of our being open together, which we usually are. If I were less guilty, I could have told her about my vacation."

Remember, there are two sides to the envy coin, and it's likely to flip back and forth over the years of any friendship. As long as you recognize this two-sided coin and the partial assumptions that make it land first one way and then another, as long as you can talk and laugh with your friend about this frequent tossing, your friendship is likely to endure.

Should You Downplay Your Achievements?

Laura felt she had to downplay her pleasures to keep Joyce's envy at bay. But she saw the cost of this action: her friendship with Joyce ran into trouble.

Almost every woman I interviewed admitted she downplayed her achievements. We are taught the importance of modesty. There are many ways to downplay your successes:

- Don't talk about your achievements.
- Pretend your accomplishments never happened.
- Minimize the amount of effort you put into getting where you are now. The "oh, it was nothing" or the "I was just lucky" approach.
- Focus on the hardships, the amount of work, your sleepless nights, your fights with your mate, the weight you gained or lost.

For many people, how much they hide their success has to do with what they want from others. Some women report they would

rather be liked than respected. Others reported they would rather
be respected than liked. Which is more important for you? People
who want to be liked more than respected are apt to downplay
their achievements for fear of being envied and thus robbed of
their pleasures.

A thirty-four-year-old attorney in private practice, who has a
good life, would rather be liked than respected. She writes that
"even with good freinds, in order to be liked I have to downplay
my happiness, material success, academic achievements, or pride
in my children's achievements."

She is more cautious with people she doesn't know. "I have to
put out feelers first, to see what the other person is like, before I
let it all hang out. I try not to tell people that my husband and I are
both lawyers, or they usually dislike us immediately.

"I prefer to let them get to know me and like me before I let
them in on the details of our life. Even when I do, if they are
envious of what I have, then I feel they don't like me. I hate that."

This attorney's reservations when meeting strangers make
sense. Why flaunt what you have or show off when you have no
idea how it will affect the other person? You might feel tentative
about a hard-won success, ready to lose it at any moment. If you
are not good at holding on to what you have, it may be better not
to risk showing it off—especially when you don't know the envy
level of the person to whom you're revealing yourself.

But I question this attorney's attitude with good friends. You
can *create* distance with a good friend if you are always
downplaying your achievements, hiding, measuring what you
should say, or feeling that your friend is so vulnerable to your
success that she couldn't possibly bear to hear the truth of your
life.

At times distance might be a relief. But if it's closeness you
want, be aware that fear of your friend's envy can keep you from
getting the support and appreciation you're after.

Even downplaying your achievements doesn't always stop
envy. *There are some people who are going to envy no matter how
much you try to prevent it.* They will always find something to
envy, so don't be surprised and disturbed by it. No amount of
fancy footwork will avoid it.

Fay, a fifty-four-year-old woman from South Dakota, wrote
about a forever envious friend. "I have a friend who certainly has
things I want. She's very pretty, thin, she doesn't work, her kids

are 'together.' I don't particularly feel envious of her, but I do feel she has enviable qualities.

"But as far as she's concerned, I always have it better than she does. When my mother was dying, this friend would talk about how lucky I was because she had such a terrible relationship with her mother. She thought her life would be better if her mother did die!

"Last year my husband was laid off from work. This was right after my mother had died, and it was a very difficult, hardly enviable time. During Christmas vacation, my husband still wasn't working, and this friend asked who was going to take care of my kids when I was working. I told her, 'John. He still isn't working, so he'll be home.' She actually said, 'I envy that!'

"I blew up at her. 'In every situation, you think I have it better than you.' More and more I see that her envy has nothing to do with me—my life can be in the worst place, and she will still envy me. She needs to envy me. *If she wants to hate me because of my 'happy' life, that's her problem*. Maybe she envies me so I will never envy her whatsoever."

The Catch-22 of Envy

Envy has a paradoxical nature: *you invite envy and dislike being envied at the same times*. Earlier we met the attorney who chooses friends who will envy her in order to boost her ego, so she can feel better about herself. Like her, you may feel that being envied is a compliment or a signal that you have something of value, that you have done something right. Being envied may raise your self-esteem momentarily. If this is so, beware . . . next comes one of envy's poisons, your fear of being disliked.

The paradox of envy: If you are envious and you get what you envy, you will probably be envied. Yet if you are envied and are scared of being envied, you won't be able to enjoy what you have. Therefore, you will remain envious.

If discomfort with being envied makes you unable to enjoy what you do have, you may remain an envious person. You may want what others have because you feel you have very little. This is the catch-22 of envy.

For example, Annabelle lives in Texas in a nice house, with a rich husband, cute kids. She has an *au pair* girl, a good job, a fine garden, the whole shebang. Yet she never thinks what she has is good enough.

Annabelle burns with envy for her friend's garden. "My friend moved into a huge home. She hired twenty men full time to completely redo her garden. Two or three times a day, I would drive from where I live on the other side of town, miles out of my way, to watch her garden grow. Then I'd come home having a three-year-old's temper tantrum. 'It's not fair, it's not fair!' I'd call up my friends and cry."

What if Annabelle took action in order to become less envious of her friend—what if she made a more beautiful house and garden for herself and developed her own talents?

Here is the problem. Annabelle *hates* being envied. She told me a story about a party at her house: "The day before the party, I ran around after work buying stuff and cutting flowers from my garden, got the house looking great. I stayed up late cleaning and preparing.

"During the party, my *au pair* innocently came downstairs, and I imagined one especially curious woman thinking, Oh, of course everything's so nice here, Annabelle's got a cast of thousands. And I had done it all myself! Yet here she was envying me my *au pair*. I was furious." Because of her guilt over wanting to be envied and her fear of being envied, Annabelle imagined this woman's envious thought.

Annabelle feels unseen, unreal, and uncomfortable when people envy her. Yet she also wants people to envy her so she will feel better about herself. She sets the stage to be envied, like getting her house in tiptop shape, and then hates it when someone does envy her. If she had an even better garden, she would be more envied and then would be even more anxious.

How does the catch-22 work?

(1) Annabelle is so afraid of being envied that she plays herself down.

(2) Since she plays herself down, she believes she is less than she is.

(3) Then she envies others for having what she imagines to be more than she has.

(4) Because she feels she doesn't have enough of what she wants, she needs to be envied in order to feel better.

(5) When she does get envied, she can't let herself enjoy what she does have: her garden, her *au pair*, her self. Catch-22.

* * *

A woman tries to look beautiful for a party by wearing lots of makeup and fancy jewelry; she wants to be noticed by her friends. But when she goes to the party and is complimented, she feels awkward with the attention she's receiving. Because she feels uncomfortable, she declines that she looks good. Now, believing her own denial and really feeling ugly, she looks at other pretty women at the party and wishes she were as lovely as they. In fact she is. But her fear of being envied, her need to diminish herself, and her envy of them keeps her from feeing good about the way she looks. She remains envious and doesn't have a good time at the party.

Beware of using envy to bolster your self-esteem. If you try to be envied and hate being envied at the same time, you will be stuck in the same envy rut. To get out of this fundamental paradox, Annabelle and the woman at the party should learn to be more comfortable being envied. Then they could better enjoy what they want so much to have. Why push yourself to have something when the fear of envy won't allow you to enjoy it anyway?

WHEN ENVY COMES BETWEEN FRIENDS

Let's look at the contrast between how we act when we're comfortable being envied and when we're not.

I was in a good mood when Ellen called to invite me over one afternoon. She greeted me at the door, offered me coffee, and we sat down to some neighborly gossip.

Suddenly Ellen jumped up. "I forgot to show you my new washer and dryer. The latest Maytags. Look at all the buttons. And they're noise free. We plan to really fix up this place. We're going to remodel the kitchen with a central island, indoor greenhouse, track lighting, Italian tile, Vegemix, extra-large Cuisinart, the works. We have two experts, a kitchen consultant and a color consultant for the outdoors paint, which of course we'll have to do next. We're tired of living in such mediocrity."

BETSY (*feeling envious and upset*): Wait a minute, Ellen, won't all this be expensive? I thought you were having financial troubles.

ELLEN: Oh, no. It won't be too hard. Didn't I tell you Jim's aunt died?

BETSY: Yes, you mentioned it. Was she rich?

ELLEN: I feel funny talking about it. Yes.

BETSY (*upset*): Thanks for the coffee. Guess I'll be going back home to hear the house rattle as I put a load of wash through.

When I left, we both felt bad. Often there is no way to avoid evoking envy when you have a sudden change of fortune that your friend does not share. Ellen and I had been equal; now she's received a windfall. In what better ways could we have handled this delicate turn in our friendship?

Ellen might have focused on some of my special qualities. Ellen, who can't sit still and has to be in the company of others to be happy, envies my capacity for self-reflection and quiet; she might have chosen this time to talk to me about her own envy. Since in Ellen's kitchen that afternoon I was primarily feeling my envy of her, I might not have been receptive to her praise.

However, Ellen's positive comments would not be in vain. In my own time, I could think more about the situation. Do I really want track lighting and Italian tile? If so, what can I do to earn the money to purchase them? If a remodeled kitchen is not truly on my priority list, perhaps Ellen's words will come back to me and I'd remember my last quiet weekend on the beach with pleasure and gratitude.

Let's put Ellen and Betsy in a few hypothetical situations.

1. Let's say I am in a good mood. I see a friend of many years, Ellen, at the supermarket. I have just lost ten pounds after two months of difficult dieting and deprivation. Ellen is not her thinnest.

ELLEN (*feeling envious*): Hi, Betsy. Gosh, you look so thin. Your diet really paid off. Maybe I should try it. Although now that I look more closely, do you think you look too thin? Don't you think you could stand to gain a couple of pounds?

BETSY (*not feeling comfortable in being envied or better off than Ellen*): Do you really think so? Maybe you're right. I pushed it too far. I guess I look too skinny. That's what I was afraid of.

(She moves her cart to the cookies aisle, feeling bad about herself.) OR:

BETSY *(feeling comfortable with being envied and with feeling better off than Ellen, recognizing the envy)*: Thanks a lot. No, I don't think I look too thin. I love being thin, wearing whatever I want. I feel lighter when I walk. I'm having more fun. The diet was really worth the effort.

Ellen is more likely to go on a diet herself, if she wants to, when she sees that her envy has not been harmful to Betsy. If Ellen believes her envy hurt Betsy, she feels mean and is less likely to be able to take good care of herself.

2. Let's say I have taken off two days from work. I am relaxing at the beach in the summer. I am somewhat tan and I feel good about how I look. I see Ellen, who has just arrived at the beach.

ELLEN *(feeling envious)*: Betsy, you're so dark! Did you know that sun causes skin cancer?

BETSY *(not feeling comfortable in being envied or better off than Ellen)*: Oh, no! You're right! I forgot. Even though I used a sunscreen, I'm worried. I think I'll go inside and watch some TV. It's too bad. I was so enjoying the weather and the water. *OR*:

BETSY *(feeling comfortable with being envied and with feeling better off than Ellen, recognizing the envy)*: Thanks for the reminder. I've been careful—always use sunscreen. You'll get tan, too. I'm having fun. Want to borrow some of my sunscreen?

3. Let's say that after years of procrastinating, I've started to jog. I'm slow but proud.

Ellen and I are at a friend's party. Ellen is dressed in bright skirts and scarves and begins to read palms.

ELLEN *(feeling envious)*: There's a darkness here, something unclear. Your health line is so . . . Wait, I think maybe it's your back, you must be careful about your back. Remember? You told me you started jogging. . . .

BETSY *(not feeling comfortable in being envied or better off than Ellen)*: Really? My mother has a bad back, and I'd hate anything like that to happen to me. Maybe I'd better give up jogging; I've read that it can be bad for the knees and back. (*She slouches a little.*) *OR* :

BETSY (*feeling comfortable with being envied and with feeling better off than Ellen, recognizing the envy*): I bet I do have a tendency to back problems. I'll make sure my running shoes are always the best, will stay on soft surfaces, and take extra care with warm-ups.

4. Let's say Ellen and I have gone shopping together for straight-legged blue jeans. We are in the dressing room. I have tried on two pairs. One looks good; the other, corduroy, does not. Ellen is upset because nothing fits.

ELLEN (*feeling envious*): I like the corduroy ones. Go for them.

BETSY (*not feeling comfortable with being envied or better off than Ellen*): I feel chunky in the cords. But since you know more about fashion than I do, I'll take your advice. *OR*:

BETSY (*feeling comfortable with being envied and feeling better off than Ellen, recognizing the envy*): I disagree: I'll stick with the first pair, the ones I can sit down in better. The cords just don't do it for me. (*To herself*): Beware of going shopping with an envious friend.

Taking Action: What Works in Dealing with Envy in a Friendship?

These hypothetical Ellen-Betsy scenarios suggest situations that occur between friends and indicate possible responses. They show how assessing your own feelings and values can affect the power that envy has in a friendship.

Here is a real-life example of how to deal with envy in friendship. Karen, a thirty-two-year-old lobbyist for a woman's political organization in Seattle, has learned not to let envy be destructive.

Karen reports, "Recently I envied my best friend's opportunity to go back to school. At first, I found myself vaguely depressed and finding excuses not to do things with her. I started getting into that full-fledged envy stuff, saying bad things about her to other people. But I caught myself.

"This time, thank goodness, I saw why I felt that way and decided to do something for myself. I took a two-week vacation, the first in a long time. *She* had the chance to go to school, but *I* had opportunities of my own. All I had to do was take advantage of an opportunity. Sitting on my can and feeling envious wouldn't have gotten me off to Vancouver for a rest.

"I also envied a friend's new house and saw myself starting to make snide remarks about her capitalism. Catching the envy as it started to flow, I decided to start saving either for a house of my own or to redecorate the one I have. **Wanting something someone else has isn't bad unless that's all you ever do.**"

For Karen, *catching her own cattiness toward her friends was the clue that let her know she was envious*. If all she had done was sit around and mope about where her fancy friends were taking education courses or how many of these friends had new homes with old Persian rugs, she'd still be sitting. She realized she could easily get stuck in the envy, building it far out of proportion. Once she recognized how envy could define the friendship rather than be an unavoidable part of it, she took action.

So did Marlene, a flamboyant friend of mine, a therapist and writer who allowed her normal feelings of envy to help her become more creative, to change her life. At first, Marlene admitted, "My problem comes when I don't recognize my friends' envy. They never say straight up, 'I hate you, you bitch, for having X, Y, and Z.' That would be easier for me to deal with. Instead, they weave their envy into the fabric of the conversation with little jabs or unsolicited comments about my looks—'You look like a clown,' because I wear such bright colors. Or they'll say, 'Only you could wear that,' punctuated at the end with a little laugh. You know it's envy, and you feel one step from the sewer."

Marlene then talked about her own envy. "If you have enough success, you can temper your envy. It is only the defeated who feel that lethal envy. They feel their possibilities are closed. It is the rage of the helpless. I saw that my mother envied me because of her helplessness, and I vowed, 'Not me. Never will I feel my possibilities so closed. Never will I do to my friends what my mother and others have done to me.'"

Marlene has a close friend who is a successful fashion photographer in New York City. She lives the artist's life in Soho, has many exciting artistic friends, and attends exhibits and late-night parties.

Marlene visited this friend. Although she was writing, Marlene hadn't published any work. "I was a mother, a psychotherapist, and I felt like Mary Middle Class. I was really envious and felt awful. I was angry at myself for a long time after returning to Berkeley. I would conjure up mean fantasies about my friend's life.

"But I remembered my other friends' envy toward me, and I stopped myself. I told myself that this feeling of envy pointed out something I wanted in my life. I could either sit around and feel bad or make my life more like hers. It was a turning point for me, a fork in the road. I could see all the years ahead I would spend justifying myself by cutting down other people's successes, like 'They come from money' or 'Their husbands helped them.' That way I'd never have to feel I hadn't tried hard enough. If I didn't do something, I knew I'd become embittered.

"So I started making my life more creative, writing in a more serious way. I am still a mother and psychotherapist. But now, five years later, when I visit my friend, I'll have two published books under my belt." Marlene was able to transform her wanting what someone else had into her own struggle to get something similar for herself.

LOSING A FRIEND TO ENVY

Sometimes you aren't able to come up with the proper action, and envy wins: you lose your friend.

One reason envy is disruptive to a woman's friendship is that, along with the Ten Commandments and the Golden Rule, you are taught the importance of relationships. Envy gets you where you live, connected to your friends. You fear the rupture of your friendship, your source of nourishment, and when envy invades, you throw up your hands in panic. What should I do? I can't stand it. She's not supposed to feel that way. She's supposed to help me, to like me. She's my friend!

Jean, a thirty-two-year-old free-lance production assistant in video and multimedia, writes about the loss of a friendship. She dared to become different from her college friend of four years.

"Nancy, my friend, precipitously and coldly ended our friendship in a good-bye letter. Although I was in too much pain to pick up all the signs, my friends I showed the letter to were quick to point out how envious Nancy was. I was surprised, because Nancy was the secure one, the one who liked herself, the one who, in addition to everything else, was the object of *my* envy. I had felt secure in our friendship because we were so much alike.

"Nancy had made allusions to being bored with the politics I was involved in. She ridiculed and scoffed at my political involvement, saw politics as an area I had 'staked out,' where she didn't belong. Nancy thought she wasn't smart enough. She claimed she couldn't live up to the person I had become.

"I had always praised her and hoped she would fit in—when she didn't, I thought I could keep both her and politics in my life, albeit separately. Nancy didn't want that. She couldn't stand to 'compete' either with me or for me.

"Not wanting to compete, her response was to dissociate herself from me. I don't think that during our friendship either of us recognized the envy, and therefore there was no way to deal with it. Then it was too late, and I was simply astonished by the envy in her letter."

Nancy wanted Jean to be just like her. It wasn't that Nancy disagreed with Jean's politics, but as Jean became different, more political, Nancy could no longer acquire her sense of identity from Jean.

When your friend changes and you feel she is no longer just like you, your identity can be threatened. You feel threatened when she dares to be different. You envy that daring even more when you don't know how to get it for yourself.

Will Success Spoil Friendship: Letty Pogrebin and Susan Anspach

Now that women have a greater variety of opportunities in life, there are more arenas in which they can envy each other. Your friends' achievements and recognition can make you feel left out, left behind, bad. Since close friends often desire equality between them, you may wonder why your friend "succeeded" and you didn't.

Also, we fear our friends' envy when we are successful. In covering up our success, we create distance. In broadcasting our success, we create envy. What do you do when you become more successful than your friend or vice versa?

It is important to recognize that your friend's success is not something she does to you. It says nothing about you as a person, since you and she are separate people. Her success does not mean you fail. Her success may even reflect positively on you, since you have chosen her to be your friend, since she likes you.

Letty Cottin Pogrebin and Susan Anspach are successful women. Their stories illustrate ways they have tried to deal with envy, success, and friendship.

Letty Cottin Pogrebin is a writer and editor of *Ms.* magazine and the author of five books, including *Growing Up Free, Family Politics,* and the forthcoming *Having Friends, Being Friends.* She was an editor/consultant of *Free to Be You and Me,* the popular children's record. As a feminist-activist, much published writer, and popular lecturer, Letty's prominence has given her some insight into the isolation experienced by people more famous than she.

She learned from her friend, the late Groucho Marx, how success can create distance between people and how other people's envy cheated Groucho of many of life's ordinary pleasures. But she hadn't really understood what he'd meant until months later.

It was a Sunday, and she and her husband were enjoying a sunny day in Manhattan's Central Park within view of the Plaza Hotel, where Groucho was staying. "Let's go up and ask Groucho to join us," said Letty. "Are you crazy?" Her husband laughed. "Do you think he's got nothing to do in New York but stroll around the park with us? With all the important people he knows, he's probably juggling a dozen invitations for brunch today."

Letty decided her husband was right; it *was* arrogant to imagine that the legendary comedian would be either available or interested in such "nobodies" as the two of them. But later in the week, when Letty saw Groucho in the course of business, she asked him casually, "What did you do last Sunday?"

"Nothing," he replied. "I stayed in my room and watched television."

Letty and her husband realized they had done Groucho a disservice by imagining his life to be an enviable round of social occasions when in fact he had been alone and lonely. This was what Groucho had meant when he'd told her earlier that being envied robbed him of ordinary pleasures—in this case, of the spontaneity of having friends drop by.

For Letty herself, the problem can be summarized as "Will success spoil old friendships?" She explained, "I have a childhood friend from Toronto who treats me as if I'm some sort of golden object. She assumes I can't be bothered with her, just as my husband and I assumed Groucho was too important to be bothered with us."

Here is an excerpt from my conversation with Letty:

LETTY: Whenever I talk to this friend, she asks when she can next see me on television. I tell her she can see me in the flesh, but she actually seems less interested in getting together in person than in admiring me from afar.

BETSY: Do you ask her, "How would it be for you to see me on television?" Do you try to understand her better?

LETTY: Not exactly. She doesn't really give me access to her feelings. My friend has changed our relationship into her being the observer of someone famous. She believes that I am big and she is little.

BETSY: Can you talk to her about her personal pain at feeling smaller than you?

LETTY: She doesn't acknowledge it as pain. She simply says matter-of-factly, "This is how life is. You and I have little in common anymore." She's not angry or sad. She's just moved herself into the category of "a friend from long ago."

BETSY: Are there special qualities she has that you would like? Do you tell her about them?

LETTY: Yes, but she doesn't hear me. I don't push it. I sense she can't budge. She feels my success creates a gulf between us, and that's just how it is. It's a loss for me. For both of us.

I talked with movie star Susan Anspach for three hours about envy. We sat on sumptuous leather couches in her Santa Monica home, eating Fig Newtons after she had returned from a gymnastics class. Susan, who has acted in the movies *Five Easy Pieces*, *The Landlord*, *Blume in Love*, *Play It Again, Sam*, *The Big Fix*, *Running*, and *Montenegro*, is a likable beauty. Long strawberry-blond curls fall over her innocent and thoughtful face. Her son's father is Jack Nicholson, and her teenage daughter's father is Mark Goddard, an actor on *General Hospital*. Susan is bright, intelligent, informed, and has thought seriously about the subject of envy.

The day we met, Susan wore a piece of Scotch tape on her forehead. I didn't mention it. (My mother convinced me I am not tactful, and I am still trying to learn that art.) In the course of our conversation, Susan put her hand to her forehead and realized the tape was there. I was about to envy her for her unwrinkled skin when Susan, without embarrassment, explained that an acting instructor had taught her to place the tape between her eyebrows twice a month to protect her skin from wrinkles. That's a good way to avoid being envied, I thought. Share what you know.

Susan says she does little to evoke envy. She doesn't brag about being an actress. Her daughter had spent lots of time with her mother at movie sets and theaters, and was six years old before she realized her mother was a movie star.

Susan explained, "I am deeply offended by the whole thing of celebrity, stardom, being considered a more exciting, fantastic, incredible human being because I happen to do this job compared with that job. A person's specialness is in their goodness, not in their job. I don't expect or want people to fall down on their face and treat me as special simply because I'm in an occupation our culture reveres. I would rather have lunch with Marina, the person who cleans my house, who is genuine, kind, humorous, and saintly than with almost anyone I know.

"As far as material things or adoration, they're like the devil to me. Awfully scary. I didn't know it at the time, but I was afraid of people envying me, especially my friends. Being envied has hurt me.

"So as not to hurt my friends, I fought my own success. I remember that when *Blume in Love* came out, we were supposed to attend the opening. Most people would love that—a big movie, and I'm the star. But I was so upset, I told my husband I didn't want to go, that I didn't want any part of it." Susan doesn't even see her own movies.

"My husband asked, 'What's wrong?' I told him, 'I made the movie, we did the work. I don't need all these parties, all this attention. They can take it all and put it in a plastic bag and throw it in the ocean.'

"I was afraid of losing people's love if I became too successful. The minute you achieve that kind of success, you are distancing yourself from people. They are afraid of you. They assume you no longer need them. And with my closest friends, that proved to be true.

"I had a really close friend whom I loved. We were beatniks together. Our whole relationship to acting, to art, to the world, was 'beat philosophy.' What they called hippie in the seventies. I told her I was going to try for success, to see how it feels. I realized I had been a hypocrite all along, pretending I didn't care about success. Who wants a Cadillac to spit on it?

"I worked harder, and with that came more money. I would buy things, and she started being cold, cold, cold, really cold. I began mentioning her coldness, and she said, 'No-no-no, it's your imagination.' I pointed out exactly how she acted toward me, and she admitted, 'You're right, I have to confess, I'm envious of your success.'"

When Susan finds a close friend being envious of her, she alerts her friend to the envy. If the envious friend continues to be mean, Susan tables the friendship until there is a change in the envy level.

Susan told me that after pointing out her friend's envy, she was set for battle, for restoring the friendship, but she realized she was too fragile for combat. If her friend needed Susan to fail, even slightly, then Susan felt she just might. Susan's friend thought that Susan was into plastic glitz stuff (even though Susan wasn't)—and that what the friend believed in was earthy, real, and natural. Susan couldn't fight and gave up the friendship.

Susan, who has become more accomplished and less tentative about her success, would now be able to talk about her insecurity, stressing how she needs her friend's support. Susan would explain to her friend that envy and the fear of being envied have the same parents: the fear of not being loved and valued.

As Susan's professional success grew, a new close friend, also an actress, became ferocious with envy. Susan said, "Do you know I started to lie just so she wouldn't envy me! And I never lie. I would tell her an audition went terribly when it went great. But these lies came back to haunt me." For example:

FRIEND: How did it go when you met Steve McQueen? Did he want you for the movie?
SUSAN: Oh, he kept commenting on how my nails were bitten. (*I bite my nails*.)
SUSAN (*to herself*): I could never tell her he said I was the best actress he had ever seen.

Later on, someone told Susan, "I hear they weren't interested in you for that movie with Steve McQueen." Susan: "I discovered that my friend had been saying this to others, and I realized that I couldn't keep playing myself down.

"Since my friend couldn't win in the actress competition she had set up, she began competing in the size of families. She couldn't have kids and instead adopted. After adopting she got pregnant and called me to tell me she was going to have a baby in November."

SUSAN (*not saying a word about herself*): I'm really happy and excited for you.
FRIEND: What about you? Have you thought about having more kids?
SUSAN: Yes, it's due in September. (*To herself*): Oh, God, she can't win with me.

Susan's friend next tried to best Susan in recipes, husbands' careers, finances, even house painters.

SUSAN: Do you know of a good house painter?
FRIEND: Yes, but I don't think you can afford him.

Susan had had it and approached the friend's husband for help.

SUSAN: I love her, please don't let her do this, talk to her, please help her. I don't want to make her feel small. I want to be her friend. I admire her inspiration, her wit, her mind; let's keep this from happening.
HUSBAND: I can't stop it. She's crazed. She dreams about you at night. It's like *Amadeus*.

The last straw: Susan invited her friend and husband and two other couples over for lunch. The friend entered the party carrying a humongous pot roast, a Dutch oven pan, and—no exaggeration— four bottles of vodka and ten bottles of wine. For four couples. Her roast was delicious. Said Susan, "My friend is a great cook; she won that one."

Why did the friend have to bring so much? Because when an envious person controls a situation, there is less for her to envy. The party was over, and Susan started wrapping up the leftover food to give back. There were three and a half bottles of vodka, eight bottles of wine, a wonderful casserole, and the Dutch oven left. Susan gave all this to her friend, and her friend refused to take it, replying, "No, you keep it, *you* need it." To Susan, the offer did not seem truly generous.

Susan learned she was not entirely responsible for her friend's envy. This woman had an envious mother. When she visited Susan, the mother asked, "You bought this house?" When Susan replied that she had, the mother said, "And my daughter is still renting. I was sure she would own a home long before you."

If you find yourself in Letty's or Susan's situation—and you might, even if you're not a 102-pound movie star with long strawberry-blond hair—here are some thoughts to consider.

1. If you don't tell the truth about your achievements, you might make your friend wonder, "If she has to be so protective of me, she must think I can't handle my envy. Maybe I can't." You insult your friend's capacity to deal with her own feelings.
2. If you tell your friend about your fear of being envied, she may end her idealization of you and realize that, even with your success, you're *you*, her old friend, the one she used to like.
3. Respect your friend's need to deal with her feelings at her own pace. She might need a no-holds-barred talk session or, instead, many small conversations over a period of time.
4. As we saw with Letty Pogrebin, talking does *not* always change the situation. To decrease the envy level by discussing it, both friends should

- be receptive to the other person's position;
- want to change;
- quit defending themselves;
- be willing to check out their own assumptions.

5. Use humor (like "What a roast!").
6. Show compassion, particularly if you discover your friend has an envious mother.
7. If you're afraid of being envied, don't assume that your success is what everybody else wants. Success does not come in one package. From the three hundred women I interviewed, I heard three hundred different definitions of success. Not everyone thinks being rich, or a movie star, or a mother, or a corporate executive,

or married is what it takes to be successful. Is your friend's success really the one you want for yourself? Ask yourself the question that is the proverbial antidote to envy: "Do I want to put out as much time, effort, and stress as she does to get what she has?"

Remember, you chose your friend because you like her.
Let's realize that in friendship

1. envy is mutual and inevitable.
2. the more you compare, the more you will envy or be envied.
3. you may fantasize and make assumptions about your friend's life. This leads to envy, which, in turn, strains the friendship.
4. if you chose your friend to become more like her, you may envy her for having whatever it is you want more of.
5. if you deny your envy to yourself and your friend, the envy is more likely to harm the friendship.
6. if you can't stand being envied, if you can't enjoy what you do have, you may find yourself forever wanting.
7. don't judge your envy. The more you judge it, the less you understand it.
8. wanting something someone else has is fine—if that's not all you ever do.
9. if both people believe they can't live with envy, the friendship is doomed.
10. if you want the friendship to endure, commit yourselves to weathering the tough times envy will bring.

Envying a friend can either wreck the friendship or enable you to look more closely at the bond you share. Remember, the nature of a close friendship is nourishment, sharing, and mutual comfort. You don't need to conceal envious feelings with friends. Friendship provides a unique opportunity to acknowledge and look envy squarely in the face, denying it its darker power.

CHAPTER 8

Women and Envy

*Women have been taught about envy from childhood.
They hear fairy tales, like "Snow White" and
"Cinderella," which teach them if they are
beautiful, like a princess, they will be envied.
Men are influenced by Greek mythology, in
which they are portrayed as competitive, physical, active. Most often in literature, women
envy what can't be achieved, like looks and
youth, and men envy attainable achievements.*
—Anonymous, 1985

Men are taught to apologize for their weak-
nesses; women for their strengths.
—LOIS WYSE [b. 1926],
American advertising executive

What *is* women's particular problem with envy? Many women,
like many men, envy people with a high income, financial
security, job status, material possessions, and career success. But
for women, the list doesn't end here.

What else do women envy? Beauty—good looks and a trim
body—is near the top of the list. Women have traditionally
counted on their looks as a source of pride and success in the
world. Now they are finding other avenues for success—in

particular, careers. While men have characteristically dealt with their envy by being competitive, women have been taught that competition is not ladylike. But competition, as we shall see, can ease envy's grip, allow you a positive discharge for your envy, and help make envy work for you.

BEAUTY

A thirty-year-old paralegal worker from Louisiana writes, "People envy me immediately because of my looks, before I ever do or say anything."

One difficulty with beauty as a cause for envy is that it can't be measured. Whereas everyone agrees that an income of $100,000 a year is more than an income of $13,000 a year, how do you measure the degree of beauty—whether a blonde is more beautiful than a brunette or whether someone with bigger eyes is prettier than someone with smaller eyes? We can quantify the blueness of an iris but not the twinkle in the eye. Since there is no single objective standard of beauty, each of us can easily feel our looks are lacking, inadequate, somehow not what they should be. Women tend to envy the superficial, the intangible— and this creates a certain powerlessness. You can envy high cheekbones, but if you don't have them, what can you do? Also, as history has shown, our ideal of feminine beauty can change unpredictably with time, or even with the season.

Perhaps the Miss America contest, begun in 1922, was an attempt to make scientific sense of the wicked queen's mirror, to determine once and for all who is the "fairest of them all." Now, with fifty contestants, ten semifinalists, five finalists, and "the fairest," the winner, are we finally quantifying beauty? In 1983, the contest winner had plastic surgery. Is beauty to be determined by nature alone? How *do* we measure beauty?

JULIE HARRIS

Even a woman as beautiful as actress Julie Harris sees herself as fairly plain. Julie, now of *Knots Landing*, lives a simple, independent life and greatly admires Mother Teresa. Julie says,

"People don't envy me because they see me as like them, not above them."

Julie Harris allows you a peek into her soul. She hates envy. "Envy is a confining, enslaving emotion. When you are envious, you try to suppress it. Any emotion you suppress most of the time goes inward and gives you bile. Envy has a bitterness, a rancor, that makes you sick." Julie knows because she has felt envy. I was surprised that what she envies in others is beauty, *physical beauty:* "The first thing when I was little that I was attracted to was physical beauty. I thought, If only I could look like that! It's what I've always been envious of."

She never thought of herself as beautiful but confessed, "I think of women I have adored and admired, like Anna Magnani, as beauty. Vivien Leigh seems to be the perfection of beauty. Or Merle Oberon, Elizabeth Taylor, Marilyn Monroe. That's beauty. Jacqueline Onassis—not strictly beautiful, not a patrician beauty like Vivien Leigh, but Jacqueline is beautiful because there is a grand aura about her. Also Jessica Lange, and darling Sissy Spacek."

When I suggested that she had qualities similar to those of Sissy Spacek, she replied, "I am a plainer version. I don't have good eyes, my features aren't good by themselves. In high school, there was a composite for the girl with the most beautiful eyes, hair, neck, legs. I was chosen for the girl with the most beautiful mouth, before I got it smashed. So I could say, 'I'm not beautiful, but I do have a mouth!'

"My mother was always glamorous and charming, and it was so impossible for me to be. She didn't encourage me in the direction of beauty; she didn't bring me out.

"A long time ago, when I was fourteen, I saw Helen Hayes do Shakespeare's *As You Like It.* She looked like a little page boy, and her hair was short, all curly, a little crown of curls. I thought, Isn't that beautiful! My hair is straight. I went to the hairdresser and said, 'I want that little crown of curls!' In those days, they gave you a very hard permanent. When I saw it, it looked awful. I had tried to look like my idol, but . . .

"Next time, I'd understand better. I would still say to a hairdresser, 'I want to look like that.' But what I would really be saying is, 'I want that face to be there, too.' The hairdresser has no control over your face. She'd do what she could and I'd say, 'That's not what I meant.' What I really meant is, 'Why can't that face be changed too?' Now, I know I can't do that. I've learned to live with my face."

* * *

Julie Harris, a wise woman, has learned to live with what can't be changed. For many of us, though, the modern focus on beauty churns up feelings of inadequacy, insecurity, and envy. Was it always this way?

No, says Dr. Robin Lakoff, co-author of *Face Value*. Before 1839, the year the camera was invented, there wasn't such an emphasis on beauty. The general public's obsession with beauty flowered in the 1920s when photography, still and movie cameras, had an enormous effect on our imagination.

Before the nineteenth century, only rich people had access to portraits of individual beautiful women. Then the artist's conception of what was beautiful represented an ideal. Formerly, a woman's beauty was spread by word of mouth, then later through print or portraits. The ideal of beauty was vague, imprecise, open to interpretation. A woman could believe that her looks *did* match the ideal.

But today, by making feminine beauty specific, as modeling agencies bombard us with Christie Brinkleys, women have a specific ideal standard that they actually fail to meet. *Now,* according to Dr. Lakoff, "The Venuses of today remind us of what we are not; they make us feel, by the human color of their eyes, the warmth of their flesh, that we might be like them if only we bought this cosmetic, that face lift."

Reminded continually of what you are not, you envy. Since the camera can lie, and the photograph can be touched up, you are continually being manipulated to envy even more. With photographic reproduction, women now believe that with time, money, good intentions, and lots of effort, they, too, can look like that. Beauty is within their reach.

With the proliferation of photography and fashion magazines, envy of beauty has been on the rise. In the 1930s, an art director of *Vogue* magazine summed it up and foreshadowed the future: "The gist of every modern photographer is the ability to transform every child of the street into a momentary goddess and object of envy and desire."

In the 1950s, *Vogue* magazine described a woman's face in terms used by investment bankers. A beautiful face meant security, "economic security, money, position, status." By the 1970s, a beautiful woman was no longer only wealthy, as *Vogue* had originally portrayed her; now she was happy with herself, looked as though appearance wasn't uppermost in her mind. She was portrayed as active, athletic, a traveler who also went back to school for her master's degree. The passive beauty was replaced. The woman of the seventies sported the "natural look" and was taught to wear makeup that didn't look like makeup. In the 1980s, you are, at all costs, also to look fit and healthy. This is a tall, unrealistic order to fulfill, replete with ways to make you feel inadequate.

We have thus arrived at a time in history where the emphasis on appearance is extreme.

There is a connection between beauty and the different ways we treat attractive and unattractive people. Studies have shown that teachers judge attractive students as having more positive personality traits. Even very young children would rather have an attractive child for a friend. Families seem to favor their attractive children over unattractive ones. Furthermore, in courts of law, attractive defendants are convicted less often and receive lighter punishments than unattractive defendants.

Another problem these days, since we don't take time to get to know each other, is that we rely more on superficial observations. Easily thrown back to the uncertainties of adolescence, we immediately judge each other on attractiveness, using a narrow definition of good looks. Because of our focus on beauty, we envy before we get to know a person. We may never even get to know the person. Envy precedes knowledge.

Of course, being beautiful doesn't insure happiness. A fifty-year-old housewife from Massachusetts reminds us, "Girls who have more than average good looks should be told early in the game not to be surprised if they find disloyalty. They might find beauty a burden. Blondes don't necessarily have more fun, and plums don't always drop into our laps if we are shapely or have dimples. It's silly to envy. Being beautiful is no gateway to paradise—especially when others are envious of you and give you a hard time in so many different ways."

Women everywhere envy each other's looks. As one friend told another, "When you moved here to Minneapolis, it's a wonder any of us became friends with you at all. You were too pretty."

Beauty can come between friends. A thirty-year-old real estate agent recounts, "My best friend is a skinny, blond, blue-eyed WASP. A couple of weeks ago, we were out at a bar. As we were leaving, two guys called out to us. We ignored them, but they were persistent. Finally, I said, 'No, we're not interested.' This guy turned on me and said, 'I didn't want you anyway, you fat slob.'

"I started crying, but my friend was furious. She tried to talk to me, but I couldn't speak to her. There was a definite rift. I knew they'd never say that to her. A few days later, she told me, 'If you had been out with Nancy, you'd have sat right down and talked it out.' Which is true, because neither Nancy nor I are that attractive." Here, beauty and the male response to attractiveness separated two good friends who didn't want to be divided.

A twenty-five-year-old secretary from Utah writes poignantly about being envied for her good looks. "At the college dorm, girls envied me for being more attractive and thinner than they were. Of course, if you've been a second-class citizen, you're bound to envy. They gossiped about me. I was deeply hurt, devastated. Now, I am cautious not to 'look too good' and often won't do things I want to do, like acting on a stage, because I am fearful of arousing envy in other women.

"In the morning, if I want to put on makeup, I will think about it for fifteen minutes, saying to myself, Will my co-worker Lulu be envious and make some remark? I know I shouldn't care, so I fix myself up. Then, if Lulu does express some envy and I enjoy it, I tell myself, Boy, you must be unhappy inside. It's false to fix myself up just to get compliments or envy from other women, just so I can feel better about myself."

This woman can't win. She's not a false person because she wants to look good. One reason she's unhappy is that she is so uncomfortable being envied, she can't take in positive regard from others. She can never feel satisfied. It's like anorexia, the disorder that causes you to refuse food. Fear of being envied is a psychiatric disorder—you can't take in positive feedback from others.

The "Snow White" fairy tale tells you that preoccupation with looks comes from or can create vanity and inner emptiness. If another woman is beautiful, does that subtract from your beauty? If you focus too much on your looks, do you apologize for being superficial? And if you don't focus on your looks enough, do you apologize for not looking up to par? Are you striving to receive just the right amount of envy, not so much that you fear being disliked, and not so little that you feel unnoticed—the perfect balance?

In a youth-worshiping culture, you know you will "lose your looks," that you will get older. You learned from Snow White's stepmother about using beauty as your only source of power in the world. Relying on your looks to define who you are, or as your way to be appreciated by others can create terror and destructiveness toward yourself and others.

Aging is a source of fear and despair. You might feel you are over the hill when your face begins to wrinkle. Men can have wrinkled skin and gray hair and still be considered appealing and vital. Our society believes that generally a man remains attractive to women until a much later age than a woman to a man.

Since beauty is in the eye of the beholder, beauty should be an addition to your life, not a goal or a one-way street toward self-esteem. You can overcome the fixation on looks through cultivating achievements and skills that develop with age. Dr. Lakoff offers a helpful suggestion of what beauty should be:

"Beauty must be understood as something achieved through individual experience, which shows in the face as a badge of a thoughtful, interested, and competent human being. The criteria for good looks in women must no longer be so dissimilar to the criteria we use for men. . . . Beauty is what shows in the crinkles around the eyes, the set of the chin, the stance of one who knows where she has been, where she is going, and how to get there. Whether the body is plump or muscular is not the issue. The issue is autonomy, being one's own person."

Nora Ephron

In her best-selling novel and subsequent movie *Heartburn*, Nora Ephron describes a problem shared by many women:

"Brenda and I had been friends since kindergarten. I was five years old. . . . I looked at her and decided she was the most beautiful thing I'd ever seen. Her flaxen hair came to her waist, her eyes were deep green, her skin was white as snow, just like a stupid fairy tale. *I always hoped Brenda would eventually lose her looks—my theory being that I would grow up and gain mine, she would lose hers, and we would grow up more or less even*—but she never did. . . . the truth is that I was secretly pleased when she slept with Charlie [my husband] because I was exonerated from the guilt of all those years of feeling jealous [envious] of her and [I] plunged suddenly into a warm bath of innocent victimization."

This story sums up what we've talked about—the envy of looks, the wish to spoil, the fallacy that there is a limited amount of good looks available. And it also points out the preference for being a guilt-free victim rather than an envious loser.

Even the Women You Envy Are Envious

If you're not already convinced how pointless this envy over looks is, here are examples from six more women. The clincher is that these six women are all successful, accomplished, and lovely, the very women the rest of us spend our time envying. Yet even these women can find something to envy about the way another woman looks. Remember, at a different time in history we would be envying fat, rather than thin, thighs.

Barbara Corday, president of Columbia Pictures Television, envies somebody for losing twenty pounds, having a baby, or looking great in a swimming suit. "I certainly have the everyday kind of small envious moment," she reveals.

When she envies, she brushes the feeling aside. "I talk to myself. Tell myself how foolish I am. This envy is not going to get me anywhere, so I might as well be happy with who I am. I tell myself that the person I envy would probably love what I have."

Sharon Percy Rockefeller, married to a Rockefeller and active with her own work, envies thinness and people with bony faces. Because she's not proud of feeling envy, she tries to get rid of the feeling. "I acknowledge I will never be thin, tell myself, You can't be thin, so grow up! Or I try to be rational and logical. But that's hard because society dictates to women that we should be thin. Even though I know I'm not going to change all that much, seeing the problem with less emotion does not lessen my wish to be slimmer."

Journalist Sally Quinn envies "fleeting things" like great legs. "In another life, I think I should have great legs. But I can laugh about it when I realize what a small thing it is compared to health and life."

Director Sara Pillsbury, Pillsbury heir, also envies women with thin thighs, but then she tells herself how stupid that is.

Congresswoman Lynn Martin tries to joke about her envy. "I envy women with tans. Tans indicate they travel to exotic places. But tanning booths have removed that source of my envy. If I see someone with beautiful naturally curly hair, I think about kicking them."

Women envy what they imagine brings fulfillment. Our research shows that after financial security and material possessions, women envy beauty above all else. But there are other symbols of fulfillment—such as babies, pregnancy, the all-American girl, and clothes.

Who's Having the Baby

A Berkeley friend told me she envies women with babies so much that she avoids places where she might see them. In other words, most places. Berkeley's favorite coffee hangout, Peet's, is known for catering to women with their baby strollers. The word in Berkeley is that many forty-year-old women, when they first notice a gray hair, decide to have a baby. This leap into pregnancy creates envy for single women who want babies, married women who can't have babies, or older women who wish they could do it over again.

What about the woman who does not have a choice, the woman—more common these days with working women starting families after their careers are launched—who cannot, for medical reasons, become pregnant? Janice, thirty-five, writes from Spokane, Washington, that she deeply envies people who have children. "Adopt a baby," people counsel her. The adoption agency told her she couldn't adopt a baby by herself—she is divorced. Janice tried for fifteen years to get pregnant before she accepted the fact that she was physically unable to conceive. She tries to reassure herself that she is fortunate not to be tied down, that anyone can be a mother, that "it's no big deal." Still, she can't find comfort in clichés.

Janice suffers. "Being childless, I sometimes feel like I'm not a real woman. I ignore the children of my friends. That hurts my friendships. I don't want to appear envious, so I tell everyone that I have no children because of choice, or that it doesn't really matter to me anyway.

"I've accepted that I can't have children, but my envy does not go away. This envy is powerful, yet power*less*; there is nothing I can remedy. I can't adopt a child, I can't get pregnant, and I can't feel enough love for my friends who do have babies. All I can do is concentrate on other goals."

People have suggested that Janice work in child care or become a teacher, but these easy solutions rarely take away the pain and loss of having an unfulfilled desire.

When you are pregnant, you are special. Jody, age 30, told me that when her friend was pregnant, her friend insisted that everything about being pregnant was wonderful. When Jody became pregnant two years later, when specialness and attention were focused on her, Jody's friend enumerated all the terrible things that would now happen. This friend, who envied Jody's specialness, wanted to spoil Jody's excitement about her pregnancy.

Tammie, a twenty-four-year-old office supply store manager, writes about a friendship that dissolved when she became pregnant: "When I was employed at a large four-star hotel, I got the boss to hire my friend. She was extremely pretty. Before she came, though, I had been the pretty one.

"Both of us were married, and she had a small baby. I became pregnant a few months later. With the usual extra weight, I tended to swell enormously. I became uglier, and she became prettier all the time, especially to the guys. The bigger I became, the uglier was her attitude toward me. One day for seemingly no reason she lashed out at me verbally. (I later realized that Tammie badly wanted another baby, but her husband was opposed.) Of course I retaliated with a few obscenities of my own, and we never spoke again. Now, I tell myself a great personality rules over beauty anytime."

Let's Hear It for Cheerleaders!

Cheerleaders represent the youthful ideal of popularity, prettiness, athletic ability, extroversion, femininity, sexuality, and acceptance by successful men—the gorgeous football stars. The quintessential high school ideal girl. Yesterday's cheerleaders were the forerunner of today's women who seem to "have it all": the successful career woman with a helpful husband and children; the suburban housewife, content with motherhood and working inside the home, enjoying her activities and the company of a loving husband. Yesterday's cheerleaders, especially the ones who could afford the fancy outfits, resemble the women of today who seem to be in society's inner circle.

One woman, a dean of student affairs at a nursing school, spoke to me about cheerleader envy. "In the little town of Oklahoma where I went to high school, being a cheerleader is *it* in importance. There is a career route which begins in junior high. I was head cheerleader. Once you have been head cheerleader in junior high, you are expected to be a substitute cheerleader in the tenth grade."

She was an excellent head cheerleader. She wiped herself out preparing for the substitute cheerleader tryouts. But as hard as she tried, she didn't get the position. The head cheerleader in high school simply explained, "We didn't want it to be too easy for you. You have it too easy. You have to earn your way to us. You have to serve your time, put in your dues to become one of our gang." Sound familiar? Many teachers have made similar comments to their students.

So our dean of student affairs joined the pep squad, which is the apprentice, second-rate cheerleader group. "I didn't like it very much, but I was peppy and did well." The next year at the tryouts, she became one of the chosen cheerleaders. She didn't let envy stop her from moving along her cheerleader career path.

Other women offered stories of cheerleader envy. A black woman doctor told me that she was a counselor to younger women in her junior year at college. The football team went on strike because there were no black cheerleaders. She had no cheerleader training, had not taken the career path described above, but she had taken dancing.

"The girls I counseled bribed me. They told me if I just tried out for cheerleader, they would buy me Sunday dinner for two months. I was skinny then, but I ate a lot. I agreed. The deal was I only had to try out. The trouble was—I passed, I was chosen.

"I started getting hate mail. One letter from the National States Rights accused me of miscegenation. I even got death threats. The dean of women alerted the FBI, whose security people followed me around the campus. There was also envy from black women who had practiced harder than I had, who wanted to be chosen but weren't. I was pledging a black sorority then, and they were more humiliating to me than to other pledges, none of whom were cheerleaders."

CLOTHES ENVY

Clothes, like cheerleaders, represent the fantasy of success. A well-put-together outfit, an attractive, daring dress, a designer's whatever, all give the impression that you are well put together, that you know who you are and feel good about yourself. Stylish clothes imply fun. When a woman buys a new outfit, she may imagine a new adventure. She envisions the possibility of something different happening to her.

Colombe Nicolas

Colombe is both an attorney and president of Christian Dior, New York. She lives in a world of clothes envy—who wore what at which party? If Colombe is seen in a ten-thousand-dollar dress, people will murmur, "Did you see Colombe in that dress? She was afraid to sit down in it because if she spilled something on it, she'd have to buy it." Or people will say Colombe didn't look relaxed at a party. "If you were wearing a ten-thousand-dollar dress, would you be relaxed?" asked Colombe.

Jill

Jill, who works for Exxon, doesn't own many clothes, but what she wears is top drawer. She told me she is envied for her clothes. Women will ask her, "Is that all wool?" "How much did that cost?" "Who bought you that?" "Another new . . . ?" In other words, "How come someone like you, who isn't very high up in the company, dresses so nicely?"

   Jill told me this story: She wore a Christian Dior outfit to work that she had purchased in Italy for fifty dollars. At eight A.M., a secretary commented, "There is something wrong with your outfit." Jill couldn't figure it out. The secretary said, "Oh, that purse, does it match your suit?" Later that day someone asked Jill, "Is your sweater too tight?" The receptionist overheard and retorted, "You're just jealous, honey. We all wish we had more right below the shoulders."

The people at Jill's office envy her style because it stands for an expression of her individuality. Many of her co-workers dress for success, in what Jill calls the "Susie Corporate" look. Jill believes these women use their clothes to conform and fit in. Jill's clothes express her autonomy and sense of self. If you don't take the time to get to know the person behind the appearance, you may find yourself envying clothes as much as looks.

WOMEN AND SUCCESS

How have women felt successful? Good looks, a husband and children, popularity, and a closet full of high-class clothes have equaled success for women for many years. But now women are achieving success in ways that have been open primarily to men. Becoming successful because of your work, not your looks, is active rather than passive, more under your control. Yet job status brings up as much envy as good looks do.

At the heart of the Snow White syndrome, a poignant manifestation of women's fear of success, is the underlying and hidden fear of being envied. Women fear being envied more than men do. Why?

Matina Horner did the pioneer research in this area. She asked, Why do women hold themselves back from their fullest potential? She did *not* find that women wish or will themselves to fail, nor that we feel satisfaction in failure. Instead, she discovered that women are motivated to become successful, but that success makes them anxious.

Dr. Horner defines anxiety as "anticipating negative consequences." *She found that 65 percent of the women tested were anxious about negative results that might result from being successful* and avoided success because of external and internal reasons:

External: social rejection, unpopularity
Internal: the fear of not being feminine (feminine women should not be achievement-oriented or overly ambitious)

She asked female graduate students to continue a story that begins like this: "After her first-term finals, Anne finds herself at the top of her medical school class." Here's an example from a woman who feared success:

"Anne starts proclaiming her surprise and joy. Her fellow classmates are so disgusted with her behavior that they jump on her in a body and beat her. She is maimed for life."

Another woman responded, "Anne is pretty darn proud of herself, but *everyone hates and envies her.*"

FEAR OF SOCIAL REJECTION

You may want to spoil a woman's success. Or, you may want to reject her so you don't have to experience the envy her success causes you. Women particularly fear this rejection. Anne's classmates envy that she is at the top; the envy becomes destructive as she brags and brings her "superiority" to their attention.

Ninety-two percent of the men responding to the above question (when the person at the top of the class was a man) provided answers that demonstrated they felt being successful was positive; success would bring happiness and fulfillment, not social ostracism. Only 8 percent of the men had a fear of success. According to Dr. Horner, success inhibits social life for the girls even more than it enhances social life for the boys. Men are less fearful of being envied.

LOSS OF FEMININITY

Dr. Horner found that many fears about success began to surface during a girl's junior year in college, when her parents wanted her to "be securely married, rather than take the unconventional and risky course of becoming a serious working person. The contradictory message the girl gets, from her parents and society, is that if she is too smart, too independent, and above all, too serious about her work, she is unfeminine and therefore never able to get married." Dr. Horner mentions the *Peanuts* cartoon in which Sally, at age five, says, "Do I really need to go to kindergarten? I just want to become a good wife and mother. I don't want to *become* somebody!"

Fear of Not Being Pleasing

For women, being pleasing to others becomes the reason to achieve. Even in preschool, little girls show more of a desire to please than boys do; little girls work for love and approval, and if they are very bright, they tend to underestimate their competence.

We fear not being pleasing because we have such a deep need for connectedness; if we are not pleasing, we run the risk of disturbing our precious connections with others. The fear of not pleasing someone plays a large part in why women don't fulfill their potential and why they envy those who *are* able to achieve and fulfill their potential.

Worrying About the Opinion of Others

Psychologists have shown that women have a greater need for feedback than men and are more concerned with the opinions of others. *The concern with being liked is even more important for a woman than being feminine and winning a man.* While little boys are learning that success means mastery of skills, independence, and gaining confidence in coping with their environment, little girls are learning that being effective lies in their relationships with others and their feelings about these relationships. Little boys try to "figure the task," and little girls try to "figure the teacher." When you are dependent on the need to be liked, you are more likely to fear not being liked—the Snow White syndrome.

Judith Bardwick, psychologist in female development, asks the following question: "Does a person strive to achieve because he has an internal standard of excellence, a self-image and feeling of self-esteem dependent on how he perceives himself performing— or does he achieve primarily in order to receive praise from others?" It has been shown that boys have more of an internal standard of excellence, but that for girls, external praise is paramount. For men, the motive to achieve is more internalized, a need to achieve in its own right.

Doubting Your Competence

We have predictable social characteristics because of our early conditioning. Parents tend to be more encouraging of a son's achievements than a daughter's. Daughters' achievements make mothers more anxious because they fear their daughters' separation from them, and because, as we have seen, mothers often have conflicts about their own achievements. When your mother shows anxiety about your competence, you begin to doubt it yourself. Doubting your own competence, you are less likely to do well and are more prone to envy.

Studies have shown that women are lower in self-confidence than men in almost all achievement situations. Is this really true? Dr. Ellen Lenney has looked closely at the results of these studies and discovered that when women receive immediate, straightforward, and unambiguous feedback about how they are doing, they *don't* expect to do worse than men. If a woman, after finishing a test, gets immediate feedback— "You passed" or "You failed"— even if she failed, she will exhibit more self-confidence for the next test. Dr. Lenney also found that when women are told their work will be *compared* with someone else's, or *evaluated*, they won't do as well.

The problem in the research on achievement motivation and success is twofold. First, *What is "achievement"?* "Intellectual, athletic, mechanical, artistic" achievements are the standard categories. Women don't display low self-confidence in *all* achievement situations—their confidence is higher in areas of interpersonal relationships and internal development.

Second, *What is "success" for a woman?* In the Women and Envy study, women defined "success," in order of frequency, as personal happiness, satisfaction with work, having enough money, professional accomplishments, a good home life, having the respect of others, a workable combination of personal and professional lives, independence, friends, the ability to cope, and power.

For women, success doesn't necessarily mean doing better than someone else or scoring better than others. Recent feminist literature—for instance, the award-winning book *In a Different Voice*, by Carol Gilligan—tells us that women see the world differently from men because of women's early identifications with mothers as caretakers. Men supposedly transfer these identifications to their fathers; women less so. Women tend to find meaning in life in terms of maintaining interpersonal relationships, and boys find meaning in the rules of the game. Women see things more in the context of how they are with others; men see things more individualistically, more absolutely. Women care more about preserving and maintaining relationships.

If little girls, as young as three years old, argue while playing a game, they will choose another game to play but still play together. When little boys argue, they tend to choose another game and then play separately. Women don't fear all types of success; they fear success in competition and in winning, less so in their relationships.

However you define achievement and success, Dr. Horner's results validate the female stereotype that "competition, independence, competitiveness, and leadership . . . are inconsistent with femininity." These qualities, however, are considered consistent with masculinity. Dr. Horner told journalist Vivian Gornick that the one time she felt comfortable speaking in front of a crowd was when she was seven months pregnant, for then she felt secure in being a woman.

FEAR OF COMPETITION

If you have fear of success, you find it difficult to compete. You lose an important means of managing and tolerating your envy.

You may have been taught that if you compete, you are a bad person who wants to hurt others. For women, "out-performing a competitor may be antagonistic to making him a friend." Therefore women, who value having a friend more than doing well at something, will be less competitive. This is double jeopardy. Besides being taught not to be competitive, you fear competition, because you fear losing your relationship.

Women have a real problem with competition. Dr. Horner's results showed that 77 percent of women did better working alone than in competitive situations. More than two-thirds of her male subjects did better in competitive situations than when working alone. Dr. Horner believes that men are less fearful of competition because for a man to surpass an opponent is, in fact, a source of pride and masculinity.

The key to success for women might be the ability to be competitive *and* maintain concern for the relationship at the same time.

COMPETITION

> If I could have success without envy, that's how
> I'd order it.
> — *Newsweek* reporter, Los Angeles, 1985

Previously you read about a negative side of competition, how competition in the workplace contributes to envy. But we find in the root meaning of the word "competition" an aide to circumventing envy: "com" plus "petition." "Petition" means to obtain, to seek. The literal meaning of "competition" is "to meet the requirements," to seek along with another, *"to strive together."*

What is the connection between competition and envy? In any situation, the process that focuses on and works toward performance based on an internal standard of excellence lessens the possibility for envy. If you can focus on this form of competition, you're less likely to be debilitated by envy. When you focus on someone else, you're like a person who runs a race and watches another runner so much that she trips, stumbles, and falls. If you concentrate on your competitor, winning will be harder.

Joyce Lindenbaum, a psychotherapist who writes about envy and competition, suggests that in competition women could "motivate each other toward some heightened capacity without fearing damage to one's self, the other, or the relationship."

In a competitive situation, partners are both separate and connected to one another. In a tennis game, a net separates you from your partner, but you are still playing one another, together. You can compete without hurting one another. You can play. Every competitive situation is *not* like one in which two women are competing for a man and hurting one another.

Many women fear competition for a number of reasons. One, it isn't ladylike. Two, they are afraid someone will envy their doing well. Three, they see competition as a process whereby someone gains at the expense of another. Four, they fear that if they compete with a friend, they will lose the friend. Yet competition can extract the venom from envy by encouraging the expression of those poisonous feelings in a less harmful way. How does this happen?

Competition discharges envy, gives it a needed outlet. In telling yourself, I can have that, too. What do I do to get it? you are already thinking competitively. In negative envy, you don't realize that you, too, may have the quality you wish for in the other person. In competition, you try to connect with the quality in yourself that, until now, you have only attributed to the person you envy.

Let's say you are attracted to a friend because of her athletic ability. You can either stay stuck in your envy of that ability or try to develop your own athletic skill. The competitive person is usually not held down by the Snow White syndrome.

In competition, one is provided with the opportunity to become competent. In envy, you remain passive, wishing, longing, hoping, but doing little to better what you have. Competition implies action. Competition is improving what you have and gently encouraging your friend to better herself. "When one gets better, the other doesn't have to get worse."

Changing Envy into Competition

Barbara, a friend who plays on a woman's soccer team, told me how she learned to change her envy into competition: as an adult, she envied people who played sports as she had as a child. But she grew tired of merely wishing to play, so she joined a local soccer team, even though she wasn't a good player. She practiced. The better players—their control of the ball, the beauty of their passes—were inspirational. Slowly Barbara learned to go for the ball, to rush a player, to play at her maximum.

Once, her team lost to a tough team whose members refused to shake hands at the end of the game. According to Barbara, "We found their whole approach the opposite to ours. Certainly we'd become more competitive as a team, winning was a lot better than losing, but not everything."

It wasn't easy for Barbara to learn to be a competitive player—individually and with a team: "It's my feeling," she told me, "that women, coming late to sports, in general not having been encouraged, either, to work with a team, to forgo all vanity and play something physically full out, very naturally would have difficulties. There is also the unpleasantness of possible rejection—one plays badly and gets pulled out, or doesn't get to play at all. And you know how women feel about rejection.

"For me, it's been a revelation to find I am without excuses. I have been on the line as a physical competitor and nothing else. No one cares if you have your period, either. We have all had periods and strained muscles. There's no talking one's way out of awkward moments, and it surely doesn't matter how cute you are or how likable. Success rests on the way you play, something boys have learned from an early age. I've also had to learn to accept criticism and not to deal it out too harshly. What I've gotten from the team is the real drama of those games, moments outside of daily family life, extraordinary elation at running, even a remaking of something like my girlhood, the thrill of competition and companionship."

The Importance of Competition: Billie Jean King

Since fear of being envied obviously holds women back, we need to pay attention to steps that lessen this fear. One step is converting envy into competition. Billie Jean King is a woman whose life is dedicated to doing precisely that.

Billie Jean King has done more for women's sports than any woman alive today. In 1974, she started the Women's Sports Foundation, whose purpose is to encourage women's participation and training in sports and fitness activities for their health, enjoyment, and personal development. There are now women champions in basketball, judo, gymnastics, tennis, skiing, swimming, boxing, running, wrestling, and horse, car, and dog-sled racing.

As a great athlete herself, Billie Jean King sets an example for all women. She has fought for equality in athletics, as other feminists have done for women in the workplace, schools, and home. She trains women to compete with men through her efforts as commissioner of Domino's Pizza Team Tennis. And she also finds time to serve as an ambassador for AIM—Adventures in Movement—which helps handicapped children.

A Lifetime of Competition.

Billie Jean has played hard. In 1959, at age fifteen, she was ranked nineteenth among the women players in the United States Lawn Tennis Association. In 1961, the first year she was invited to Wimbledon, she and Karen Hantze won the women's doubles title. In 1962, she upset the number-one seeded player in the Wimbledon tournament, Margaret Smith, in the first round of play. In 1966, she won Wimbledon and was ranked the number-one player in the world. In 1970, she won her second U.S. Championship. Even with suffering through one foot and five knee operations, losing eight years of good tennis, Billie Jean has won 20 Wimbledon titles and played full-time tennis until she was thirty-nine years old. How did she become so good?

Billie Jean always knew she would be great in something: "I remember when I was five, I told my mom, 'I'm going to be able to do something really special in my lifetime.' And my mom looked at me like 'Oh, sure.' "

Billie Jean has always loved sports. When she was four, she played baseball and longed to become professional. As she put it, "We're talking big leagues, but there was no place for me." She also enjoyed track, basketball, and football, but when she was ten, her mother objected, explaining, "These sports aren't ladylike." Her father suggested tennis.

It clicked. "The first day I hit a tennis ball, I knew that's what I wanted. That same day I told Mom, 'I found what I want to do.' My mom said, 'That's wonderful,' and I could tell she didn't believe me. I said, 'Mom, yoo-hoo, I'm over here. I really want to do this. This is it. I love tennis. I get to run. I get to hit a ball. It's like dancing, and I love dancing.' I realize now that tennis gave me the true athletic experience of being able to express the mental side and the physical side of myself as one. Mom said she and my father would support whatever I wanted to do. Two months later, I told my parents, 'I'm going to be the number-one tennis player in the whole world.' "

Billie Jean King sensed she was special. She wasn't so afraid of envy that she had to mask her greatness. To see a woman so assuredly claim her self-worth presents a model, a possibility for other women to be great themselves.

Finances.

Her father was a fireman, her mother a housewife; they lived in Long Beach, California. It was the 1950s, and they didn't have much money. They couldn't afford fancy tennis outfits, so her

mother sewed a white blouse and shorts for a tennis tournament.
The tournament director scorned Billie Jean's outfit and wouldn't
include her in the picture with the other girls. "Little girls wear
tennis *dresses*, not shorts," he admonished. "Someday," Billie
Jean decided, "tennis won't be so stuffy."

In 1970 she entered the Pacific Southwest Championships. First
prize for men was $12,500; for women, it was $1,500. Billie Jean
and eight other women boycotted the tournament. Then she
helped promote the Virginia Slims Circuit, which for the past
fifteen years has become one of the largest income producers for
women tennis players.

Beating Boys.

Beating Chris Evert in 1973, she retained her Wimbledon title.
Also that year, she defeated Bobby Riggs in the "Battle of the
Sexes." It hadn't come naturally for her to beat boys in tennis. "If
I played against boys when I was growing up," she told me, "I
always let them beat me. It wasn't worth the hassle to have the guy
suffer humiliation from his peers. But I wasn't reaching my full
potential. Now I always tell my students, 'Never think of yourself
as losing to a boy or a girl. You lost because the other person was
more skilled than you that day. Today I watch the girls out there
going full blast, and I just love it.' "

When asked about all the emphasis placed on winning, Billie
Jean answers, "Winning can't connect with your whole personality. I don't have the feeling of good or bad attached to winning.
I see losing as another stepping-stone to trying harder next
time."

Dealing with Envy from Teachers.

"Growing up, I was discouraged from tennis by some teachers
at school. In junior high school, they wouldn't allow my participation in tennis outside of school to count for points in the Girls
Athletic Association. Physical education teachers in my senior
year of high school were more concerned that I was going to miss
school than that I was going to Wimbledon. They could have been
envious that I was an upstart, upstaging them, challenging their
authority.

"There were some exceptions. One was my third-grade teacher,
Mrs. Hunter. She wrote on the back of my report card to my
mother, 'Your daughter is very exceptional in sports. You should
let her grow in that area.' Mrs. Hunter was so observant it was
unbelievable. She made everybody believe in themselves."

Competition Begins with Yourself.

"Since acceptance was in the minus column for me, I think I played more for the love of the game, wanting to do the best for me, than for winning. *You have to have the courage to try. That is a large part of competition. You have to first compete with yourself.*"

You'd think someone with the killer instinct would be out to win partly to impress others. But Billie Jean says, "I don't keep a trophy case. What matters to me is not 'I did it! I did it!' but what I'm doing today and tomorrow."

This is the secret to her success. We know about ways in which women had been hindered by focusing on recognition and approval, but for Billie Jean, doing well was more important than recognition and approval.

"I want to change women's socialization process and their relation to competition, and I think team tennis is a good place to start." Billie Jean feels it is important that girls and boys learn to play together, on the same team, with the same goals, the same experience in sports together. She believes that when women and men are trained to build up their similarities, rather than their differences, women will be less handicapped in business. "Girls have been trained to worry about everybody else first. I'm preparing girls and women for what I call the real world. The work force."

Billie Jean informed me, "The newspaper *U.S.A. Today* gave the results of a huge survey. It reiterated what I've been saying for twenty-five years: The only way girls get into sports is by playing with boys when they're children. When girls play with girls, they very rarely get into sports. That's why team tennis is so important. There are two girls and two boys on a team. Every game you win counts for your team, so your contribution always counts in the final outcome. Boys and girls practice together and learn to help each other. Gender doesn't matter. You can play the supportive or the leadership role, and they can change throughout the match or practice."

Billie Jean explained, "I think men and women are the same because we all go through the same emotions—joy, anger, sadness, grief; every human has these feelings. Each person is sensitive in different ways. If we can be trained to play together, we'll communicate better, we'll have more compassion for each other, we'll feel closer, we'll enjoy each other's differences because we'll realize how similar we are. Women have to go out and experience the ways in which they are similar to men. They can't learn about it on a video. They have to experience competition."Billie Jean King is helping women be more comfortable about winning and losing—to learn to care less about being liked, about what others think—by providing them with outlets for their envy. "Sports reflect society," she points out. "Research shows that women who have been in sports do much better in leadership, self-esteem, and success. One of the best things I've done is help women athletes be appreciated, admired, acknowledged, and accepted."

As we have seen, many women who are not Billie Jean King avoid competitive situations and undermine their own success in order to avoid being envied. Since it's such a persistent problem, let's review what does and doesn't work to find comfort when you are envied.

You are now familiar with what doesn't work:

- You remain in the Snow White syndrome, holding yourself back from your fullest potential.
- You ignore the envy; deny it.
- You put yourself down, play down your successes, or fail to recognize your achievements.
- You feel guilty. You apologize for doing well.
- You avoid, withdraw from, or become nervous around an important person in your life who is envying you.
- You get angry and attack the envious person unproductively.
- You don't take responsibility for evoking envy.
- You get an exaggerated sense of your own importance. You believe someone else's impression of you. Your bubble is then easily burst.
- All of the above.

You've also learned the worst of what happens when you try to maneuver out of being envied: You are accused.

- You try hard to be nice; you are accused of being patronizing.
- You try to explain yourself; you are accused of being defensive.
- You act as though being envied doesn't bother you; you are accused of being cold and aloof.

- You act as if you were the same as the envious person; you are accused of losing your identity or being self-critical.
- You try whatever you can to rise above the envy. You are envied even more.

Now you're ready to see what does work when you're envied.

CHAPTER 9

Twenty Well-Known Women Reveal How They Deal with Being Envied

The greatest of all secrets is knowing how to reduce the force of envy.
—CARDINAL DE RETZ, *Memoirs*, 1673–6

"I have so much honey, the bees envy me."
—"MY GIRL," The Temptations

Sally Quinn, Constance McCashin, Barbara Corday, Julie Harris, Lynn Martin, Christine Craft, Rona Barrett, Julia Child, Rona Jaffe, Carolyn Kizer, Billie Jean King, Susan Merzbach, Judith Crist, Jean Bolen, Janet Leigh, Sara Pillsbury, Anne Isaak, Sharon Percy Rockefeller, Peggy Hora, and LaDonna Harris are women *not caught in the Snow White syndrome; they are all extremely successful.*

These women are in the limelight; they *have* to deal with being envied and have found ways to deal with it without holding themselves back. Even though each one of these twenty women feels hurt when envied, she is not afraid of being hurt and pushes forward regardless. She finds ways to live with envy more contentedly, although she cannot make it disappear.

How do these women become comfortable enough to allow themselves to live up to their fullest potential? When an interviewer meets a more well-known person, there is an immediate potential for envy. I was fortunate in being able to see firsthand how these women handle such a situation. They were remarkably consistent.

They showed great respect for me. They did not appear to judge me; each of them made me feel important. Each tried to learn about my world. They did not show off. They had a clear, inner sense of self-worth and seemed at ease with who they are. They were open about their problems, not feigning to have it all together.

Before I interviewed them, most of these women had *never* thought about how they handle being envied. But they do handle it, unknowingly. Clearly there is no perfect way, and even famous people don't always deal with envy successfully. But read their stories carefully: you can learn from them.

SALLY QUINN

Sally Quinn is a journalist who wrote extensively for the *Washington Post* "Style" section. Her autobiography, *We're Going to Make You a Star,* describes her experience of being pitted against Barbara Walters for the morning prime-time television spotlight. Sally was the first woman anchor on *The CBS Morning Show.* Barbara Walters had been a hostess on *The Today Show*, and CBS tried to create the illusion that Barbara was envious of Sally's moving into her territory. In reality, Sally and Barbara were friends. But while CBS spent time and money publicizing this nonexistent rivalry, it neglected to teach Sally Quinn the job— what to do as an anchorperson. The show bombed in a few months. Sally then married Ben Bradley, the powerful editor of the *Washington Post.* Her most recent book, *Regrets Only,* was a best-seller.

She detests being envied—something surprising for a person so often in the limelight. "Envy is the most frightening, the most ugly emotion when it surfaces in friends or relatives. It is so scary to me that it actually makes me not want to be successful."

How so?

"My way of dealing with being envied is to be as self-deprecatory as possible," Sally explained. "When on *The Morning Show*, the public perception of me was, 'There's a big star.' I needed to allay any possible envy of me. To do so, I made fun of myself in my book. I presented only the down side of being a television star: exhaustion, humiliation, a broken romance, acne."

Why was that?

"Because I believe there is a balance in life. There is no such thing as having it all. If I have too much, I will have to lose something. If good things happen to me, I will have to pay for my success."

Sally needs to protect herself if she does too well. She is superstitious. "Do you believe in the evil eye?" I asked.

She wasn't sure what I meant.

"In societies that believe in the evil eye," I clarified, "anyone having more than another person is vulnerable to the evil eye. If anything bad happens to them, they know why— the evil eye."

Sally understood. "Here's an example. Nora Ephron is my good friend. When her book *Heartburn* came out, I had a party for her—twenty-six people. People wondered if I was envious of Nora's success. Not at all. I gave a speech to the effect that I feel total relief when my friends are successful. I want my friends to be successful, rich, famous—then we can be friends without this ugly emotion, envy, in the way."

What is it about envy that Sally fears?

"When I feel envious, I feel loathsome, unworthy, and demeaned. I don't want anyone else to have to feel that way."

Sally knows the hatred she feels when she envies someone. She doesn't want to be hated.

"That's right," she agreed. "I had an envious friend hate me. She'd criticize my work at the *Post*, on television. She'd tell me I was fat when I wasn't."

Couldn't Sally have talked to her about it?

"Never," Sally replied emphatically. "Envy is the pits. It would be better to accuse someone of stealing than to accuse them of being envious."

I suggested that Sally tell her friend, "I know how you feel. I've been envious, too. It must be hard for you. It is for me when I feel envy. But you're envying the *appearance* of my life. You know, in reality I've had some severe problems. I don't want to lose you as a friend. I don't want to hurt you."

"But I just can't say those things," Sally countered. "I don't want to sound like I'm on an ego trip. I'm not the confrontational type. I get so unhappy and depressed when I'm envied."

I explained to Sally that the envious person already feels guilty about her feelings. If that envious person thinks he or she is hurting you, her guilt is worse. But if you can talk about being envied, let the person know her envy isn't destroying you, she won't feel like such a terrible person—a big relief for her. She will more likely be able to improve her life and not be stuck in envy. The envious person needs to be reassured her feelings are human, that you accept her; that her feelings will pass as she tries to accomplish something for herself.

What we learn from Sally Quinn is that the Snow White syndrome can be internal. You can be successful in the outer world but feel paralyzed internally when envied. You may live with the fear of becoming successful or, like Sally Quinn, with the terror of what will happen to you when you do achieve success.

CONSTANCE McCASHIN

Constance McCashin plays Laura Avery on *Knots Landing*. She tries to make an envious person feel more comfortable, but she doesn't usually succeed.

What does she do when envied?

"One time I was in the grocery store with my four-year-old son, Daniel. I had just gotten my period. I felt awful. Daniel was being a pain, and this perfectly groomed woman with two angelic children said, 'Constance McCutchen?'

"I said, 'Yes,' even though she got my name wrong. I thought she knew me. It never occurs to me that people know me from the show. I added, 'McCashin.'

"She said, 'I really like you on your show.'

"I replied, 'I thought you knew me.' I was really hassled and harried, and I kept going.

"I ran into her five minutes later in the produce section, and she said, 'You know, if I were in your shoes, I'd be a lot nicer to my fans.'

"I think to myself, What am I supposed to do? I got this kid, I feel wretched today. I think people don't realize you are the same as they are.

"Here's another example. I was at the park with a group of friends, sitting on a blanket. Some people I didn't know came over and plopped themselves on our blanket. They wanted to take my picture. I didn't want to be rude. These envious-type fans try to take away your mystique."

I explained, "They intrude. When you feel the person is trying, in one form or another, to obliterate you (as Snow White's step-mother tried to do with Snow White), or spoil your nice day, then you know it's envy. Why not assert yourself and tell them, 'I'm enjoying the day, this is my blanket, nice to meet you, but I want to talk to my friends now'?"

Constance replied, "But I feel so violated I don't know what to say. I feel an obligation to the public; how I am with them might be the one experience of me they will remember. When people are obviously uncomfortable with me, I think it's my responsibility to make them comfortable. I try the female, middle-class way—I try to make it nice for the other person, smooth things over, make them feel good. But when the person is hostile or envious, I feel hurt and misunderstood. I'm caught off guard."

What can we learn here?

If someone makes you feel guilty and bad about yourself, that intrusion on your mood can alert you to the presence of hostility and envy. Once you identify the envy, you need to protect yourself against their desire to intrude. Protected, you may be more able to make the other person feel comfortable.

BARBARA CORDAY

As president of Columbia Pictures Television, Barbara Corday is one of the most influential women in Hollywood and has to deal with being envied. She gave me an example: "In a restaurant, when I got up to go to the bathroom, I overheard two people talking about me. Something about how I was doing my job, how I was in a meeting, an innocuous conversation, but they were acting as if they knew me. In fact, neither of them knew me. I was then aware that I had become one of the people that other people talk about. It was a shocking revelatory moment. I found it very unnerving."

Barbara isn't usually bothered when others envy her. "I have been lucky. Most of my successes have come since the women's movement, in which I've been very active. The women I work with are outwardly committed to supporting other women. They are thrilled to have me as their boss. Rather than envy, it's like a new world has opened up to them."

In the rare instances when Barbara is envied, how does it make her feel?

"I don't like it, but I don't like any negative feelings. I am a positive person with a positive outlook, and any negativity is real counterproductive. Envy is something I don't want to be around."

Barbara is good at diminishing envy. "Personal style has a great deal to do with it. I operate with an open-door policy. I am very careful about including people, about disseminating information, delegating, making people feel part of the team. At a recent conference we had in Miami, everyone had the same type of room, the same everything.

"On the down side, being envied affects my enjoyment of feeling successful. I don't like having to watch what I say, how I say it, and who I am. I don't want to have to sit on myself."

Clearly, Barbara enjoys her life and wants to make success possible for everyone she works with.

Julie Harris

Actress Julie Harris handles being envied by avoiding what causes envy. She lives a simple life: that is what I first noticed about her. Neither she nor her home was ostentatious. She says she doesn't experience being envied. She did not evoke envy in me. People will say to her, "You are so much like me; you are simple, unaffected."

Julie is not caught up with the image of being an actress, an image that sets many actresses apart from other people. She tells herself it would be fun to own a Rolls-Royce or a sable coat. Then she says in her lilting voice, "Sable coat . . . when would I wear it? . . . Rolls-Royce . . . where would I drive it? . . . I can't even take care of a simple car, what am I going to do with a beautiful machine like a Rolls? I wish I could lead that kind of life, but I don't. I admire women who can, like Sarah Bernhardt. . . . She had a great house in Paris, an iron retreat in France, chinchilla coats and sables, and she'd go out to midnight suppers in Paris with her sable coat, and I think, How wonderful to live in that grand manner! But I can't do it, it's not me. Getting a lot of attention makes me uncomfortable. It goes against my basic nature."

Lynn Martin

Lynn Martin, member of the House of Representatives from Illinois, is one of the most important Republican women in Congress. She is first in her freshman class in Congress to hold a

leadership role. To assist George Bush, she played the part of
Geraldine Ferraro in a practice debate with him. Like most
women, Lynn is still learning how to handle being envied. She is
envied for being an important woman in politics, for her enthusiasm, for her ability to get along with people, for her ability to
laugh.

"Women have never been trained to accept a compliment, and
I am trying to learn how," she told me in her office on Capitol
Hill. "When someone envies me, I'll answer, 'Oh, I was lucky. If
I were born in Afghanistan, I wouldn't be where I am today.'
Women were trained to be modest. Being modest is coy.

"I am practicing saying, 'Thank you.' If you make what was
meant as a little compliment—envy or not—into a huge production, you go overboard. I want to say, 'Thank you,' and drop it
altogether."

When an envious comment comes their way, many women are
learning to say, "Thank you," or "Yes, that's true," instead of
apologizing with, "Oh, it was nothing!"

CHRISTINE CRAFT

Christine Craft was a news anchorperson for station KMBC in
Kansas City. The station's owner, Metromedia, fired her because
she didn't defer to men. They told her she was too old and too
unattractive. She was then thirty-six, and today, at forty-two, she
is still youthful and attractive, with beautiful skin. She sued
Metromedia for not providing equality in the workplace for
women. They told her, "You can't fight us. We're Metromedia.
We have a whole team of lawyers." I asked her how she had the
courage to fight this big corporation. "Growing up in Santa
Barbara, I was a competitive surfer. When you've seen real
sharks, the corporate ones don't scare you quite as much."

When the station hired her, she explicitly requested, "I don't
want to be made over." "Fine," they assured her. "We love you
the way you look." Instead, they made her over, tried to change
her face to make her more presentable. "I was told I looked like
a mutt, that my face was too square, my jaw was too square, one
eye was smaller than the other. 'Have you been in an accident?'
they asked me. They brought in makeup experts to draw brown
grease railroad tracks down my face, to try to make my face look

more symmetrical. Was I not a journalist when my face didn't look symmetrical?"

Because of the publicity she's gained from her hard-fought, Title VII lawsuit—a suit she won initially and later lost on appeal—Christine Craft has become what she calls a "dubious celebrity." She has become known politically, helped Gary Hart's campaign, has been asked to speak at prestigious dinners and to run for Congress, has been on the lecture circuit, and was nominated one of the five best collegiate speakers in 1984.

"An attractive anchorwoman put me down for being on the lecture circuit. I know that real social change doesn't occur just through endless lawsuits, but through debates, dialogues, and talking. Now I would handle her envy by challenging her to go on a lecture tour, to be in a different city every day, different motel room, no one to do her hair or nails, and large audiences to speak to extemporaneously, without a TelePrompTer. Let her do that for six months and see if she still envies my being a 'celebrity.' That anchorwoman had no grasp of the reality involved in litigating against a major corporation. But it hurt the hell out of me to have to defend my love of journalism because I'm fighting a battle that hopefully will help protect women's integrity in the future."

Could it be that Christine, like Snow White, was too threatening? Christine was told that other women journalists envy her, even though she lost her lawsuit, because they resent someone who challenges exactly what they didn't have the guts to challenge.

I asked my favorite question: "How do you handle being envied?"

"Eleanor Roosevelt understood that no one could hurt you unless you let them. I try to learn from her simple homily: 'It can only hurt as much as you let it.'

"It's not good to internalize someone's envy, to take it seriously. I know it hurt Eleanor Roosevelt to be told she was ugly. When Joan Rivers told a mean joke about me at the Emmy Awards, I actually shed a full tear, and I hardly ever cry. She said, 'Christine Craft won a half million dollars and spent half of it on cosmetics.' To be the butt of a very, very public joke, that I was really that ugly mutt—spending half the money I hadn't made on something frivolous—that was painful to hear. Joan's jokes are envy-mean jokes."

Envy is intended to hurt. You can try not to let it hurt, but don't be upset with yourself when it does. Accept that it hurts, realize

*the envier has a problem, do your best not to be brought down,
and move on.*

Rona Barrett

Describing herself as an "entertainment journalist reporter," Rona
Barrett admits that she is hard on herself. She covers television
and movies for the *Rona Barrett Report* on both TV and radio. "I
must constantly prove to myself that I am the best. I want a good
story every day. If I don't get one, I attack myself: 'How did I
miss that story? Why didn't I know that? How can I be in a
thousand places at the same time? For goodness' sake, Rona, you
should be.' As soon as I come off the air, I think, holy mackerel,
what do I say tomorrow?"

People who push themselves as Rona does are sometimes
envied by those less ambitious. She is also envied because of her
work. "I cover Hollywood, thought to be glitzy and glamorous,
never serious, and therefore I am not validated as being a really
serious person. I am still referred to as a gossip columnist. I abhor
that term. People are labeling me from my original days in
journalism when I did write a gossip column—but that was fifteen
years ago. There seems to be a need to belittle what I do."

What does she mean?

"I have a theory that when you're in the gutter, there are
thousands of people who want to help you to the sidewalk. Once
you're on the sidewalk, there are thousands of people who want to
push you back into the gutter. America wants heroes and heroines.
The minute we get them, we must destroy them."

Envy?

"Oh, yes. Envy is a frightening feeling because when you're
envious, you're not in control. Most people prefer to be in
control."

They push you back into the gutter so they don't have to envy
you anymore?

"Yes. I think any time you stand up and can be counted, people
admire and resent it at the same time. When you become
successful in a business like mine, it can be a disaster. I need to
know what's going on out there, and now people feel they can't
approach me. It's a double-edged sword to become recognizable
as a journalist. Years ago, no one knew my face, I could go into
a room, sit in a corner, and observe everything. Now people are

intimidated. They think, Why would Rona Barrett want to talk to me, she's such a busy lady. So they stay away and, out of fear and envy, don't give me stories.

"There are lazy journalists out there who think, Ah, Rona's big enough, we can sock it to her, we can let her have it. She built a big new home, she drives around in a Rolls-Royce, what difference does it make to her? Let her suffer. I try to pay absolutely no attention to it and just do what I have to for myself. When someone is truthful with me about their envy, I somehow know how to deal with it. I like it when the envy's up front. After taking time to think about it, I might share my struggles and let them know it's not easy to be as driven as I am."

Rona has been envied for having earned money on her own and for having style. "I have been very hurt when envied by people I've worked with. I don't think you know when you're envied, not right away. It's frequently only upon reflection. So when I feel hurt, I reflect upon it more and see if envy's there."

Rona places envy in a larger cultural context and is therefore less affected by it. She is reflective and philosophical about how her life and work typify envy's general cultural trends. She expects to be envied.

JULIA CHILD

Julia Child told me she rarely experiences envy from anybody. Well, maybe once in a while from "rather bitchy types." If she is envied, it's because she was the first chef to be on television. She never felt envied by her mother. "We were happy. Everything was wonderful. Anything we did, my mother thought was marvelous."

Julia confides that "certain critics, with envy dripping from their pen, have written sarcastically and vituperatively about me, saying that everything I did was entirely wrong and stupid." These critics have ridiculed Julia, the "French Chef," who, they say, is neither French nor a chef! Julia attributes such remarks to her success and popularity.

Julia deals with barbs in a characteristic way: with humor. "Such comments don't disturb me. They're kind of a drop of vinegar." Julia laughed. "In fact, it's rather nice to have someone envy you so you can talk about that person!"

Julia assured me, "Envy has never affected me. I have a 'to hell with it' attitude. I don't care what people think of me. I care about my writing, and my profession, cooking. I know what I think of myself, which is more important. I am in charge, the captain of my own ship."

RONA JAFFE

I sat with Rona Jaffe in her East Side Manhattan apartment. As she hassled with a television repairman who was trying to sell her a three-year repair contract for a TV that had never broken, I slipped in the question, "How do you handle being envied?"

Rona interrupted the repairman and answered, "I thought *you* were going to tell *me* how! I'd like not to be so hurt and angry when I'm envied. I try to get under the envious person's skin, just for five minutes, and see how annoyed she is, gnashing her teeth. I'd see she wishes she were me, that she should share my success, that maybe she has a rotten life and thinks I have a wonderful life. I'd understand her better. Then, I'd come back into my own skin, and say, 'Okay, it's okay,' and once again, I'd be glad I was me. I'd tell myself then, I'm not going to let this one hurt me. It's *her* problem."

Rona is at the heart of empathy. You get under someone's skin, and then you understand that person. Understanding the other person helps you be less affected by their envy.

Every writer is criticized. Rona, too. Once a review of her book *Class Reunion* was included on the first page of a newspaper next to a picture of Menachem Begin. It was a nasty review, the kind of personal attack you know comes from envy more than from a person's taste. Initially Rona felt hurt by the two-page review, which said what a horrible writer she was. But then Rona said, "Look who's on the first page, me and Begin. Why, I must have made it! And a two-page review is no joke!

"That critic might be imagining me on the Riviera, on my yacht, when actually I'm in my office working, writing." Rona tries to understand the critic, to get under his skin, to remind herself that he is probably paid comparatively little for his work.

CAROLYN KIZER

Poet Carolyn Kizer doesn't see much envy in her life. I said, "But there must be some additional attention coming your way since you won the Pulitzer Prize."

Carolyn responded, "Oh, if I walk into a room and everyone makes a fuss, I just ask, 'Who won the Pulitzer last year?' That stops them. No one ever knows!"

Carolyn doesn't give envy a chance to take shape. Instead she uses humor to help would-be enviers see the reality of our culture—famous today/forgotten tomorrow.

BILLIE JEAN KING

Billie Jean has felt envied by other women in two particular ways. First, some have discounted what she has done by not giving her credit for founding the Women's Sports Foundation. "I founded it, it was my idea, and I got a group of people to help organize it. I put up the money and hired the executive director. And when some women write about it, they don't tell the truth. They say, 'A *group of us* founded the W.S.F.' Most things I don't care about, but this I do, because founding it was major for me.

"So I called up the foundation: 'This is Billie Jean King. I don't like what you wrote. It hurts my feelings. I've been discounted. Was it my idea or not?' They said, 'Yes.' And I replied, 'It's important to me how history is written. Why don't you just tell the truth?' "

She dealt with the envy directly. The foundation changed what they wrote about their origins, and Billie Jean felt appreciated for a major contribution she had made. Then she herself is careful to give others credit for their ideas and contributions.

Second, some players have wanted Billie Jean to lose a match for the wrong reasons—so she won't be too successful. She has heard them say, "I don't want her to win. I'm sick of hearing that Billie Jean King's done this or that."

If she heard that before a match, could it keep her from winning?

Billie Jean told me, "I was absolutely crushed. These were younger players, and I had fought for them so they would have a better life. They had the attitude, 'If I can't have it, why should you? Better that neither of us has it, so let me make your life miserable.' I knew I needed *to refocus immediately*."

In "refocusing," Billie Jean talks to herself and tries to fight the envy with analysis and reason. "Hey, I'm a professional athlete. My job is to give 100 percent to the fans and to me; that's what I owe myself. I can't let someone's envy put me into a tailspin and not perform well. Sure I'm hurt. I'm human. But after the match I'll be more upset with myself if I let petty remarks get to me. Like do they really know me, anyway? Do I really care what they think?

"If you play like a donkey, King," she continues talking to herself, "nobody wins. How would that help anyone? What good would it do? It wouldn't be healthy if I let that envy get to me; it wouldn't make things better."

Susan Merzbach

Susan Merzbach, president of Fogwood Films, Sally Fields' production company, is a prominent Hollywood executive.

"My attitude about envy and success changed when I became vice-president of 20th Century-Fox Studios, which is a pretty heady thing to be. I fantasized about my new job: 'Oh, good, the little Jewish girl from Massachusetts will now have a fancy title, fancy office, fancy salary, visibility, seeming authority, notoriety, everything I associate with success. I will finally feel the way I believe others feel—"on top of it." ' But nothing changed. I still felt like a flop. It was a huge crash for me. I hit the existential wall and realized those things were truly meaningless. Mainly, there was just additional responsibility."

I wondered if Susan were trying to avoid being envied by diminishing what she had achieved as vice-president of the studio. But as we talked further, I discovered she didn't need to avoid being envied; she had found her own way to deal with envious people.

People now fantasize about Susan's life the same way she did when she first moved into her job. "It works to let someone see the reality of your job, to take it out of the realm of fantasy. When envied, I explain a typical day in my life, the number of hours, the kinds of responsibilities, the pressures, and why, for twelve years, I've had no personal life. Most women I know start their careers with more of a balance, and the men have wives to take care of them. And no one envies the amount of work I do."

I wondered, "What if someone tells you, 'I am a housewife, and I envy you being a movie executive'?"

Susan replied, "I ask them, 'What do you want to do?' Most of the time, when you talk straight to people and ask them to define what they want, they realize they lack definitions, that the problem is with themselves. They don't envy you because you're luckier. They just haven't figured out what they want to do and how to get there."

JUDITH CRIST

Judith Crist, now sixty-three, worked as a reporter, editor and critic for the New York *Herald Tribune* from 1945 to 1966, was film critic for *New York* magazine from 1968 to 1975 and for the *Saturday Review* from 1955–57 and 1980–84. Besides teaching at Columbia University's Graduate School of Journalism, she has been a film critic for *TV Guide* for the past twenty years.

"My mother brought me up to believe that appearances don't matter, so I've had blinders on and ignored how people see me. I was always overweight, and my mother never did a damn thing about it. Her attitude was, 'My dear Judith, if people think less of you because you're wearing a darned stocking or the same blue dress you wore last week, then you're not much of a person.' So I concentrated on being a person. I didn't worry about my figure, my stockings, or my face. One of the ironies of life is that I was on TV, *The Today Show*, for ten years, and on WOR-TV since 1981."

Judith Crist says she has been envied—"by fellow professionals who want the opportunities I have, by wives who want the husband I have, by parents who want the son I have—he's a golden boy— and by laymen who want the job I have, the very job I dreamed of having as a young girl." Many people who love movies would like to be paid, as Judith is, to watch the very movies they enjoy seeing.

Judith uses familiar approaches. "I've downgraded what I am doing so much that it's a part of my personality. I love my job, but when I'm envied for being a movie critic, I tell the person, 'You're lucky—you get to pick the movies you see, I have no choice,' or, 'You get to go to a movie, just sit there, and not have to think about it.'" She is not really downgrading her work, making less of it; she is explaining the reality of her life.

Judith says she handles being envied "in the same way I deal with people who dislike me. I go out of my way to take people into my camp, to be humble, to share my problems, and to consult with them about what they think.

"I show people that what I've got isn't that different from what they have. It's very simple. Everything I've got is because I've worked for it. I've never had an employee who thought that he or she worked harder than I do. If an employee walks in at nine A.M., they know I've been at the desk since seven A.M.

"If you haven't earned what you have, you're nervous about others' envy. But if you know that what you've got has been acquired by the sweat of your brow, then you can be extremely comfortable with your superiority. Certainly for thirty years I have felt very much at the top of what I was doing."

JEAN SHINODA BOLEN

Unlike Judith Crist, Jean Shinoda Bolen, author of the national best-seller *Goddesses in Everywoman*, stresses the innate gifts given to her rather than her hard work. She is a successful psychiatrist, lecturer, and author. When envied, she explains, "Life is like a lottery, and I was lucky, or graced, to have received what I have."

Jean believes that she doesn't *deserve* what she has received in life. She thinks she's no more deserving than someone who hasn't received the same opportunities and benefits of parents, money, intelligence, age, or looks. "I was given these gifts. I didn't do anything to get them. I don't believe in the Calvinistic idea of being rewarded for hard work. Most people who work hard aren't rewarded equally."

Jean informs me that the success of her book is *not* because of her hard work. Much depended on timing and luck. "I wrote a book about goddesses at a time when there was an interest in goddesses. The success of my book has to do with things outside myself, that have no bearing on whether I am deserving or not."

JANET LEIGH

Movie star Janet Leigh, sitting in her elegant Beverly Hills home at sunset, high above Los Angeles, does not feel deserving of her success, either. Like Jean Bolen, Janet's belief in God and her spirituality enable her to remove her ego from her success. "What has happened to me is not my doing. The circumstances of my life—the timing of when I came to Hollywood, being discovered, and the development of my career—I had nothing to do with that."

I reminded Janet, "Your acting is your doing."

"Yes, but I was given the opportunity to act," Janet countered. "I have nothing to do with the way I look. God was kind to me in terms of my physical appearance. So I just tell people who envy me either, 'I am lucky,' or, 'Thank you.'

"The part of being envied which bothers me is people assume that because you are a movie star, you are different from them. When I was making my first movie, on location in Santa Cruz, California, kids from my hometown, Stockton, came to see me. The gate guard told me they were there, and I went to talk to them. They automatically assumed I had changed as a person, become someone else. I hadn't. The same at college reunions—they assumed I wouldn't remember them. Or interviewers have come with the preconceived idea they wouldn't like me. I try to be as simple and honest as I can. I try to disarm them before they have a chance to move too much into their envy. I set down the ground rules. I am me, not a movie star."

SARA PILLSBURY

Sara Pillsbury, the woman who co-directed the movie *Desperately Seeking Susan*, inherited a million dollars from the Pillsbury family. For our interview she dressed plainly and stretched out to relax in her office full of movie posters and baby toys—she often brings her baby daughter with her to work.

Sara sees all she has—her inheritance, her hair, her height, her intelligence, her attendance at the best schools—as gifts that were given to her. "But it is up to me to make the most of what I have. I've worked hard and done a good job of combating people's envy of me."

How does she do it?

"I am open and honest about what I have. Many people who have a lot of money never talk about it. I am conscious about who I am and maintain a sense of humor. People have liked me."

By talking about what she has in a straightforward manner, Sara demystifies her wealth. When you have a truthful conversation about what you own, you're able to talk about the other person's reaction.

A friend of hers asked Sara how much money she had inherited.

Sara answered, "Almost a million dollars, but I can't touch it."
The friend burst out crying. Sara admitted, "I felt sympathetic
toward her. I was honest about how much I appreciate the money,
how much security it brings. Seeing her upset made me want to be
nicer toward her, more charitable. It must be hard for someone
who has worked as hard as she has to be around someone like
me."

The philosophy of deserving, as Judith Crist and others believe,
implies that you deserve what you have because you've worked
hard for it, implies a reward for hard work and a punishment for
sloth. This philosophy of deserving is tricky. It can lead to envy.
Let's say you and someone else both work hard. She becomes
successful, you less so. You wonder, "Why don't I have what she
has? I deserve to be rewarded. I work hard, too. What is wrong
with me? Am I not a deserving person?" Hard work is not
proportional to economic rewards.

Whichever argument you believe—that you deserve what you
have because you've worked hard for it or that fate gives you gifts
which you then make the most of—both are clearly attempts at
handling being envied. You can explain how deserving and
hard-working you are *or* hand the responsibility for what you have
over to God, luck, or fate. Either way, you are trying to make
sense out of why you have more than someone else, a feeling that
leaves a mixed taste in your mouth. Many women reported they
enjoyed being envied, until they realized it meant they were
hurting someone else.

ANNE ISAAK

Anne Isaak is the successful owner of two chic New York
restaurants, Elio's and Petaluma, where many of the "beautiful
people" socialize. Being envied forces Anne to worry about the
feelings of others. She encounters many people who have dreams
of opening their own restaurants. They tell her about how much
they want to do what she is doing, or they "ooh and aah" because
Mia Farrow dined last night at Elio's.

When she is envied, she'll respond, "It's nice to be independent," or, "Thank God the restaurant worked." Being envied
detracts from Anne's own happiness and self-fulfillment and
makes her feel less successful than she is. "When I'm not envied,

that means everyone else is happy doing what they're doing, and I don't have to worry about them. I don't like people pussyfooting around me. When I am envied, I have to figure out how to make the other person happier.

"The positive side is that I can share the money I have earned with my friends, family, and social causes. Actually, being envied enhances my feelings of social responsibility. I could never enjoy what I have if I hogged it all for myself. I wish there was an equalizing agent in close relationships."

SHARON PERCY ROCKEFELLER

Sharon is the daughter of Illinois senator Charles Percy and the wife of West Virginia senator Jay Rockefeller. She was chairperson of the Corporation for Public Broadcasting for three years, is on Stanford University's board of directors, and is raising four children. "That's what I do best," she says. She is wealthy, accomplished, attractive, and self-aware, yet she has rarely felt envied.

How could that be? Perhaps because Sharon has learned the art of warding off envy. She said she hasn't read Dale Carnegie's *How to Win Friends and Influence People*, but she behaves as though she has. Sharon does not consciously set out to prevent envy. She's a natural at "how to be popular and prevent envy at the same time." It's in her blood. "Being envied is truly alien to me. It is much less work and trouble if you just prevent envy."

Her husband was governor of West Virginia for twelve years, and as First Lady of West Virginia, living in a fifteen-acre mansion, working closely with people from other backgrounds, she had to be careful not to incur their envy.

What does she do?

"*I act vulnerable some of the time*, which prevents people from assuming I've got it all wrapped up. I am not a superwoman." Sharon lets you know her life is not perfect. "When you're needed as a politician's wife, that is the ultimate call. Your needs are secondary to his. I am a woman of the eighties, constricted by the values of the fifties all around me in Washington."

"*I don't act like I'm above people*. When I went to West Virginia, as the governor's wife, I was twenty-two years old and scared. I moved into Jay's house with a suitcase of anxiety about being out of my element and in his. I'm now forty-one, and I grew up with the state and its people. I worked on many community boards." In West Virginia, she was a Head Start teacher and chairman of the board of a company that ran fifteen arts-and-craft co-ops.

"*I was never uppity. I never tried to change people.* I eventually fit in, and people loved my children. They gave me lots of credit for having this tribe of children. In West Virginia, there is less pressure to be a career woman."

"*I do things to actually reduce the potential for envy.* On my thirty-second birthday, we went to a restaurant. We ended up spending the evening signing autographs. You've got to be nice to others. So, in order not to disappoint people and wreck our personal life at the same time, we stopped going out for dinner."

Sharon doesn't view people in a hierarchy. "There is nobody in the world I wouldn't talk to, whether it's a homeless person in West Virginia or president of the United States. They are pretty much the same to me. Important people are not more innately interesting than anyone else.

"*I try hard not to evoke envy.* External appearances are important. Clothes make a statement. If you present yourself dramatically and dress up in fur coats, too much jewelry, it puts people off and creates envy. But if you dress down, you make a terrible statement. It means you don't respect the people you're talking to. And you can be envied for that."

These are other guidelines that work for Sharon:

- I prevent envy by how I talk to people.
- I talk about my children, a common denominator.
- I smile a lot.
- I act friendly, casual, informal.
- I give lots of gifts.
- I reach out to others. "At the Corporation for Public Broadcasting, I talked with each of the one hundred people who worked there. I knew the names of their wives and husbands, how old their children were. I sent every person there a Christmas card."

"But Sharon," I said, "you're a Rockefeller, a multimillionaire. Don't people envy that?"

She understood immediately. "The money creates a lot of distance between people. But not having a sophisticated eastern patrician accent helps. *I refused to be a debutante.* I've revolted against that sort of stuff all my life—what in the world would being a debutante accomplish? It's the ultimate phony waste of time. I don't feel the need to be built up by other people as much as meet my own standards."

Sharon takes care of two residences: their Charleston home of fourteen acres and their Washington, D.C., fifteen-acre home. I asked her, "How do you make people feel at home in your mansions?"

"People have usually decided beforehand whether they are going to like you or not," Sharon replied. "But niceness matters. Sometimes I think I am overly nice, more nice than I ever should be. I carry the Rockefeller tradition: *permanently generous and gracious; professionally nice, permanently nice.*"

PEGGY HORA

Judge Peggy Hora explained, "I try to spend time with the person who envies me and share what I have. Share my knowledge or offer to take the person to a meeting and introduce them to so and so. You disarm when you say, 'Hey, what I have is not mutually exclusive. I really love power, and I love it so much that I want to share it with everybody. So come with me, I'll share it with you. Do you want to meet Hippity-Hop?'"

Say you envy Peggy because she is a judge. Peggy will tell you how to become a judge and help you along the way. She'll tell you to join the Bar Association, suggest what kind of work you should do, what committees to join, whom to contact in the community, how she did it.

If you respond, "But I'm not as aggressive as you are, Peggy," she'll tell you, "Judge Hippity-Hop isn't aggressive, either. You don't need my personality to be a judge. There *are* ways to enhance the possibility of reaching your goal. You have to be political. You either have to be in electoral politics or know the governor or make people the governor knows promote you."

"But Peggy," I ask, "what if someone doesn't respond to your help and just outright envies you? Do you fear you won't be liked if you're too successful?"

"I work on the assumption that I'm a pretty nice person," she answered. "I think most people will think I'm nice. I think most people will like me."

I explained to Peggy that many of my patients and other women fear people won't like them when they do well, that they remain in the Snow White syndrome. Peggy does not. She lists her strategies:

- I wouldn't be happy if I held myself back. If I purposefully sabotaged myself so somebody might like me, I would not like myself.
- I trust my instincts that I am not going to hurt someone.
- What I do has a good basis. I am a good person.
- *My* having something doesn't mean *you* can't have it. There's enough of the good things, of love and happiness, to go around for everybody. It's out there for the grabbing. It goes beyond the galaxy. That's how vast love is.

LaDonna Harris

A dynamic, gracious, soulful Comanche Indian woman, LaDonna Harris heads the nonprofit American Indian Opportunity Organization. The organization works together with two million Indians from five hundred tribal entities. LaDonna was married to Senator Fred Harris for thirty-one years and ran for vice-president of America on the Citizen's Party ticket with Barry Commoner in 1980. LaDonna exudes warmth and motherliness.

For LaDonna, the word "envy" conjures up evil, discontent. "It immobilizes you. Indians have their own philosophy on how to deal with being envied." First, Indians do little to create envy in the first place. Second, leaders of Indian tribes emerge because of their particular qualities. If they fail to exhibit these qualities, people turn their backs on them and they are no longer leaders.

What are these qualities?

You are taught to be selfless and not show off. LaDonna said, "If you show off, people put you down. There are appropriate social ways for showing off, like games, dancing, competitions, headdresses, art work."

You are taught to be fair, to share, and to give away what you have. You can give away skills, deeds, songs, your name. You don't keep your own ideas for self-aggrandizement. LaDonna told me that during a visit to her cousin, her husband admired a painting, so the cousin removed the painting from the wall and gave it to him.

LaDonna explained, "We establish everyone as equal in a

group. We don't have somebody on a podium talking down to the group. We sit in a circle, equal. People at meetings share information, no one knows all the answers. We are struggling for the same purpose."

A friend of LaDonna's told me that LaDonna is one of the few publicly visible women she knows who is not openly attacked for her successes and achievements.

"Why is that?" I asked.

LaDonna's friend explained, "Because LaDonna touches people. She knows how to elicit the best from them. She doesn't speak in derogatory terms about others, she treats people well regardless of who they are or what they have said or done. She gives to people who come her way. She is warm and gracious to almost everyone."

"Don't people envy that about her?" I questioned.

"They just don't," replied her friend.

"As a Native American woman in our society," LaDonna explains, "I grew up feeling so much discrimination that I am sensitive to other people's discomfort. When I'm envied, I try to include the person who feels excluded so they won't direct their envy, their frustrations, at me. For example, at a reception, if someone is not talking to anyone, if they are being left out, I put them together with someone compatible."

It would be unrealistic to say LaDonna is never envied. She has worked closely with women who, despite her generous qualities, have found her threatening when they felt she surpassed them. They showed their envy by making it hard for her to do her work. LaDonna, like every well-known woman I talked to, felt hurt when envied.

LaDonna realizes she is not the only one hurt by envy. The envious ones, those who feel "left behind" and rejected, are hurt, too. Indians call this the crab syndrome. When crabs are clambering along, if one starts to get ahead, the others will pull it down.

LaDonna said, "I'm a Pollyanna. I didn't want to believe in the crab syndrome. I thought that if I gave back what I learned in my travels, no one would be hurt or envy me. But now I see that in the Indian community, because we are a tribe and so interdependent, one weak link is upsetting."

"I give much back to my community. I acknowledge the strength I feel comes from them. My culture tells me that when good things happen to you, you are supposed to give back. We believe that those who have the most have the greatest obligation to give back to the community."

Here LaDonna uses the important technique of giving credit where credit is due. Since the envious person usually wants credit, or a boost in self-esteem, this helps combat envy.

She points out, "Comanche values honor that if someone succeeds, the other person rejoices. Another Indian's success will reflect on all of us. I never believed in the crab syndrome. I was horrified by it. To hurt someone is disgusting."

The crab syndrome operates in every community; it is everywhere. You saw how it functions in the "Snow White" fairy tale, with your mother, sister, co-worker, boss, helper, friend, and mate. The best way you can deal with it is to *accept that it exists*. As much as Indians encourage each other to feel equal, there is always one crab who goes off on her own. As much as she gives back to the community, there may be other crabs left hurt and envious.

All of these women work to avoid being pulled back by the other crabs or by a single crab who feels rejected. There is no formula to make someone else's envy go away, but remember some of the possible responses you can have. Perhaps you'll devise a few of your own.

1. Address the envy head on; talk openly and directly about the problem.
2. Put the envy into perspective; realize it's not your problem—unless you have purposefully caused it.
3. Feel moderately complimented.
4. Let the envious person get to know you as you are.
5. Make the envious person feel important. When people feel good about themselves, their envy lessens.

Also, it helps to keep in mind what is positive about being envied: although 32 percent of the women I interviewed reported nothing good about being the target of envy, 63 percent reported something positive about the experience.

When envied, you learn about yourself. You're given the chance to take a fresh look at what you may have taken for granted, to realize how much you have to be grateful and thankful for. You're able to appreciate your unique qualities and accomplishments, to feel validated and valuable. You may also, for the moment, enjoy the secret and forbidden pleasure of arrogance. You can gain perspective, and you're encouraged to keep on with what you're doing, even if it's a struggle. Of significance, you learn to be sensitive to your effect on others.

When envied, you don't learn only about yourself—you also learn about the person who envies you. You can sympathize and empathize with that person. You know how awful it feels to envy; you can imagine the envier's pain and unhappiness and feel closer to her. As a role model, you can help the person who envies you to use her own capabilities to move forward in life, suggesting, "If I can do it, you can, too." You can help the envious person by opening the door to a discussion of envy and allowing her to see who you really are. Finally, you are given the chance to express and practice human kindness and empathy in its fullest sense when you help the envious person and share what you know.

Envy is not going to disappear, but you do have the power to work with an envious person to identify what you're each feeling. You also have the power to alter your own response to being envied. And you certainly have the power to deal with your own envy—to change your experience of looking at the world through green-tinted glasses.

CHAPTER 10

Making Envy Work for You

Love without desiring, all that you are not.
—W.H. AUDEN, "Many Happy Returns"

I ask not good fortune . . .
I myself am good fortune.
—WALT WHITMAN, "Song of the Open Road"

Every woman wants envy to go away; then we could brag that no one is ever threatened by someone else's success, that we aren't upset when someone gets a leadership position that we wanted, that we are never petty, that we are supportive. That is our goal.

We *can* create conditions where we have less need to envy, where we find ways to make ourselves feel better about what we have, where we have better outlets for our envious feelings, where we admire and learn from others, where we understand how universal and mutual the feeling is. We should all attempt to work toward this goal.

You have learned what doesn't work when you are envied. **Here is what doesn't work when you are the envier.**

- You hurt yourself.
- You ignore or hide your envious feelings from yourself. You're like an artesian well—if you repress your feelings here, they inevitably pop up there.

- You focus on the external. You think if you had what someone else has, you would feel better.
- You discount your own accomplishments.
- You put yourself down, feel self-critical.
- You pretend that what you want doesn't matter to you.
- You are so worried about not getting enough that you don't get what you need.
- You act like a shrinking violet.
- You feel "I'm so lucky that she's being nice to me."
- You feel that life is unfair, that you are equally deserving as the person you envy.
- You stop yourself from fulfilling your potential. You imagine the good thing you want resides only in the person you envy.

When you envy, *you also hurt the person you envy*. Your envy may make you cold, judgmental, distant, and causes you to withdraw from the person you envy, even when she is important to you. You may criticize, gossip, or try to wreck her accomplishments. You may find an ally to dislike the person you envy. Since you feel you deserve to have what the other has, you use this feeling of "deserving" to bypass your conscience, as a justification for domination, greed, or stealing. You blame the other person for what you don't have, believing it's his or her fault that you feel deprived. If you can't have it, she shouldn't, either.

Handling your envy: We've seen what happens when women say, "I wish that were mine. I deserve to have it," rather than, "Is it possible to obtain? If so, what can I do to get it?"

Realize the solution is not only external. Do you want exactly what she has, or do you envy what you *imagine* will make you feel good? Do you want something because advertising tells you it will make you feel better or because a more realistic appraisal tells you this particular item is necessary?

You envy because there is a difference between who you are and who you feel you should be. But where does your idea of who you should be come from? Is it based on what your family and society, siblings, teachers, coaches, and relatives wanted for you, what they felt they could not themselves obtain? Or is it what *you* truly want for yourself?

The destructive consequence of envy is that you *devalue* yourself and others. The constructive consequence is that you *reevaluate* yourself and what you want. You question what makes you happy, what you like to do. Through evaluation, you learn to *value* yourself and the person you envy.

One woman wrote, "The only *truly positive* thing I see about women envying is that it's so obvious—so strong, such a deep part of our being, powerful and prevalent, that it draws our attention. That's good, because we really need to assail it, take it by the horns and examine it, find out its sources. We need to know *how* to change ourselves."

Before you were aware of your envy, you did not have the capacity to change. Now you do. By listening to what envy has to tell you, you can understand the richness and variety of human possibility. No matter how bad a situation you're stuck in, envy can be a force for change.

Envy can work to encourage you to improve your life.

MOVING THROUGH THE CONTINUUM OF ENVY

The Wish to Harm→Self-Hatred→Resentment→Covetousness→Admiration→Emulation

This continuum represents a staircase to valuing yourself and others, a way out of destructive envy. You do not have to pass through each stage. You could move directly from the wish to harm to positive envy emulation, or beyond. These stages underscore the varieties of reactions you can have to your envy. They are presented as a guide, to enable your envy to work for you. However, for a specific explanation, you will observe Nora as she moves step by step through the entire continuum.

Nora's envious mother made her give her only baby up for adoption. When you've had an envious mother, you know envy will be a problem in your life, and it was not surprising Nora needed therapy. In the workplace, Nora had to learn how to handle being envied by her manager. She also went through a dose of the "all or nothing envy blues" with her friend Holly.

When Nora came to therapy, she was a very envious person, although she didn't know that was her problem. She felt hateful toward her friend, embittered, with little self-worth. I asked Nora, "Do you want to get better, or do you want to get even?"

You, like Nora, will be offered suggestions to help you pass through each of these difficult stages. With time, effort, and application, you can find a similar path.

THE WISH TO HARM

Nora got divorced. After a year of casual, unfulfilling affairs, she was depressed. She began to feel intense rage at her friend Holly, who enjoyed a pleasurable sex life with her boyfriend. Nora seemed to believe that if Holly's sex life got worse, Nora's would mysteriously get better. Nora maligned Holly and told Holly's boyfriend about Holly's past affairs.

With the wish to harm, you feel angry. What the other person has is more than you can stand. You believe that her having what she has means you can't have the good things you want. Hurting her feels like your only satisfaction.

AWARENESS: Nora realized the absurdity of the situation, that there was no point in harming Holly. Hurting Holly or wishing her harm would not get Nora what she wanted; Nora would not find a lover just because Holly lost hers.

You, too, may find yourself wanting to hurt someone who has what you want. Instead, why not ask yourself:

• Is hurting her really going to help me get what I want?
• Is hurting her going to make me feel better?
• Does hurting her actually wreck what she has?
• Isn't this wish to harm ridiculous?

SELF-HATRED

Seeing her wish to harm Holly as ridiculous keeps Nora from further acting meanly to Holly. Trying to hurt Holly had made Nora feel worse about herself because she actually cares about Holly. Feeling worse about herself, Nora was less able to go after what she wanted. She felt even less worthy of a good sex life.

Nora still had hateful feelings, but now they were directed at herself. She over-ate and withdrew from situations where she had the potential of meeting someone for herself. When Nora saw that she was damaging herself, she also realized it was envy she was feeling. She tried to get rid of her awful feelings in other ways:

She wrote Holly a poison pen letter but didn't send it. She no longer gossiped to Holly's boyfriend. Instead, she *imagined* talking to him. She wrote in her journal about the unfairness of Holly having a better sex life, describing her anguish and fear about never having someone to love her as she wishes to be loved. Writing about your feelings helps distance you from the need to hurt yourself.

AWARENESS: Nora realized that the harm she wanted for Holly was instead happening to herself, so she found other ways to get rid of her hateful feelings. She became aware that she envied Holly, and with this awareness, she was able to forgive herself for hating Holly.

When you find yourself acting self-destructively, you have to find ways to soothe yourself:

- Try to act kindly toward yourself.
- Look at what you're doing to hurt yourself and substitute something you enjoy doing instead.
- Find supportive friends who encourage you and teach you to forgive yourself.

Once you can accept your envy and forgive yourself for it, you are ready to enter the next phase.

RESENTMENT

Nora began to feel resentment, a milder form of envy than the wish to harm or self-hatred. Rather than actively damaging anyone or herself, Nora allowed herself just to experience bitterness and anger.

When you feel resentment, you do nothing. You feel paralyzed, stopped in your tracks, unable to get•what you want, defeated. You get stuck in thinking, If only I had this, everything would be okay. You are convinced you will never have what you want, so why bother trying? Instead of living your own life, you spend your time wishing you were living someone else's. You feel sorry for yourself, believe you are less than you actually are. You know the feeling—you're in an elevator of a fine hotel, feeling elegant. Another woman enters with a phony aloof air, and you feel like a shlump.

Nora began to reason with herself: "Am I going to stay trapped or become conscious enough to choose something other than resentment?" The next step is to use reason to *separate* what you envy about the person from the person herself. What you envy is not the whole person but something you're missing or wanting.

AWARENESS: Nora understood that she didn't envy all of Holly's life, but just one aspect—Holly's satisfying sex life. She identified what it was she envied about Holly and separated this from Holly as a whole person.

Whatever it is you envy about a person—look at it—ask yourself:

- Do I need to hold on to bad feelings?
- Do I envy everything about the person or just an aspect of her life, a quality, possession, or temporary success?
- Am I willing to trade places with her; am I willing to become her?

When you separate what you envy about a person from the whole person, you are freer to concentrate on what you want.

COVETOUSNESS

As Nora moved out of resentment into covetousness her envy provided a barometer for her appetites. She stopped concentrating on Holly and began to focus on her own desire, hunger, and longing—on *what*, specifically, she wanted: a better sex life.

In covetousness, you will feel greedy, petty, and shameful. And since brooding over what you don't have is a waste of time, Nora looked for the way out of covetousness. To do so, as she had done when stuck in self-hatred, she reflected on the nature of envy. She remembered our discussions about envy being universal, normal, and endless. If it wasn't "this" she envied, it would be "that."

Nora also told Holly about her sexual envy, which made it more acceptable. Nora told me, "I talked to Holly because she is important to me. If she weren't, I'd talk to someone else about my feelings." After hearing Nora's feelings, Holly was able to reveal her envy of Nora. Then the two women learned about envy's mutuality.

AWARENESS: Nora realized that her focus on Holly's sex life was itself a disguise for what Nora really wanted for herself. Nora understood she felt lacking inside herself and wanted something to fill that lack.

To move out of covetousness, focus on your desire. Ask yourself:

- How much do I really want what I envy?
- Is what I want obtainable, within my reach?
- Can I talk to the person I envy about my feelings?

When you understand that what you covet may be a disguise for something lacking in you, you are more able to motivate yourself to admire or achieve what you covet in someone else.

ADMIRATION

Eighty-two percent of the women surveyed found something positive about their envy.

Admiration is not idealization. When you idealize, you feel small and separate. When you admire, you observe and appreciate the other person's good qualities, the strengths and uniqueness of the person you envy. You can't own someone else's success or achievements but you are a part of the achievement just by observing it.

Nora and I discussed the importance of admiration. "I disliked a woman at work who was straightforward," Nora recalled. "I used to say, 'That bitch; she's real aggressive.' Once I realized it was envy, that *I* wanted to be like her, more aggressive myself, I got to know her better and figured out how to become more like her."

Since envy comes in part from not looking deeply enough into yourself, I explained to Nora that in order to learn from her envy, she had two tasks:

1. *Locate what she likes about herself.* Nora tells herself, "Okay, Holly has a good feeling about herself that I would like. I remind myself that I have a good life; remind myself what I do have, what I can do, and that I don't always need to be doing what someone else is doing. Sometimes I make lists about what I like about myself, rather than self-improvement lists. I feel grateful for my own gifts, essence, values. I like that I relate well to people, have a good sense of humor, vitality, and enjoy the outdoors."

2. *Explore where her envy comes from.* Envy is, after all, admiration gone sour. When you admire someone, you begin to see how you had been distorting the true picture. In admiration, you learn from your envy. Many women reported, "I'd never try to learn from someone I didn't envy at least a little. If I never envied, I'd never learn." Or, "I become closer to the person who has what I want. I get to know her better and try to be with her more."

To discover if what she wants is within her reach, Nora has to figure out what it is she really envies. When she looked more closely at her envy of Holly, she saw what she wanted was not sex per se, but intimacy. It was Holly's excitement about herself, her vulnerability in a trusting relationship and openness to loving someone, that Nora actually envied. Nora realized that what she envied about Holly's sex life was something within Nora's reach, something she, too, could achieve.

AWARENESS: In admiration, Nora was more connected to possibilities inside herself. She explored where her envy came from. She evaluated what she liked about herself and Holly. She no longer felt that what she envied was out of reach, but that she, too, had something good inside of her—it wasn't located only in Holly, the person she envied.

Explore your envy by asking yourself these "how to deal with envy" questions:

- How did I get the expectation that I *should have* whatever I envy?
- How and when did I stop feeling good about myself?
- Do I envy what *I* want or what someone else wants for me?
- What made me imagine something outside myself would make me feel better?
- If I buy a BMW, will I want a Mercedes in two years?
- Am I afraid of acknowledging what I do have?
- What is good and unique about me?

When you know what is good about you, you are able to admire and emulate.

EMULATION

Nora told me, "Now the person I envy is a role model rather than someone I'd like to wipe off the face of the earth." Admiration and emulation are closely linked. You can pleasantly observe something good in the person you envy, work at finding it inside yourself, admire it, or emulate—polish to the very best what you have. Admiration takes less initiative than emulation does. Admiration is enjoying and appreciating. Emulation is an action approach; you do something specific to change yourself or your situation.

However, emulation does not mean become *the same as* the person you envy. It means you strive to improve who you are, become like the person you admire. If emulation makes you want to outdo your child, sibling, mate, co-worker, or friend, it won't work for you. If Nora gave up her basic personality, her own special qualities and habits, in hopes of becoming like Holly, she would only end up feeling emptier and more envious. It just doesn't work to *always push yourself* to become forever better and better in order to match someone else. Have you seen the T-shirt emblazoned with, "He who has the most toys when he dies, wins"? Isn't being equal or, a little less than, good enough?

A woman from South Carolina wrote, "Just making an effort was a tremendous force against feeling envious. Envy has something to do with passivity, with forbidding oneself to try to change or get what you want."

When you emulate someone, remember that the world will not stop turning if you make a mistake in trying for what you want. Have you seen the sign that reads, "I didn't fail. I discovered I did something that didn't work"?

Nora makes an effort. Nora realized she had a choice, a chance to change. She focused on an area of self-confidence: her bubbly personality, the fact that she relates well to people. She decided to do more of what she enjoys. She became more available to her friends and made efforts to meet new people.

AWARENESS: Nora makes up her mind to go after what she wants, and figures out how to do it.

Ask yourself:

• Am I willing to give up something to work for what I want?

- Am I willing to pay the price, expend the effort?
- If so, what can I do to get it, or something similar, step by step? Who can help me along the way?
- If I can't have the very thing I envy, can I have something else that will make me feel good?

Nora now strives to get what she wants rather than hurting her friend. She has learned, through the sometimes painful process of struggling with not having everything she wants, how to take better care of herself. But the resolution of what Nora is looking for is not this neat and simplistic. This search, this conflict goes on for life. We're always caught between feeling we need to change ourselves on the one hand and accepting who we are on the other. Nora learns about her complexity as a person, the opposites that are within her. She comes to accept the worst of her feelings.

Through therapy, Nora moved from her hateful envy of Holly toward being more open to people, toward confidence in herself as a person who could receive love. At the end of our therapy, Nora was proud of herself: "I use my envy to make me go for what I want. I accept who I am. I say, 'My life is not Holly's. It is my own.'"

How a mother taught her daughter to make envy work for her. Nora learned her lessons, step by step. LouAnn, a fifty-eight-year-old doctor from San Diego, was given a similar education early on. LouAnn related the following story. "My mother would listen to my problems, then ask questions. When I'd come home from school and complain that Henrietta was so much prettier than me and that I hated her for it, my mother would say, 'Yes, Henrietta is pretty. But what do you mean by pretty? Do you means looks, behavior?'

"My mother's questions would guide me to the root of what I was really feeling. If I said, 'Oh, Henrietta just thinks she's so cute!' my mother would ask, 'Well, don't you think she's cute?' I'd respond, 'Yeah, but she's so stuck up about it.' Mother would keep asking questions, and if she heard envy, she'd ask me, 'What is it about her that bothers you? What do you think she has that you don't have?' If what I envied was looks, my mother would say, 'Well, those are her natural gifts. Here are your natural gifts. Make the most of the gifts you have.' If the envy was for talents, acquired traits, my mother would say, 'Then emulate it—if you admire ability, try to develop that in yourself.'"

LouAnn's mother didn't allow her to wallow in envy. Instead, she taught her daughter to question her feelings thoroughly and accurately. Now, when LouAnn feels envy, she questions herself before getting stuck.

MAKING ENVY WORK FOR YOU: WELL-KNOWN WOMEN

Many well-known women have learned the same lessons as Nora and LouAnn.

LaDonna Harris

Since LaDonna was taught that envy is "not nice," she tells herself she does not envy any person; only something about them, like nice clothes or a good figure. "When I see something I envy, I try to incorporate it into myself. Like, look how that jacket makes her look slimmer, I'm going to try that. If I don't do anything to change, I remain envious. And besides, Indians are taught not to want things. We say, 'If they are feeling envious, they are acting like white people.'"

Billie Jean King

Billie Jean's envy takes the form of nostalgia. "Women starting in sports now have a much better opportunity to become a good player than I had. They have better coaching and more money. I wish that were happening to me now. My friends tell me it's too bad I couldn't be younger today, just starting out, because I'd thrive. I'd love the challenge of being the constant professional athlete. It's great that Martina and Chris are making lots of money. It's just that I, too, would have fit in well today. When I was coming along, nothing fit.

"I was always the first—the first to lift weights, the first into nutrition. I got Martina and Chrissy into weight lifting. And Martina and Chrissy would have made me a better player. The younger ones always end up beating you over the long haul because as you're on the way down, they're on the way up. So it never works out quite right."

When Billie Jean envies, what does she do?

"I tell myself 'It's okay to dwell on this for a moment.' Then I remind myself, 'This is how it is.' It's important for me not to dwell on what could be because I'm not going to be fifteen again. I'm not going to have a chance to put on a circus."

As much as Billie Jean knows she "could eat it up, take more and more of what there is today for women athletes," she realizes we wouldn't have this situation without her, either.

She reassures herself, "I don't have it so bad. I'm not afraid. I just think out my envy—that helps me get rid of it, let it go. If the envy keeps repeating itself, I know I'm in trouble. Then I talk to a friend or get help. It's not healthy to just let it sit inside my gut and not try to deal with it. I use it as feedback and learn."

Susan Merzbach

In her first twelve years attempting to make it big in Hollywood Susan felt a lot of envy. She asked the typical envier's questions: "Why is that person moving faster up the ladder than I am?" "What's wrong with me?" "Why did he get something done when I didn't?" "What do they have that I don't have?"

But Susan saw the light. "I realized each person had a particular career route which did not guarantee them direct access to stardom. It just meant that at that particular time in their life, they were doing one thing and I was doing another. Especially in Hollywood—success rides a roller coaster.

"I also saw the reality that in Hollywood, only the executive head of the studio with his green stamp of the board of directors has absolute authority. All the rest of us have the same, lesser, authority. So what was I screaming about?"

As successful as she is, Susan, surprisingly, envies anybody with a million dollars. She is afraid of becoming a bag lady— "being alone with no money, in the street, nowhere to go. It's paralyzing, and it's the biggest fear of women in this town. When I can get rid of that fear, I'm home free. I'll be able to laugh again—you know, the kind of laugh that makes your side hurt."

This is how Susan deals with her envy. "I see that my envy is always in direct relation to how I feel about myself. What is it that is really making me unhappy? Why do I need outside validation?

I know that the person I envy is only serving to bring something into focus for me, that I have to deal with myself. When I envy a huge stock portfolio and pretend that's what brings security, I think, Fool! You'll just be a bag lady who's had a greater fall."

JUDITH CRIST

"I envied more when I was younger. Thirty years ago, when I worked at the *Herald Tribune*, it was more elegant to be a theater than a movie critic. I joined the *Tribune* dying to be a theater critic. Walter Kerr was then the theater critic for the *Tribune*. I became the reviewer for off-Broadway plays, and working under him was like being the handmaiden to God. I deeply envied him because he had the exact job I had dreamed of all my life.

"Then one day, the way a lightbulb goes up over your head on comic strips, I suddenly saw the light. I realized: Walter Kerr is ten years older than me, ten times as brilliant. He is in perfect health. I will never get his job as long as he works here. Facing reality brought the end of envy for me."

RONA BARRETT

You might expect that someone who interviews the stars—the Jane Fondas, Joan Collinses, Sylvester Stallones, and Robert Redfords—might feel some envy toward them. Not Rona. She has never interviewed anyone of whom she's been envious.

"Whenever I feel envy, I feel rage and anger. It is a waste of energy. I also realize that if you get what you envy, you exchange one set of problems for another.

"I understand that what appears to be greener over there really isn't. I don't know what is happening at his or her house since I don't live there. How do you really know what Sylvester Stallone feels at night when he closes his door and has to face not only the good things but the demons he knows that exist?

"I've had so much struggle in my life that I don't envy anyone who is struggling. I have more compassion than envy. When someone struggles to become successful, to get to Mount Pinnacle, there is a huge price to pay. No one has obtained an enormous success who hasn't struggled to get there. Nothing happens to anybody overnight, and if it has been overnight, that person isn't properly prepared.

"So I don't envy, because I know that everyone struggles."

JEAN BOLEN

"I envy people who lead a less structured life with free time to travel. I like my life, but I'd like to lead another life at the same time. I'd like to live out the artist part of my life, but I have artist friends and have lived vicariously through them and their accomplishments. I can't do everything I want to do."

PEGGY HORA

I told Peggy about a woman I interviewed who had bone cancer and asked Peggy, "What would you have said to this woman who, of course, envied healthy people?" Peggy would tell her, "What you are envying you will never have. But in the time you have left, and with the energy you're not going to spend on envy, what can you have instead? You can have something that most people might never have. You can have peace with yourself, with who you are. You have your memories and experiences. When it matters how long you have to live, you can live more fully."

CAROLYN KIZER

Carolyn Kizer views envy more from a political than personal perspective. She talks about situational envy. "When I was a young girl visiting Oxford and Cambridge and women were just not around, I felt an envy for the unfairness of it all. It made me livid. Or, like every woman, I envy men's ability to go to a bar or to take a walk late at night, the greater freedoms that they have. Also, when I read about the lives of Henry James and his circle, I envy people who have a constant circle of people doing work like their own. These examples seem situational to me. My father thought that envy was a totally illegitimate emotion. He hated the emotion so much, he wouldn't even see *Othello*. I love to see *Othello*, but I've never consciously envied any particular person. That must be a terrible burden to carry with you."

What to do about envy? "Personal envy is caused by a narcissistic focusing on oneself. My parents were always reaching out to other people, looking for their point of view. That approach to life is an envy killer."

SUSAN ANSPACH

The closest Susan has come to ever feeling envy was when Meryl Streep made *The French Lieutenant's Woman*. Susan had walked around for three years with the script for the movie under her arm. "It's a great part, a great book. I identify with the essence of the leading character in her line, 'I chose my shame for my freedom.' I could never convince a studio to produce the movie. They told me, 'Women aren't in.' Can you believe it?"

But Susan has such respect for Meryl Streep's ability that she changed her envy from resentment into admiration: "I have such a love of talent that I thought, God, Meryl deserves this. She's terrific. She should do good movies. I gave up on getting the movie made. She made it happen. Forget it, Susan.

"I know that life is what you give it each day. It's not what you could be doing, that 'if you could do this, you'd feel better.' I don't care who you are, where you are, what's happening, life is what you bring to each moment, your own capacity to get out of bed in the morning, to get the ball rolling. The peace and love around you, the harmony. I believe that's what life's about. Just let your feeling happen, let it come out strong, and it will be over with. Something else will happen. That's what I did the day I read about Meryl making the movie."

Making Peace with Envy

The goal of your work with envy reaches beyond emulation. You learn how to become less driven and to make peace with your own envy. Nora and these more well-known women have gleaned what envy has to offer them: they value themselves and the good in others.

SNOW WHITE REVISITED

The question remains, since we all end up like our parents in some way, will Snow White make peace with envy or will she become like the wicked queen? If we interviewed the adult Snow White, I could imagine asking her, "Have you learned to make envy work for you?"

Snow White might reply, "The wicked queen never knew that envy that ran her life. I, on the other hand, had time to heal in the glass coffin, to think about my stepmother's envy and how it almost killed me. When I left the coffin, I felt nourished by my helpers, the dwarfs. I was changed. I was ready for marriage, a real bond of the male and female parts of me. I did what I needed to do—kill off the evil of that wicked queen. I had the courage to confront envy, to allow myself to live a life in which I valued myself and others."

TWELVE KEYS FOR MANAGING ENVY

1. *Observe whatever envy you feel and watch it quietly.* Either it passes, or it becomes a guide to live more completely.

2. *Be satisfied with what you have.* "A little of what you fancy does you good." You don't have to have everything you envy.

3. *Accept inevitable limitations.* Remind yourself that you just can't have some things. You're not going to have different parents, different genes, a different past.

4. *Know that someone else has it worse than you do.* "I used to feel sorry for myself because I had no shoes until I met a man that had no feet."

5. *Share what you have.* Know there are enough of the good things in the world to go around.

6. *See envy's truth: that envy and being envied are two sides of the same coin.* The envier and the envied have much in common; in either case you may feel small, isolated, hurt.

7. *Put yourself in the shoes of the person you envy.* As novelist Rona Jaffe put the Golden Rule of envy, "I know what it's like to be envied. When I envy, I tell myself I never want to do the bad things that have been done to me or make that person feel the way I have felt."

8. *Know that the cure for envy is originality—being true to who you are.* Value yourself as you are, your own strengths, your own goals. Focus on what you have, not what you lack. You have your own style, your own confidence. Don't feel that you have to become someone else.

9. *Be fully engaged in life, absorbed in doing what gives your life meaning.* According to the late actress Rosalind Russell, "Taking joy in life is a woman's best cosmetic."

10. *Know the world doesn't center around you.* Have a spiritual connection with something larger than yourself. Appreciate the little things in life. Rejoice in the ability of someone else.

11. *Laugh and joke about your envy.* Know that everyone is full of self-doubt. Know that even people you envy envy others. We're all in it together.

12. *Feel gratitude for your life of beauty and the beauty of life.*

When you're aware of your envy, you're freer to change. When you learn from your envy, you see envy as something common to all. You are freer to live the life you want, to use your envy to challenge yourself and strive for something more. When you feel appreciation for what you do have, however small, you are more able to transform envy into love. When you see the other person suffering from similar dark emotions, you're more likely to reach out to the person you envy rather than try to hurt her or yourself. Let's remember St. Augustine: "If you love, you are not one that has nothing."

Appendix

THE ENVY QUESTIONNAIRE

General

1. What kind of work do you do?
2. How do you feel about your personal life at present?
3. How do you feel about your professional life at present?
4. How do you generally feel: self-confident or self-critical?
5. What does it mean to you to be successful?
6. Do you feel successful as a person?
7. Do others see you as successful?
8. Are there areas in your life you plan on changing in the near future? If so, what?
9. Where do you hope to be in your life five years from now?
10. What is your economic background? What type of work did your father do? Your mother?
11. How old are you?

Being Envied

12. How would you describe or define envy?
13. Have you ever felt envied?

14. Did you experience envy from your mother? If yes, for what? How did your mother feel about herself?

15. Have you felt envied by your husband (spouse, significant other)?

16. Have you felt envied by a co-worker? Why?

17. Have you felt envied by a sibling? Why?

18. Have you been envied by other helping professionals (therapist, doctor, teacher)?

19. What have you been envied for? (If not for a long time, when? What? Keep questioning.)

20. What do you do when you feel envied?

21. How did it feel to be envied?

22. Can you give an example of how you dealt with being envied?

23. What ways of dealing with envy did not work for you?

24. Does being envied affect your feeling of success?

25. Do you feel you hold yourself back for fear of being the target of envy?

Envying

26. Did you or do you find yourself envying others?

27. What do you envy?

28. Do you recall feeling envious of your mother? Is she happy now?

29. How does envying someone make you feel about yourself? Is it positive or negative? What is negative about it?

30. What do you do to deal with your envious feelings?

31. Would you please give an example?

32. What way of dealing with envy did not work?

33. What might you do differently next time?

34. Does your envying someone affect your feeling of success?

35. What do you see as the cause of people envying one another?

36. How prevalent does envy seem? How much envy is there around you?

37. Can you find anything positive about envying?

38. Can you feel anything positive about being the target of envy?

39. Do you feel men or women envy more? Why?

40. Is there anything else you would like to say?

41. Would you be interested in reading a book on envy?

RESULTS OF WOMEN AND ENVY RESEARCH SURVEY*

1. THE PROFESSIONS OF WOMEN SURVEYED ARE:

Actress, administrator, antique dealer, architect, architectural manager, artist, assistant magazine editor, assistant radio producer, babysitter, baker, banker, broadcast journalist, carpenter, cashier, CPA, clerk, community organizer, comptroller, computer operator, congresswoman, consultant, cook, copy editor, counselor, customer service representative, data processor, day care teacher, doctor, deputy tax assessor, educational administrator, editor, executive, exercise instructor, farmer, film producer, graphic artist, hairstylist, historian, homesteader, hospital manager, housecleaner, housekeeper, housewife, human service worker, investor, investment banker, journalist, judge, landscape architect, lawyer, literary agent, lobbyist, manager, masseuse, mental health professional, model, movie reviewer, musician, news anchorperson, newscaster, nurse, nursing assistant, nutritionist, paralegal, park ranger, philanthropist, photo lab assistant, pianist, poet, political consultant, prison guard, professor, program developer, psychiatrist, psychologist, psychotherapist, public relations officer, publisher, purchasing agent, ranger, real estate broker, receptionist, rehabilitation counselor, researcher, restaurateur, retired, salesperson, screenwriter, secretary, self-employed, social worker, software tester, software writer, speech pathologist, stage manager, stockbroker, structural engineer, student, swim coach, systems analyst, talk show hostess, teacher, technical editor, technical writer, TV producer, tennis professional, typist, unemployed, union organizer, unskilled laborer, vice-president/marketing, video producer, waitress, writer.

*The results of the survey do not correspond on a one-to-one basis with the questions. In some instances they were combined and in others correlated.

2. MOST FREQUENT PROFESSIONS WERE:

Writer, housewife, psychotherapist, student, graphic artist.

3. HOW MANY WERE HAPPY IN PERSONAL AND/OR PROFESSIONAL LIFE?

PERSONAL LIFE		PROFESSIONAL LIFE	
Happy	58%	Happy	45%
Okay	21%	Okay	24%
Unhappy	20%	Unhappy	19%
In transition	1%	In transition	5%

4. ARE YOU SELF-CONFIDENT/SELF-CRITICAL?

Self-confident	33%	Both	48%
Self-critical	19%		

5. IF SELF-CONFIDENT, HOW DO YOU FEEL ABOUT BEING ENVIED?

Positive about being envied	10%	Negative about being envied	80%
Neutral about being envied	10%		

(Even if you feel good about yourself and self-confident, you will likely still feel negative about being envied.)

6. IF SELF-CRITICAL, HOW DO YOU FEEL ABOUT BEING ENVIED?

Positive	18%	Negative	77%
Neutral	5%		

7. WHAT DOES IT MEAN TO YOU TO BE SUCCESSFUL?

Happiness in general	32%	Independence	3%
Happy with work	18%	Having friends	3%

Money	16%	Coping well with your life	2%
Accomplishments	10%	Having everything	.36%
Good home life	6%	Improving present situation	.36%
Gain respect	5%	Power	.72%
Good personal and professional life	4%		

8. ARE YOU SEEN AS SUCCESSFUL BY OTHERS?

Yes	69%	Partially	21%
No	7%	Don't know	4%

9. IF SEEN AS SUCCESSFUL BY OTHERS, HOW DO YOU FEEL ABOUT BEING ENVIED?

Positive	18%	Negative	70%
Neutral	12%		

10. WHAT IS YOUR ECONOMIC BACKGROUND?

Middle class	35%	Varied	7%
Lower middle/blue collar	27%	Upper	4%
Upper middle	22%	Lower/poor	4%

11. HOW OLD ARE YOU?

0–20	2%	51–60	9%
21–30	21%	61–70	4%
31–40	44%	Over 70	2%
41–50	19%		

(There was no statistical difference between the age categories as to how respondent felt about being envied or envying.)

12. HAVE YOU EVER FELT ENVIED?

Yes	95%	Maybe	2%
No	3%		

13. WHAT IS MOST ENVIED?

Mate or boyfriend	16%	Relationships	2%
Personal characteristics*	15%	Success	2%
Life-style	14%	Opportunity	2%
Physical attractiveness	10%	Nothing	.40%
Income	8%	Power	.40%
Talents, abilities	7%	Happiness	.40%
Professional		Leadership qualities	.81%
accomplishments	6%		
House	4%		

14. HAVE YOU EXPERIENCED ENVY FROM YOUR MOTHER?

Yes	57%	Maybe	4%
No	37%		

15. WHAT DID YOUR MOTHER ENVY YOU FOR?

Opportunity, education	20%	Easier life, security	3%
Relationship with father	11%	Talents, abilities	2%
Social, sexual freedoms	11%	Material comforts	2%
Youth	7%	Life-style	2%
Relationship with your husband	7%	Everything	1%
Physical attractiveness	7%	Personal and professional life balance	1%
Accomplishments	6%	Better home life	1%
Independence	5%	Happiness	.48%
Intelligence	5%	Power	.48%
Personal characteristics	4%	Health	.48%
Other	3%		

---

*Assertiveness, competence, friendliness, and self-assuredness.

16. HOW DOES YOUR MOTHER FEEL ABOUT HER-
    SELF?

Bad	55%	Combination	10%
Good	32%	Don't know	3%

(It was statistically significant that Mom was more likely to envy
daughter when Mom felt bad about herself.)

17. IF YOUR MOTHER WORKED, DID SHE ENVY YOU?

Yes   63%   No   37%

18. HAVE YOU FELT ENVY FROM YOUR MATE?

Yes   70%

(It was statistically significant that self-confident women were
more likely to be envied by their mates.)

19. HAVE YOU FELT ENVY FROM CO-WORKERS?

Yes   82%

20. HAVE YOU FELT ENVY FROM A SIBLING?

Yes   71%

21. HAVE YOU FELT ENVY FROM SOMEONE IN THE
    HELPING PROFESSIONS*?

Yes   57%

22. WHAT DO YOU DO WHEN ENVIED?

Avoid showing off   24%   Avoid the other   6%

*Helping professions include therapists, teachers, coaches, lawyers, nurses,
and good doctors.

Put things into perspective	16%	Other	5%
		Do nothing	4%
Ignore situation	13%	Act defensive	3%
Try to win other's favor	12%	Feel guilty	.8%
Discuss it	10%	Try not to feel guilty	.8%
Feel complimented	6%		

23. HOW DOES IT FEEL TO BE ENVIED?

Bad	61%	Both good and bad	11%
Good	17%	Other	7%

24. WHICH WAYS OF DEALING WITH BEING ENVIED DO NOT WORK?

Ignoring envious feelings	26%	Being direct	9%
Negativity	18%	Overcompensating	4%
Playing things down	13%	Avoiding person	4%
Other	12%	Withdrawing	1%
Feeling guilty	12%		

25. DO YOU HOLD YOURSELF BACK FOR FEAR OF BEING ENVIED?

No	56%	Yes	43%

26. DOES HOLDING YOURSELF BACK RELATE TO ENVY FROM YOUR MOTHER?

Yes, it was statistically significant that those envied by their mother are more likely to hold themselves back for fear of being envied.

27. DO YOU ENVY OTHERS?

Yes	84%	Don't know	7%
No	9%		

28. DO/DID YOU ENVY YOUR MOTHER?

Yes	30%	No	70%

29. IS THERE A CONNECTION BETWEEN ENVYING YOUR MOTHER AND MOTHER'S ENVY TOWARD DAUGHTER?

Yes, it was statistically significant that if your mother envied you, you are less likely to envy her.

30. HOW DOES ENVYING SOMEONE MAKE YOU FEEL ABOUT YOURSELF?

Bad	81%	Look at self harder	3%
Good	6%	Neither good nor bad	.95%
Other	3%	Accept	.95%
Encourage self to change	3%		

31. HOW DO YOU DEAL WITH YOUR ENVIOUS FEELINGS TOWARD OTHERS?

Accept them	29%	Other	6%
Put things into perspective	19%	Isolate self	6%
Suppress them	15%	Compliment envied person	4%
Talk to others	9%	Drive self harder	2%
Make resolutions	8%	Joke about feelings	2%

32. WHAT MIGHT YOU DO DIFFERENTLY NEXT TIME?

Be more effective	29%	Be more careful	6%
Be realistic	12%	Focus on positive	4%
Act naturally	10%	Get help from friends	4%
Other	8%	Don't be critical	2%
Attain that which is envied	8%	Be direct	2%
Ignore feelings	6%	Use envied person as role model	2%
Recognize feelings earlier	6%		

33. WHAT DO YOU CONSIDER TO BE THE CAUSE OF ENVY?

Feelings of deprivation	36%	Not knowing one's limitations	4%
Low self-esteem	26%		

Seeing others as better		TV and advertising	2%
off	13%	Perfectionism	2%
Feelings of failure	9%	Competition	.9%
Other	8%		

34. WHAT IS POSITIVE ABOUT ENVYING?

It motivates you	58%	Learning	
Helps you look at your		Experience	6%
own values	16%	Other	3%
Nothing	15%		

35. HOW MANY FEEL THERE IS NOTHING POSITIVE ABOUT ENVYING?

Nothing positive about envying   15%

36. WHAT IS POSITIVE ABOUT BEING THE TARGET OF ENVY?

Gain validation,		Allows emotional	
self-esteem	42%	closeness	5%
Nothing	32%	Learning experience	3%
Model to someone		Motivation	.48%
else	12%		
Other	6%		

37. DO YOU THINK MEN OR WOMEN ENVY MORE?

Women	57%	Don't know	8%
Women and men		Men	5%
equally	18%		
Each differently	12%		

38. CATEGORIES OF WHY WOMEN OR MEN ENVY MORE

Women, they show emotions		Women, they are more	
more	26%	envious by nature	3%
Women, they are		Women, because their	
insecure	17%	roles are changing	3%

Women, they have to try harder 9%

Women, some combination of looks, clothes, men 8%

Women, they are taught to envy 7%

Equally, men and women envy for different reasons 4%

Men, they are more competitive 4%

Women, they care more about who has what 3%

Women, they have more superficial things to envy 3%

Don't know why 3%

Equally, but women are better at expressing envy 2%

Women, they are more social 2%

Women, because men are able to diffuse envy 2%

Don't know, but women are better at expressing envy .89%

Envy is universal .89%

Men, because women are more perceptive .89%

Notes

CHAPTER 1

Page 1, *Walt Disney*. According to Jack Zipes, in *Breaking the Magic Spell: Radical Theories of Folk and Fairy Tales*, pp. 95–115, Walt Disney, in his first full-length animated movie, *Snow White and the Seven Dwarfs,* laundered the original version of the tale. Disney gives center stage to the dwarfs, who pursue the queen and cause her death. In the Grimm brothers' version, the dwarfs are minor characters, and the Prince and Snow White kill the queen at their wedding.

Disney's version is overly sweet and romantic. Snow White wishes and hopes for her prince to come; in the Grimm brothers' version, she does not anticipate a prince. Furthermore, when "Snow White and the Seven Dwarfs" was first released in 1936, America was in the throes of a depression. In his movie, Walt Disney tried to instill the image of America as "one, big, happy family"; tried to wash over the economic mess we were in, and wanted to praise the values of capitalism and the work ethic. Hence, Disney's hit song, "Whistle While You Work." Disney portrayed Snow White as an innocent "Miss America," representing the basic goodness of America's economic system, and the dwarfs as hard workers. Snow White teaches them to be neat, clean, and orderly. In the Grimm brothers' version, the dwarfs' cottage is already "neater and cleaner than can be told."

Page 3, *The Hunter*. Dr. Bruno Bettelheim, in *The Uses of*

Enchantment, p. 205 and 206, says that since most children fear being eaten by animals, the child's unconscious mind views the hunter as a protector. A child hopes that the parent-hunter can scare away frightening animals. Dr. Bettelheim also believes that the hunter is like a weak father who tries to placate his wife and daughter.

Page 4, *Stepmother's gifts*. Dr. Bruno Bettelheim, on p. 211 of *The Uses of Enchantment*, talks about Snow White's eagerness to accept her stepmother's temptations because these offerings appeal to Snow White's inner need for adolescent development.

Page 5, *Coffin*. Dr. Bettelheim, on p. 213 of *The Uses of Enchantment*, describes Snow White's time in the coffin as a period of gestation and growth necessary to develop the maturity to enter an intimate adult relationship.

Page 6, *Narcissistic mother*. The child of a narcissistic mother learns not to express much distress, for if the child's complaints are heard at all, they are heard only as an annoyance. According to Psychoanalyst Alice Miller, in *Prisoners of Childhood (The Drama of the Gifted Child and the Search for the True Self)*, patients with extremely self-preoccupied mothers like the Wicked Queen find it difficult to talk about or experience being depressed even after years of therapy.

Page 7, *Mirroring*. Dr. Heinz Kohut, in *Restoration of the Self*, says a mother's proper mirroring of an infant lays the foundation for the child's development of goals and ambitions.

Alice Miller, on p. 32 of *Prisoners of Childhood*, mentions that when a mother projects onto the child her own fears and wishes for the child rather than seeing the child's uniqueness, the "child would not find himself in his mother's face but rather the mother's own predicaments."

Page 7, *Envious mother*. Madonna Kolbenschlag, on p. 30 of *Kiss Sleeping Beauty Good-bye*, says "the image of the 'bad' mother emerges out of the 'good.'"

Page 10, *Dwarfs*. P. Zabriskie, in a lecture entitled "Issues of Life, Love, and Death in Fairy Tales," given at the C. G. Jung Institute in San Francisco, said that the dwarfs in "Snow White" not only work as miners but they actually help Snow White mine for what is special and unique in herself.

Dr. Bettelheim, in *The Uses of Enchantment*, explains: "under the guidance of the dwarfs, Snow White grows from a child helpless to deal with the difficulties of the world into a girl who learns to work well, and enjoy it."

Page 11, *The glass coffin*. Marie L. von Franz, on p. 140 of *The Feminine in Fairytales,* talks about the use of the glass motif in fairy tales. Glass, she says, illustrates a condition of being partially cut off—emotionally but not mentally. People can see a problem but not "feel" it.

Page 11, *Quiet space*. Alice Miller, in *Prisoners of Childhood,* tells us that the child of a narcisstic mother cannot know who she or he is until this child becomes independent from the mother. Snow White needed this time of concentration on herself to learn to become independent.

Page 11, *Sleep*. Dr. Bettelheim, on p. 214 of *The Uses of Enchantment,* comments that fairy tale heroes often fall into a deep sleep. Each awakening, each rebirth, symbolizes a "higher state of maturity and understanding."

Page 13, *Mastering trials*. Dr. Bettelheim, on p. 127 of *The Uses of Enchantment,* talks about the heroes and heroines of fairy tales, like Snow White, who master the trials set before them, and achieve a "true selfhood." On page 226, Dr. Bettelheim concludes that fairy tales like "Snow White" and "Sleeping Beauty" encourage the child not to be afraid of the dangers of passivity, and not to fear a quiet growth; you don't always have to be "doing" to be changing.

CHAPTER 2

Page 14, *George P. Elliott*. From the article "Buried Envy," *Harpers.* July, 1974, p. 17.

Page 15, *Maury Silver*. From the article "When Envy Strikes: How to Spot It, Ways to Cope," in *U.S. News and World Report.* November 1, 1982, Vol. 93, p. 81.

Page 15, *Joyce Brothers*. Dr. Joyce Brothers wrote this in "That Green-Eyed Monster—and What to Do About Him!" *Good Housekeeping,* August 1969, Vol. 169, p. 46.

Page 15, *Are You Feeling Envy?* The following sources were helpful in the formulation of this section. Mary Williams, in her article "Success and Failure in Analysis. Primary Envy and the Fate of the Good," *Journal of Analytical Psychology,* 1972, Vol. 17, No. 1, p. 17, describes envy as pain felt at another person's success. Maury Silver, in *U.S. News and World Report* (November 1, 1982), p. 81, discusses envy as a vice that involves people feeling demeaned by the success of another—success they would like for themselves. Suzanne McNear, in "Coping with

Envy," *Cosmopolitan*, July, 1980, p. 213, says women envy people who are leading lives they feel *they* ought to be leading. Also, Dr. Hal Sampson, in a personal communication, said that people who envy usually have feelings of entitlement. Walter G. Joffe, in "A Critical Review of the Status of the Envy Concept," *International Journal of Psychoanalysis*, 1969, Vol. 50, p. 543, describes the difference between the perception of the self and the ideal self as a critical aspect of what causes envy. Maury Silver (like almost every other theorist on envy), in the *U.S. News and World Report* interview cited above, discusses the envious person's need to hurt and put down the object of their envy. Judith Hubback in "Envy and the Shadow," in the *Journal of Analytical Psychology*, Vol. 17, No. 2, p. 153, informs us that after the repeated failure to get what you want, envy becomes colored with hate and the desire to spoil.

Page 16, Philip M. Spielman, M.D., in "Envy and Jealousy: An Attempt at Clarification," *Psychoanalytic Quarterly*, January 1971, Vol. 40, No. 1, pp. 60–61, talks about the envious person's wish to rob the person of the envied thing.

Page 16, *Anais Nin*. Anais Nin, an American diarist and writer, is quoted in *A Woman's Notebook, III*, edited by Amy Shapiro.

Page 16, *Dante*. Leslie Farber, in *Ways of the Will*, mentions that in Dante's *Inferno* (from *The Divine Comedy*) the punishment for the envious is that their eyelids be sewn together. Says Dante, "an iron wire pierces all their eyelids and stitches them up." Canto XIII, *Purgatorio*.

Page 17, *Joke*. The envy joke is from psychologist and expert on the theory of envy, Albert M. Shapiro, Ph.D.

Page 17, *Snow White's stepmother*. Helmut Schoeck, on p. 21 of *Envy: A Theory of Social Behavior*, mentions that if one is envied, and "stripped of every possession, such a demonstration of goodness would still humiliate (the envious person) so that his envy would be transferred from one's possessions to one's character."

Page 18, *The Continuum of Envy*. Reading Dr. Philip M. Spielman's comprehensive and clarifying article, "Envy and Jealousy: An Attempt at Clarification," enabled me to conceptualize a continuum of envy. I am indebted to him for his ideas.

Page 18, *Admiration*. Steven Frankel and Ivan Sherick, in "Observations on the Development of Normal Envy," *The Psychoanalytic Study of the Child*, 1977, Vol. 32, pp. 257–281, inform us that envy has a role in personality development as a motive for introjection and identification.

Page 20, *Primal wanting*. In "Envy and the Shadow," *Journal of Analytic Psychology,* 1972, Vol. 17, No. 2, p. 163, Judith Hubback writes about the hungry, wanting aspect of envy as an essential part of normal personality development.

Page 20, *Jealousy*. George Foster, in "The Anatomy of Envy: A Study in Symbolic Behavior," pp. 167–168; Peter Titelman, in "A Phenomenological Comparison Between Envy and Jealousy," p. 194; Philip Spielman, in "Envy and Jealousy, An Attempt at Clarification," p. 59; and Harry S. Sullivan in *The Interpersonal Theory of Psychiatry,* pp. 346–348 and 355; all discuss differences between envy and jealousy.

Page 21, *The baby's envy*. Melanie Klein. *Envy and Gratitude and Other Works 1946–1963,* New York, Delacorte Press, 1975.

Page 21, *Envy-Gel*. The term Envy-Gel is from David Matthews, a friend in San Clemente.

Page 22, *Denying envy*. This quote was paraphrased from George P. Elliot's "Buried Envy," p. 14.

Page 22, *The costs of envy*. Laurence Shames, in "The Creeper: How Did a Little Sin Like Envy Get Such a Bad Reputation?" *Esquire,* August 1982, p. 16, mentions the heavy costs of envy.

Page 22, *Self-pity*. Harry S. Sullivan, in *The Interpersonal Theory of Psychiatry,* p. 354, discusses self-pity as a way to avoid feeling envy.

Page 23, *Injustice*. George P. Elliott, in "Buried Envy," p. 12, writes that envious people hide their self-dissatisfaction by commenting on the injustice in the world.

Page 23, *Indifference*. Suzanne McNear, in her *Cosmopolitan* article "Coping with Envy," quotes a psychiatrist who says we pretend indifference or become vindictive in order to mask our true feelings.

Page 23, *Avoidance*. Suzanne McNear in "Coping with Envy," pp. 212 and 237, reflects upon avoidance as a way to deal with envy; but that being open about your envy works better than avoiding the person you envy. On p. 212, she talks about Marilyn Monroe's rephrasing of Joan Crawford's comment: "Joan called me a 'sleazy whore.' "

Page 24, *Criticism*. Maury Silver and John Sabini, in "The Perception of Envy," *Social Psychology Quarterly,* June 1978, Vol. 41, No. 2, pp. 108–109, discuss the need to undercut the person you envy as a method of self-protection.

Page 24, *Fake praise*. My paraphrase of Harry Stein is from "Thy Neighbor's Life," *Esquire*, July 1980, p. 17.

Page 24, *Devaluing others*. Silver and Sabini in "The Perception of Envy," p. 109, mention that congratulations which arise from envy come out forced and choked, diminished and cool.

Page 24, *Gossip*. G. Medini, Ph.D., and E. H. Rosenberg, Ph.D., Tel Aviv, in "Gossip in Psychotherapy," *American Journal of Psychotherapy*, 1976, p. 457, say that gossip is a method used to obtain relief from envy.

Page 24, *Evoking envy*. The concept of the need to *evoke* envy as a defense against *feeling* envy comes from two sources. The first is a personal communication with Albert M. Shapiro, Ph.D. The second is the quote from Leslie Farber's *Ways of the Will:* "One of the favorite stratagems is the attempt to provoke envy in the envied one." It is Leslie Farber's notion that the envier heaps a barrage of compliments onto the envied one, to pretend he is not envious.

Page 25, *The wish to help*. In a personal communication, Albert M. Shapiro, Ph.D., talked about the need to see through a person who only wants to help, for no one is totally selfless.

Page 26, *Projection*. Judith Viorst provided the basis for this story in her humorous article "Envy Feels Awful," *Redbook*, December 1983, Vol. 162, p. 26(2).

Page 28, *Becoming a clone*. Judith Viorst, in "Envy Feels Awful," *Redbook*, December 1983, Vol. 162, p. 28, relates this vignette about Joan and Emily.

Page 28, *Suffer quietly*. Laurence Shames, in "The Creeper," *Esquire*, August 1982, p. 15, reminds us that we're all in it together.

Page 28, *Wicked Queen envy*. Suzanne McNear, in "Coping with Envy," *Cosmopolitan*, July, 1980, p. 212, says that envy involves resentment and desire, and on pp. 196 and 213, she mentions the term *all-consuming envy*.

Page 29, *Cycle of envy*. Suzanne McNear gives us this familiar envy story in her *Cosmopolitan* article, "Coping with Envy," p. 237.

Page 29, *Destructive envy*. Rob Haeseler, in the *San Francisco Chronicle* (March 13, 14, 1985), and Michael Covino in "Borderline," *East Bay Express*, April 5, 1985, pp. 10 and 14, both write about this murder.

Page 30, *Envy Is Universal*. Envy's universal nature is discussed by most theorists of envy. Two particular sources are

George Foster in "The Anatomy of Envy: A Study in Symbolic Behavior," *Current Anthropology*, pp. 165–202, and Helmut Schoeck in *Envy: A Theory of Social Behavior*, pp. 1 and 2.

Page 30, *Self-interest*. William Evans, in "The Eye of Jealousy and Envy," *Psychoanalytic Review*, says that people envy because of a natural self-interest, a wish to have their own needs met.

Page 31, *Infants and envy*. Melanie Klein, *Envy and Gratitude and Other Works 1946–1963*.

Ann and Barry Ulanov, in *Cinderella and Her Sisters: The Envied and the Envying*, p. 43, describe Kohut, Winnicott, and Farber as believing that envy doesn't exist in the infant from birth, but rather, results from an early disruption in the infant and mother's relationship.

Walter G. Joffe, in "A Critical Review of the Status of the Envy Concept," *International Journal of Psychoanalysis*, p. 540, mentions that, developmentally, envy occurs after the child develops the capacity to fantasize what would happen if the child were to get what he or she desires.

Page 32, *The ideal self*. Walter Joffe, in "A Critical Review of the Status of the Envy Concept," p. 543, explains that envy is a consequence of the discrepancy between who we actually are and who we want to be.

Page 32, *Why we envy*. A personal communication with Steven Joseph, M.D., helped me conceptualize what Heinz Kohut might have said about the reason we envy.

Page 33, *Mirroring*. I am indebted to the following sources for helping me to formulate my ideas in the section about mirroring.

In *Prisoners of Childhood (The Drama of the Gifted Child and the Search for the True Self)*, p. 9, Alice Miller provides an insightful and accessible analysis of the narcissistic mother. On p. 16, she explores how a child who is adequately mirrored feels about his parents. She also discusses a mother who is an inadequate mirror. This mother seeks what she lacks in herself from her own child, a child who is dependent on her and therefore has little choice in the matter.

In a personal communication, Florence Irvine, M.D., suggested the appreciation of a child's artwork as an example of positive mirroring.

Heinz Kohut, in *Restoration of the Self*, gives an excellent analysis of the importance of mirroring in child development.

Page 35, *Feeling superior*. Harry S. Sullivan, in *Clinical Studies in Psychiatry* (S. W. Perry et al., eds.), p. 130, notes that envious people have often been given an irrational and extravagant picture of themselves as children.

Page 35, *Change in status*. Maury Silver, in an interview in *U.S. News and World Report*, says that in a relationship which has been constant, envy is provoked when one person improves and the other doesn't.

CHAPTER 3

Page 38, *Social Proximity*. Helmut Schoeck, in *Envy: A Theory of Social Behavior*, pp. 40 and 156, discusses the importance of the relationship between social proximity and envy: as social proximity increases, so does the possibility for envy. You envy more what you feel is within your reach.

I am indebted to historian Roberta Seid, Ph.D., for sharing her knowledge about the increased visibility and social proximity between classes of people, the relationship between envy and narcissism, and the effect of our consumer economy on the current explosion of envy.

Page 38, *Limited good*. George Foster, in "The Anatomy of Envy: A Study in Symbolic Behavior," *Current Anthropology*, 1972, p. 168, discusses the concept of "Limited Good." He explains that envy is more common in deprivation societies, societies which are based on an image of limited good. In these societies, says Foster, "life is played as a zero-sum game, in which one player's advantage is at the expense of another . . . some people are poor while others are not . . . the well-being and power of those with plenty is visible to, and resented by, those with little."

Page 39, *Sexual equality*. In a personal communication, sociologist Arlie Hochschild explained that Ivan Illich, author of *Gender*, believes that when men and women lived separately and differently, before the present "gender divide," they didn't compare themselves to each other, and there was no envy. It is Mr. Illich's opinion that since men and women are so different, they should keep their separate places in society. Today's breakdown of the gender divide causes more envy between the sexes. However, the inequality still inherent in how men and women are treated needs to be addressed as a prominent cause for the amount of envy we have between the sexes.

Page 39, *Segregation*. George Foster, in "The Anatomy of Envy: A Study in Symbolic Behavior," p. 185, discusses *encap-*

sulation, a device which produces subsocieties whose members ideally have the same access to what are considered to be the good things in life. He believes there is less envy with encapsulation because the person who has less does not assume he could realistically ever attain as much as the person who has more.

Page 39, *Consumerism*. Christopher Lasch, in *Culture of Narcissism*, pp. 30 and 139, observes that today "to live for the moment is the prevailing passion—to live for yourself." On p. 23, he writes that "our cravings have no limits."

Page 40, *Unrealistic expectations*. Christopher Lasch, in *Culture of Narcissism*, focuses on the problems in a society where its members have inflated and unrealistic expectations of themselves.

Page 41, *Social protections against envy*. I am indebted to George Foster, "The Anatomy of Envy: A Study in Symbolic Behavior," and Clarence Maloney (ed.), *The Evil Eye*, for much of the following information on the compliment, and the fear of praise and the Evil Eye.

Cultures where the compliment is feared are found in the Near East, Turkey, Ireland, Italy, India, Mexico, Latin America, Greece, Tunisia, Ethiopia, and other parts of South Asia.

Clarence Maloney (ed.), in *The Evil Eye*, p. 135, mentions that it is culturally unacceptable for Indian parents to praise their children as American parents do.

George Foster, in "The Anatomy of Envy," p. 176, informs us that in non-Western society, compliments—quantitatively far less frequent than in the United States—are routinely discounted. In Mexico (Foster studied the village of Tzintzuntzan), a person who is told he looks well becomes most uncomfortable and assures the speaker that appearances are deceiving, that last week he was at death's door.

In a personal communication with psychologist Judith W. Klein, Dr. Klein illuminated some confusion about compliments and envy. Many women feel being complimented is a sign of being envied, others don't. For Dr. Klein, if the person complimenting does so from a position of strength, then the compliment feels pure, like a nourishing gift. If the complimenter is in a position of weakness and requires a response and your response builds up the complimenter, then the compliment is not a real gift. You feel the envy, hurt and self-criticism behind the compliment.

Cultures where the Evil Eye is feared are found in the Near East, the Mediterranean, southern Asia, northern Europe, all across

North Africa, and among ethnic U.S. populations, such as Italians, Spanish, Jewish, and Slavic Americans.

Information about the Evil Eye is found in Clarence Maloney (ed.), *The Evil Eye*.

Assuming that people who are different are always envious is an unjust accusation and leads to the real oppression of those who already have much to endure. I thank Matt Holdreth for his careful reading of this material.

George Foster, in "The Anatomy of Envy: A Study in Symbolic Behavior," p. 183, comments that in some societies a sneeze symbolizes the loss of the soul which, if not recovered, can lead to death. Other societies recognize the sneeze "more realistically," says Foster, "as the possible early warning of illness . . . perhaps produced by witchcraft or some other envious feeling. To wish a sneezer 'health' is thus an elementary precaution." You assure the sneezer that you hope he remains in good health. He also offers another example of a protection from envy—the postcard from the traveler, who shares symbolically in his journey by saying, "Having a wonderful time, wish you were here."

Page 45, *Pregnancy*. In a personal communication, Albert M. Shapiro, Ph.D., observed that there is more envy today because the modern woman flaunts her pregnancy.

Page 46, *Gift-giving*. George Foster, in "The Anatomy of Envy: A Study in Symbolic Behavior," lists many ways we protect ourselves from being envied. Also, George Foster's is only one possible interpretation of behavior. His paper contains 14 pages of rebuttal by reputable anthropologists. For anyone interested in pursuing this subject further, his paper and these rebuttals are well worth reading.

Page 46, *The Snow White Syndrome*. Ancient Greeks feared *hubris*, excessive pride; a human being should not exceed the limits imposed on him by the gods. The fear of hubris acted as the principal sanction against arrogance and the possibility of being envied. As an ancient Greek you wouldn't wish to be more than a god. Lightning strikes the mountaintops and if you're visible, you get struck. Therefore, the safe path is to remain mediocre and average.

Page 48, *Male chauvinism*. Sherwyn M. Woods, in "Some Dynamics of Male Chauvinism," *General Psychiatry*, January 1976, Vol. 33, p. 63, discusses the etymology of the word chauvinism.

In her article "Early Origins of Envy and the Devaluation of

Women: Implications for Sex Role Stereotype," *Bulletin of the Menninger Clinic*, November, 1974, Harriet Lerner discusses the male's stereotype of women as being a reversal of the little boy's need and dependency on the mother. If a little boy were made king, his childish wishes for power might be expressed as "no one is superior to me." Many of the stereotypes of masculinity and femininity indeed come from the little boy's envy of his mother's power over him and his subsequent need to devalue her. In the stereotypes, the woman is passive, waiting, less aggressive, less intelligent, weak, and childish. According to Lerner, these images of woman are actually what the little boy felt when he was dependent on his mother. The images of masculinity—aggression, intelligence, power, strength—are experiences the little boy had of his mother. If he takes on these qualities for himself (and the little girl identifies with the helpless female stereotype) the boy, as a man, no longer feels inferior.

Page 48, *Male envy*. Throughout this next section, I am indebted to Wolfgang Lederer's highly recommended book, *Fear of Women*. His research into the history of male envy of women has been invaluable to my study. His book is well-documented, fascinating and informative reading.

Page 49, *Fear of the vagina*. Dr. Bruno Bettelheim, in *Symbolic Wounds: Puberty Rights and the Envious Male*, pp. 51 and 53, says that viewing menstruation not as debilitating but rather as having extraordinary magical powers may allow genital sexuality to become more acceptable.

Wolfgang Lederer, in *Fear of Women*, p. 45, notes that North American Indian tribes, New Mexican Jicarilla Apaches and some tribes in India, believe in *vagina dentata*.

Page 51, *Penis envy*. Wolfgang Lederer, in *Fear of Women*, writes about the envy men feel for women's power. Dr. Lederer calls into question the role of penis envy as a major force in women's lives.

CHAPTER 4

Page 56, *Housewives*. The housewife is still being devalued. Collette Dowling's *The Cinderella Complex: Women's Hidden Fear of Independence*, which told women they cannot be fulfilled while remaining at home and dependent on their husbands, sold 3 million copies.

I am indebted to Glenna Matthews for sharing material from her book, *Just a Housewife* (Oxford Press, 1987), which promises to be an important and ground-breaking treatment of the predicament of the housewife.

Nathaniel Hawthorne, in *House of the Seven Gables* and *The Scarlet Letter,* glorified the importance of the housewife.

Page 57, The direct quotes from Philip Wylie are taken from pp. 201 and 204 of *Generation of Vipers.*

Page 59, *Altruistic surrender.* According to Arlie R. Hochschild, in *The Unexpected Community,* pp. 107 and 110–111, altruistic surrender is connected to how deprived the mother feels in the first place. People with few social rewards are more likely to feel altruistic surrender. I am grateful to Dr. Hochschild for teaching me about altruistic surrender, and for proofreading the sections on the sociology of envy in this manuscript.

Page 60, *Mother's opportunities.* Betty Friedan, in *The Feminine Mystique,* prompted many women to realize that they had thought little about what they wanted to do with their lives other than be a wife and mother.

Page 70, *Fear of mortality.* In a personal communication, Susan Griffin, poet and author of *Women and Nature* and *Pornography and Silence,* reminded me about the connection between a mother's fear of mortality and her envy of her daughter for having much of life ahead of her. I thank her for her encouragement about this project.

Page 73, *Queen Bee mothers.* Much of my information in this section was gleaned from Ruth Moulton's "The Effect of the Mother on the Success of the Daughter." *Contemporary Psychoanalysis* 1985, Vol. 21, pp. 266 and 269. Dr. Moulton defines success as "a sense of satisfaction in utilizing your own resources." My research was confirmed by Dr. Moulton's statement, "Thus mothers can defeat daughters, but later try to live vicariously through them."

Page 74, *Mothers as the source.* This quote is from a *San Francisco Examiner* article by Scott Winokur about Dr. Ruth Moulton's study on Queen Bee mothers.

Page 79, *Denise.* In a personal communication, Dr. Arlie Hochschild explored a mother's need to identify with her daughter's rewards rather than seek unique rewards of her own.

Page 80, *Compassion.* This definition of compassion was taken from *Origins: A Short Dictionary of Modern English* by Eric Partridge. Compassion is essential to life, as well as to psychotherapy. People need to understand others and have an innate need to feel understood. The therapist shows empathy and understanding for the patient, and the patient often reciprocates by feeling compassion for the therapist. The same holds for all relationships that allow growth and love to develop.

Page 82, *Mother's feelings*. Alice Miller, in *Prisoners of Childhood (The Drama of the Gifted Child and the Search for the True Self)*, examines what happens to the child who worries more about her mother's feelings than her own. This child develops little ability to know her own feelings.

CHAPTER 5

Page 85, *Parents and change*. Stephen P. Bank and Michael D. Kahn in *The Sibling Bond*, p. 10, explain that parents are not static. The ways they change affect how they raise children of different ages.

Page 91, *Rivalry*. Peter B. Neubauer, in "Rivalry, Envy and Jealousy," *Psychoanalytic Study of the Child*, 1982, Vol. 37, pp. 122 and 123, also illuminates the differences between rivalry and jealousy. Furthermore, the definition of "rivalry" comes from *Origins* by Eric Partridge. In a personal communication, Albert M. Shapiro, Ph.D., observed that envy results when your sibling, in fantasy or reality, has more than you do.

Page 91, *Envy between siblings*. I am grateful to Stephen P. Bank and Michael D. Kahn, *The Sibling Bond*, p. 197, for much of the following information on the nature of siblings. Bank and Kahn agree that parents need to set limits on how much aggression the older child shows towards her new sibling.

It is a complicated task for the older sibling to adjust when a new child enters the family. How the parents handle this adjustment period will influence the siblings' future relationship. Bank and Kahn discuss the "lumping" process as a parental attempt to avoid sibling rivalry. They mention how avoiding playing favorites can actually create more jealousy and identity confusion. The natural aggression of sibling rivalry can actually help children to grow. The earlier the access between siblings begins, and the more prolonged in contact, the more intense will be the sibling relationship, especially when it is stressed by the issues of separation, death and social comparison later in life. The sibling rivalry in the Freud family, as elucidated by Bank and Kahn, is an extreme example of favoritism and its effect on a family.

Page 92, *Inadequacy*. Dr. Bruno Bettelheim, in *The Uses of*

Enchantment, pp. 103, 106, writes that every child feels "hope-lessly outclassed" at some point in his relationship with his sibling and his parent.

Page 106, *Mate envy.* Nancy Friday, on p. 154 of *Jealousy,* provides a highly researched and well-documented account of the intensity of envy and jealousy in dependent relationships. As she says on page 159, "the closer the person is to you, the hotter the resentment of the other person's success."

Page 107, *Working women.* The man doesn't want his wife to be the man. He's confused. He often had no role models to help him understand this modern woman, especially if his father was the chief breadwinner. From Deidre S. Laiken's "When Couples Compete," *New Woman,* March 1986, p. 38.

Page 107, *Destructive envy.* The quotes from Nancy Friday are from her book, *Jealousy,* pp. 142 and 144. From page 40, she examines the necessity of being able to admit to your envy before you can feel remorse or say you're sorry.

Page 114, *Working as a team.* Deidre S. Laiken, in "When Couples Compete," reminds us of the importance of couples working as a team in order to lessen a "you won, I lost" competitive attitude.

CHAPTER 6

Page 116, *Competition in the workplace.* Betty L. Harragan, in *Knowing the Score,* pp. 52–53, suggests that it is the work itself and the structure of the workplace that needs to be examined. She thinks a psychological approach to the problem could be harmful. But she also believes that "one bad apple" and "obnoxious behavior" can cause more job dissatisfaction than the work itself. We will be examining envy as a major reason why the "bad apple" behavior exists.

Page 128, *Being defensive.* In a personal communication, Albert M. Shapiro, Ph.D., provided insight into what to do when someone calls you "defensive."

Page 133, *Debt to feminists.* I suggest Betty Friedan's article "How to Get the Women's Movement Going Again," *The New York Times Magazine,* November 3, 1985, for a reminder that women who have benefited from the women's movement have an obligation to continue its efforts.

Page 133, *Women and power.* Marilyn Loden, in *Feminine Leadership or How to Succeed in Business Without Being One of the Boys,* says that feminine leadership relies heavily on personal power.

Page 136, *Envy and the Helper.* In a previously published article, "Fear of Envy in the Psychotherapy Relationship," I explain that when a helper envies her patient, she does to herself what the envier wants to do to others. The helper believes she cannot help her patient and spoils what she has accomplished. Then, feeling less competent and insecure, the helper is actually less able to help her patient. The play *Equus,* by Peter Shaffer, deals with this theme. A psychiatrist manages his own envy of his patient by turning the envy against himself. He compares himself to his patient, and says, "That boy has known a passion more ferocious than I have felt for any second in my life. And let me tell you something: I envy it." This psychiatrist tells himself, "I settled for being pallid and provincial, out of my own internal timidity." He loses sight of the good work he has done for others. Ann and Barry Ulanov, in *Cinderella and Her Sisters: The Envied and the Envying,* p. 77, shed light on envy among people in the helping professions. They quote Dr. Harold Searles, a well-known psychoanalyst, who envies a patient for her youth and health: "I feel personally, in contrast to my patient, overwhelmingly puny and socially inferior, and (would) have no sense whatever that I had made any contribution, however small, to the improvement in her."

CHAPTER 7

Page 152, *Women and friendship.* I appreciate and acknowledge psychologist and author Lillian Rubin for the scholarship and research of her book, *Just Friends: The Role of Friendship in Our Lives.* The following section on the nature of friendship is replete with information from her book. For anyone interested in exploring the subject of friendship further, I highly recommend her book.

Page 155, *Equality.* Aldous Huxley in *Brave New World,* and George Orwell in *1984* describe a society which aims to eliminate differences between people. There is no envy in a totally equal society.

Page 161, *The need to envy.* In a conversation with Hal Sampson, Ph.D., I learned that the need to envy someone regardless of her life situation is often a defense against being envied. You envy the other person first in order to avoid her envy of you. If you envy her, and put yourself down, she is then less likely to be envious of you.

Page 171, *Friends' successes*. Luise Eichenbaum and Susie Orbach, in *Understanding Women: A Feminist Psychoanalytic Approach,* p. 144ff, say that women tend to focus on how their success makes a friend feel badly. These authors suggest the need to experience your own success first, not push it away, *not* focus on how your friend is feeling. Only then can you cope with the difference in your achievements and those of your friend without having to deny your own success.

Page 176, *Envy and control*. In *Jealousy,* p. 516, Nancy Friday says in order to avoid feeling envy, an envious person becomes possessive and controlling. When we control someone, we are less envious of that person.

Page 177, *Handling a friend's success*. Susan Gervasi, in "Will Success Spoil Friendship?" *Washington Post,* April 4, 1985, p. C5, offers clear guidelines on how to handle a friend's success.

CHAPTER 8

Page 179, *Epigraph*. The quote from Lois Wyse is from *A Woman's Notebook III,* edited by Amy Shapiro.

Page 182, *Beauty*. I am indebted to linguist and author Robin Lakoff for her personal communication about women and beauty and for her insightful book written with Raquel Scherr, *Face Value: The Politics of Beauty*. I also thank writer Mandy Aftel for her help in connecting me with Robin. Quotations from her book are on pages 6 and 10.

Page 185, *Nora Ephron*. This quote is from Nora Ephron's *Heartburn,* p. 179.

Page 192, The comment about Anne is from Dr. Matina S. Horner's article "Fail: Bright Women," *Psychology Today,* page 38. The results of Dr. Horner's research appear in another of her works, "Toward an Understanding of Achievement-Related Conflicts in Women." *Journal of Social Issues,* 1972, p. 171.

Page 193, *Pleasing others*. The relationship between pleasing others and achievement is discussed in Lois W. Hoffman's "Early Childhood Experiences and Women's Achievement Motives," *Journal of Social Issues,* 1972, p. 130. She also talks about women's needs for feedback and parental ambivalence about their daughters' achievements.

Page 193, *Internal Standards*. Judith M. Bardwick's discussion of an internal standard of excellence is found in Chapter 10 of her book *The Psychology of Women: A Study of Bicultural Conflicts*, on p. 169. By "internal standard of excellence," she means judging and making decisions based on what you want rather than what someone else wants for you.

Page 194, *Dr. Ellen Lenney*. The close examination of the results of these studies is found in Ellen Lenney's article "Women's Self-Confidence in Achievement Settings," *Psychological Bulletin*, January 1977, p. 5.

Page 195, *Fear of success*. Georgia Sassen, in "Success Anxiety in Women: A Constructivist Interpretation of Its Source and Its Significance," *Harvard Educational Review*, February 1980, p. 16, says that women fear success primarily in their relationships with others, and that Dr. Horner was testing for success particular to competitive situations rather than interpersonal situations.

Matina S. Horner in "Toward an Understanding of Achievement-Related Conflicts in Women," *Journal of Social Issues*, 1972, p. 158, observes that the research results from the men and women she tested are consistent with the dominant sexual stereotypes. In "Why Women Fear Success," *New York Magazine*, December 20, 1971, Matina Horner discusses her work with Vivian Gornick.

Page 195, *Outperforming a competitor*. The quote of Dr. Horner's about outperforming a competitor appears in Lois W. Hoffman's "Early Childhood Experiences and Women's Achievement Motives," *Journal of Social Issues*, p. 135. These results of Dr. Horner's research appear in "Fail: Bright Women," *Psychology Today*, p. 62.

Page 196, *Competition and envy*. I am indebted to Berkeley psychotherapist Joyce P. Lindenbaum for her insights into the connection between competition and envy as well as her positive approach to competition in relationships in: "The Shattering of an Illusion: The Problem of Competition in Lesbian Relationships," *Feminist Studies*, Spring 1985.

Page 200, *Tennis is stuffy*. The quote from Billie Jean King about tennis being stuffy comes from Julian May's *Billie Jean King: Tennis Champion*.

Page 202, *Being envied*. Jungian analysts Ann and Barry Ulanov in *Cinderella and Her Sisters*, p. 20, offer a thorough and illuminating analysis of the phenomenological experience of being envied. I am very indebted to them for their stimulating insights and theological approach into the nature of envy and being envied.

CHAPTER 9

The core of this chapter comes from interviews. I am grateful to these women for their giving freely of their time, their insights and interest in this study.

CHAPTER 10

Page 229, *Being deserving*. In a personal communication, Thomas W. Cohen, D.M.H., talked about using the notion of being "deserving" as a way to justify greed and domination of others. He also explained the need to use your envy to evaluate what you want in life, to find value in yourself.

Page 230, *Nora*. Florence Irvine, M.D., and Jane Burka, Ph.D., in their personal communications, suggested James Masterson, M.D.'s idea that patients must choose whether to get better or get back at someone found in *The Narcissistic and Borderline Disorders: An Integrated Developmental Approach*, p. 188.

Page 243, *Snow White Revisited*. At the end of Anne Sexton's poem, "Snow White and the Seven Dwarfs," from *Transformations*, Snow White picks up a mirror and looks into it. Anne Sexton therefore raises the question: Will Snow White become like the Wicked Queen?

Page 244, The quote of Marie Lloyd is from *A Woman's Notebook, II*, edited by Amy Shapiro. The quote from Rosalind Russell is found in *A Woman's Notebook, III*.

Page 244, *Gratitude*. Melanie Klein, in *Envy and Gratitude and Other Works*, advises us of the necessity for gratitude as a means to come to terms with envy.

Page 244, *Envy is common to all*. Ann and Barry Ulanov, in *Cinderella and Her Sisters*, show how envy and being envied have a communality of experience. They examine how to use your envy to deepen yourself. "Failing, for whatever reason, to achieve our end, we can so deepen our appreciation of the accomplishments of others that we become a critic and scholar of the moral purpose of beauty or goodness of others . . . (In appreciating others) we bring acceptance into our lives, even reverence, as we do when we are brought to awed admiration of a musician's or a dancer's or an actor's performance. This way we nurture quality in the world." The Ulanovs also provided me with the quote from Saint Augustine.

Bibliography

Allphin, Claire. "Envy in the Transference and Countertransference." *Clinical Social Work Journal* (1982) 10(3).

Bank, Stephen P., and Michael D. Kahn. *The Sibling Bond*. New York: Basic Books, Inc., 1982.

Bardwick, Judith. *The Psychology of Women: A Study of Biocultural Conflicts*. New York: Harper and Row, 1971.

Barthelme, David. *Snow White, a Novel*. New York: Atheneum Press, 1982.

Bettelheim, Bruno. *Symbolic Wounds: Puberty Rites and the Envious Male*. New York: Collier Books, 1954.

———. "Dialogue with Mothers; Jealousy in the Younger Sibling." *Ladies Home Journal* (July, 1966) 83:39.

———. *The Uses of Enchantment: The Meaning and Importance of Fairy Tales*. New York: Vintage Books, 1977 edition; 1975 copyright.

Boehm, Felix. "The Femininity Complex in Men." *International Journal of Psychoanalysis* (1930) 11:444–469.

Brothers, Joyce. "That Green-Eyed Monster and What to Do About Him!" *Good Housekeeping* (August, 1969): 144, 169.

Bruner, J. Review of "Siblings: Love, Envy, and Understanding." *New York Review of Books* (October 27, 1983) 30:8416.

Chetwind, Tom. *Dictionary of Symbols*. Chicago: Granada Publishing Co., 1982.

Circlot, J. E. *Dictionary of Symbols*. New York: Philosophical Library, 1962.

Claremont de Castillejo, Irene. *Knowing Woman: A Feminine Psychology*. New York: Harper and Row, 1973.

Coburn, Judith. "Self-Sabotage: Why Women Fear Success." *Mademoiselle* (September, 1979): 192, 225.

Cohen, Betsy. "Fear of Envy in the Psychotherapy Relationship." *Journal of the Psychotherapy Institute*, Berkeley, 1982.

Cory, C. "Power Envy." *Psychology Today* (June, 1981): 15, 29.

Covino, Michael. "Borderline." *East Bay Express* (April 5, 1985) 7:25.

Daniels, Marvin. "The Dynamics of Morbid Envy in the Etiology and Treatment of Chronic Learning Disability." *The Psychoanalytic Review* (1964–1965) 51(4):585–596.

deBeauvoir, Simone. *The Second Sex*. New York: Bantam Books, 1961.

Disney, A. "Taming the Green-Eyed Monster (Jealousy Is a Most Normal Emotion)." *Ladies Home Journal* (February, 1981): 98.

Dowling, Collette. *The Cinderella Complex: Women's Hidden Fear of Independence*. New York: Simon & Schuster, 1981.

Eichenbaum, Luise, and Susie Orbach. *Understanding Women: A Feminist Psychoanalytic Approach*. New York: Basic Books, 1982.

Elliott, George P. "Buried Envy," *Harper's* (July, 1974): 12–18.

Ephron, Nora. *Heartburn*. New York: Pocket Books, 1983.

Erikson, Erik. "Inner and Outer Space: Reflections of Womanhood." *Daedalus* (Spring, 1984): 582–606.

Evans, William. "The Eye of Jealousy and Envy." *Psychoanalytic Review* (1975) 62(3):481–492.

Faber, Nancy. "There Are Four Kinds of Jealousy, Says an Expert, and 'Sexual' is Only the Beginning." *People* (October 6, 1980) 93(3):14.

Farber, Leslie. *Ways of the Will*. New York: Basic Books, 1966.

Fisher, Roger, and Ury, William. *Getting to Yes*. New York: Penguin Books, 1981.

Foster, George. "The Anatomy of Envy: A Study in Symbolic Behavior." *Current Anthropology* (1972) 13(2):165–202.

Frankel, Steven, and Ivan Sherick. "Observations on the Development of Normal Envy." *The Psychoanalytic Study of the Child* (1977) 32:257–281.

Friday, Nancy. *My Mother, My Self: The Daughter's Search for Identity*. New York: Delacorte Press, 1977.

————. *Jealousy*. New York: William Morrow and Co., 1985.

Friedan, Betty. *The Feminine Mystique*. New York: Dell Publishing, 1963.

————. "How to Get the Women's Movement Going Again." *The New York Times Magazine* (November 3, 1985):26.

Friedman, Sonya. *Men Are Just Desserts*. New York: Warner Bros., 1983.

Gervasi, Susan. "Will Success Spoil Friendship?" *Washington Post* (April 4, 1985):C5.

Gilligan, Carol. *In a Different Voice: Psychological Theory and Women's Development*. Cambridge, Mass.: Harvard University Press, 1982.

Glamour. "What Men Envy Most in Women." (January, 1980): 144–145.

Gornick, Vivian. "Why Women Fear Success." *New York* (December 20, 1971):51, 58.

Grimm Brothers. *The Complete Grimm's Fairy Tales*. New York: Pantheon Books, 1944.

Haeseler, Rob. "Orinda Teenager Convicted of Second-Degree Murder." *San Francisco Chronicle* (March 13, 1985).

Harragan, Betty L. *Knowing the Score: Play-by-Play Directions for Women on the Job*. New York: New American Library, 1980.

Helgesen, Sally. "Sometimes You Envy Your Friends." *Glamour* (March, 1982): 80, 128.

Hochschild, Arlie R. *The Unexpected Community*. Englewood Cliffs, New Jersey: Prentice-Hall, Inc., 1973.

————. *The Managed Heart: Commercialization of Human Feeling*. Berkeley: University of California Press, 1983.

————. "Ivan Illich: Vive la Difference!" Review of *Gender*, in *The New York Times Book Review*. (January 30, 1983): 7, 26.

Hoffman, Lois W. "Early Childhood Experiences and Women's Achievement Motives." *Journal of Social Issues*. (1972) 28(2): 129– 155.

Horner, Matina S. "Fail: Bright Women." *Psychology Today* 1969 3(6):36.

————. "Toward an Understanding of Achievement-Related Conflicts in Women." *Journal of Social Issues* (1972) 28(2):157– 175.

————— and M. R. Walsh. "Psychological Barriers to Success in

Women." in Kundsin, Ruth B., ed. *Women and Success: The Anatomy of Achievement*. New York: William Morrow, 1974:138–144.

House, William C. "Actual and Perceived Differences in Male and Female Expectancies and Minimal Goal Levels as a Function of Competition." *Journal of Personality* (1974):493–509.

Hoyt's New Encyclopedia of Practical Quotations. New York: Funk and Wagnalls Co., 1922.

Hubback, Judith. "Envy and the Shadow." *Journal of Analytical Psychology* (1972) 17(2):152–166.

Jaffe, Daniel S. "The Masculine Envy of Woman's Procreative Function." *Journal of the American Psychoanalytic Association* (1968):16:521, 548.

Jencks, Christopher. *Inequality: A Reassessment of the Effect of Family and Schooling in America*. New York: Harper and Row, 1972.

Joffe, Walter G. "A Critical Review of the Status of the Envy Concept." *International Journal of Psychoanalysis* (1969) 50(4):533–545.

Jongeward, D., and D. Scott. *Women as Winners*. Menlo Park, Ca: Addison-Wesley, 1976.

Jung, Emma. *Animus and Anima*. Dallas: Spring Publications, Inc. 1957, 1981.

Kernberg, Otto. *Borderline Conditions and Pathological Narcissism*. New York: Jason Aronson, 1975.

Kestenberg, Judith S. "Outside and Inside, Male and Female." *Journal of the American Psychoanalytic Association* (1968):457–520.

Klein, Melanie. *Envy and Gratitude and Other Works, 1946–1963*. New York: Delacorte Press, 1975.

Kohut, Heinz. *The Analysis of the Self*. New York: International Universities Press, 1971.

———. *Restoration of the Self*. New York: International Universities Press, 1977.

Kolbenschlag, Madonna. *Kiss Sleeping Beauty Goodbye*. New York: Bantam Books, 1979.

Kuehnelt-Leddihn, E. V. "The Politics of Envy." *National Review* (June 24, 1977): 721.

Krueger, David W. *Success and the Fear of Success in Women*. New York: The Free Press, 1984.

Laiken, Deidre. "When Couples Compete." *New Woman* (March 1986): 36–41.

Lakoff, Robin, and Scherr, Raquel. *Face Value: The Politics of Beauty*. Boston: Routledge & Kegan Paul of America Ltd., 1984.

Lasch, Christopher. *Culture of Narcissism: American Life in an Age of Diminishing Expectations*. New York: Norton & Co., 1979.

Lederer, Wolfgang. *Fear of Women*. New York: Harcourt Brace Jovanovich, 1968.

Lenney, Ellen. "Women's Self-Confidence in Achievement Settings," *Psychological Bulletin* (January, 1977) 84(1):1–13.

Lerner, Harriet. "Early Origins of Envy and Devaluation of Women: Implications for Sex Role Stereotypes." *Bulletin of the Menninger Clinic* (November, 1974): 36(8), 538–553.

Lindenbaum, Joyce P. "The Shattering of an Illusion: The Problem of Competition in Lesbian Relationships." *Feminist Studies* (Spring, 1985) 11(1):85–104.

Loden, Marilyn. *Feminine Leadership or How to Succeed in Business Without Being One of the Boys*. New York: Times Books, 1985.

MacLeod, Sheila. *The Snow White Soliloquies*. New York: Viking Press, 1970.

Maloney, Clarence, ed. *The Evil Eye*. New York: Columbia University Press, 1976.

Mancuso, J. R. "Envy the Entrepreneur? You May Be One Yourself." *Saturday Evening Post* (May/June, 1979):58–59.

Masterson, James F. *The Narcissistic and Borderline Disorders: An Integrated Developmental Approach*. New York: Brunner-Mazel, 1981.

Masterson, J. "Pretty Eyes and Green, My Love." *Psychology Today* (February, 1984) 18(1):71.

May, Julian. *Billie Jean King: Tennis Champion*. Mankato, Minn.: Crestwood House, 1974.

May, Rollo. *The Meaning of Anxiety*. New York: W. W. Norton, 1950, 1977.

McNear, Suzanne. "Coping with Envy." *Cosmopolitan* (July, 1980):196–237.

Medini, G., Ph.D., and Rosenberg, E. H., Pd.D. "Gossip and Psychotherapy." *American Journal of Psychotherapy* (1976):452–462.

Melamed, Elissa. *Mirror Mirror: The Terror of Not Being Young*. New York: Linden Press/Simon & Schuster, 1983.

Miller, Alice. *Prisoners of Childhood (The Drama of the Gifted Child and the Search for the True Self.)* New York: Basic Books, 1981.

Miller, Jean Baker, ed. *Psychoanalysis and Women*. Baltimore: Penguin Books, 1973.

Moulton, Ruth. "A Survey and Reevaluation of the Concept of Penis Envy." *Contemporary Psychoanalysis* (1970) 7:84–104.

———. "The Effect of the Mother on the Success of the Daughter." *Contemporary Psychoanalysis* (1985) 21(2): 266–283.

Nelson, J. B. "Anlage of Productiveness in Boys: Womb Envy." *Journal of the American Academy of Child Psychiatry* (1968) 6:213–225.

Neubauer, Peter B. "Rivalry, Envy, and Jealousy." *Psychoanalytic Study of the Child* (1982) 37:121–142.

Oxford Book of Aphorisms. Chosen by John Goss. New York: Oxford University Press, 1983.

Partridge, Eric. *Origins: A Short Dictionary of Modern English*. New York: Greenwich House, 1983 ed.

Psychology Today. "The Evil Eye—A Stare of Envy." (December, 1977):154–156.

Psychology Today. "Power Envy." (June, 1981): 89–90.

Quinn, Sally. *We're Going to Make You a Star*. New York: Simon and Schuster, 1975.

Rheingold, M. D. *The Mother, Anxiety, and Death: The Catastrophic Death Complex*. New York: Little, Brown and Co., 1967.

Rosenthall, Michael. "Notes on Envy and the Contrasexual Archetype." *Journal of Analytic Psychology* (1963) 8(1):65–75.

Rosten, Leo. *Treasury of Jewish Quotations*. New York: McGraw Hill, 1972.

Rubin, Lillian. *Just Friends: The Role of Friendship in Our Lives*. New York: Harper and Row, 1985.

Rubin, Theodore I. "Myths of Jealousy." *Ladies Home Journal* (May, 1978) 95(2):44.

Sassen, Georgia. "Success Anxiety in Women: A Constructivist Interpretation of its Source and its Significance." *Harvard Educational Review* (February, 1980) 50(1):13–24.

Sanford, Linda, and Donovan, Mary Ellen. *Women and Self-*

Esteem: Understanding and Improving the Way We Think and Feel About Ourselves. Garden City: Anchor Press/Doubleday, 1984.

Schalin, Lars J. "On the Problem of Envy: Social, Clinical and Theoretical Considerations." *Scandinavian Psychoanalytic Review* (1979) 2(2):133–158.

Schoeck, Helmut. *Envy: A Theory of Social Behavior*. New York: Harcourt Brace & World, 1966.

Schoenfeld, Eugene. *Jealousy: Taming the Green-Eyed Monster*. New York: Holt, Rinehart and Winston, 1979.

Scott, William C. "Self-Envy and Envy of Dreams and Dreaming." *International Review of Psychoanalysis* (1975) 2(3):333–338.

Searles, Harold F. *Countertransference and Related Subjects*. New York: International Universities Press, 1979.

Sexton, Anne. *Transformations*. Boston: Houghton Mifflin, 1971.

Shainess, Natalie. *Sweet Suffering: Woman as Victim*. Indianapolis: Bobbs-Merrill Co., Inc., 1984.

Shames, Laurence. "The Creeper: How Did a Little Sin Like Envy Get Such a Bad Reputation?" *Esquire* (August, 1982) 98:15–16.

Shapiro, Amy, ed. *A Woman's Notebook II; A Woman's Notebook III*. Philadelphia: Running Press, 1981, 1983.

Silver, Maury, and John Sabini. "The Perception of Envy." *Social Psychology Quarterly* (June, 1978) 41(2):105–111.

———. "The Social Construction of Envy." *Journal for the Theory of Social Behavior* (October, 1978b) 8(3):313–332.

Silver, Maury. "When Envy Strikes: How to Spot It, Ways to Cope." *U.S. News and World Report* (Nov. 1, 1982): 81(2):93.

Smith, Vivien, and Whitfield, Margaret. "The Constructive Use of Envy." *Canadian Journal of Psychiatry* (February, 1983) 28:14–17.

Spielman, Philip M., M.D. "Envy and Jealousy: An Attempt at Clarification." *Psychoanalytic Quarterly* (January, 1971) 40(1): 59–82.

Stein, Harry. "Thy Neighbor's Life." *Esquire* (July, 1980) 94:17–18.

Stern, Barbara L. "Don't Let Envy Undo You." *Vogue* (March, 1981) 171:142.

Sullivan, Harry S. *The Interpersonal Theory of Psychiatry*. New York: W. W. Norton, 1953.

————. "Envy and Jealousy as Precipitating Factors in the Major Mental Disorders. In S. W. Perry et al., eds. *Clinical Studies in Psychiatry*. New York: W. W. Norton, 1956:128–145.

Suttie, J. D. *Origins of Love and Hate*. London: Paul Kegan, Trench, Trubner and Co. Ltd., 1935.

Symonds, Alexandra. "The Liberated Woman: Healthy and Neurotic." *American Journal of Psychoanalysis* (1974) 34:177–183.

————. "The Myth of Femininity: A Panel." *American Journal of Psychoanalysis*, 33(1): 42–55.

Titelman, Peter. "A Phenomenological Comparison Between Envy and Jealousy." *Journal of Phenomenological Psychology* (Fall, 1981) 12(2): 189–204.

Time. "Envy in Infants." (May 24: 1976): p. 69.

Ulanov, Ann and Barry. *Cinderella and Her Sisters: The Envied and the Envying*. Philadelphia, Westminster Press, 1983.

van Leeuwen, Kato. "Pregnancy Envy in the Male." *International Journal of Psychoanalysis* (1966) 47:319–324.

Viorst, Judith. "Envy Feels Awful." *Redbook* (December 1983) 26(2): 162.

von Franz, Marie L. *The Feminine in Fairy Tales*. Dallas: Spring Publications, 1972.

————. *Interpretation of Fairy Tales*. Dallas: Spring Publications, 1982.

Wagner, Geoffrey. "Some Reflections on Envy." *National Review* (October 23, 1962): 313–314, 330.

Webster's New World Dictionary of the American Language, College Edition, World Publishing Co., 1955.

Weigle, M. *Spiders—Spinsters, Women and Mythology in Fairy Tales*. Albuquerque: University of New Mexico Press, 1982.

Williams, Mary. "Success and Failure in Analysis: Primary Envy and the Fate of the Good." *Journal of Analytical Psychology* (1972) 17(1):7–16.

Winokur, Scott. "'Queen Bee' Mothers Stinging Successful Daughters." *San Francisco Examiner*. March 5, 1985.

Woods, Sherwyn M. "Some Dynamics of Male Chauvinism." *Archives of General Psychiatry* (January 1976) 33(1):63–65.

Wylie, Philip. *Generation of Vipers*. New York: Reinhard and Co., 1942.

Zabriskie, P. *Issues of Life, Love, and Death in Fairy Tales*. (cassette tapes) Lecture at C. G. Jung Institute, San Francisco, December 2 and 3, 1978.

Zilboorg, Gregory. "Masculine and Feminine, Some Biological and Cultural Aspects." *Psychiatry* (1944) 2:257–296.

Zipes, Jack. *Breaking the Magic Spell: Radical Theories of Folk and Fairy Tales*. Austin: University of Texas, 1979.

Index

IMPROVE YOUR HEALTH!

__**THE FOUR DAY WONDER DIET**
Margaret Danbrot 0-515-08563-4/$3.95
Lose 10 pounds in four days: It's fast, easy, and it works!

__**THE FAT TO MUSCLE DIET** Victoria Zak,
Cris Carlin, M.S., R.D., and Peter D.
Vash, M.D., M.P.H. 0-425-11060-5/$3.95
Fast, safe, permanent weight loss with the revolutionary diet plan
that boosts your calorie burning power!

__**THE 200 CALORIE SOLUTION** Martin
Katahn, Ph.D. 0-425-09668-8/$3.95
From the author of The Rotation Diet—how to burn an extra 200
calories a day and lose weight!

__**THE GOLD'S GYM WEIGHT TRAINING
BOOK** Bill Dobbins and Ken Sprague
0-425-10404-4/$3.95
From the most celebrated gym in America—the fast, scientific way to
shape your body beautifully.

__**BEYOND DIET: The 28-Day Metabolic
Breakthrough Plan** Martin Katahn, Ph.D.
0-425-09915-6/$3.95
Beat the diet game by changing your body metabolism in just 28 days
. . . and eat more than you ever thought you could!
